The Institutions of State Business Relations

Emerging Markets Studies

Edited by Joachim Ahrens, Alexander Ebner, Herman W. Hoen,
Bernhard Seliger and Ralph Michael Wrobel

Vol. 8

PETER LANG

Tamar Jugheli

The Institutions of State Business Relations

The Case of Food and Agriculture Sector of Georgia

PETER LANG

Bibliographic Information published by the Deutsche Nationalbibliothek
The Deutsche Nationalbibliothek lists this publication in the Deutsche Nationalbibliografie; detailed bibliographic data is available in the internet at http://dnb.d-nb.de.

Library of Congress Cataloging-in-Publication Data
A CIP catalog record for this book has been applied for at the Library of Congress.

ISSN 2190-099X
ISBN 978-3-631-84678-0 (Print)
E-ISBN 978-3-631-85401-3 (E-Book)
E-ISBN 978-3-631-85402-0 (E-Pub)
E-ISBN 978-3-631-85403-7 (E-Mobi)
DOI 10.3726/b18434

Peter Lang – Berlin · Bern · Bruxelles · New York · Oxford · Warszawa · Wien

This publication has been peer reviewed.

www.peterlang.com

To my parents Naili and Tamazi
and to my aunt Ciuri

Copyright Notice

I hereby declare that this research was conducted for Ph.D dissertation at the University of Groningen supervised by Professor Herman W. Hoen and Professor Joachim Ahrens. The research does not contain the materials accepted for any other degree in any other university. The dissertation does not contain any materials previously written and/or published by another researcher, except where appropriate acknowledgment is made in the form of reference.

Tamar Jugheli
October, 2020

Contents

Copyright Notice vii

Acknowledgement xv

List of Figures xix

List of Tables xxi

Abbreviations and Acronyms xxiii

Abstract xxvii

Chapter I Introduction 1

1.1. State Intervention as a Driver of Development 1

1.2. Georgia as a Locus of the Study: Increased State Intervention 3

1.3. The Puzzling Area of the Economy: The Food and Agriculture Sector of Georgia in 2004–2016 6

1.3.1. State Intervention in the Food and Agriculture Sector in 2008–2012 7

1.3.2. State Intervention in the Food and Agriculture Sector in 2012–2016 7

1.4. The Research Question and Theoretical Argument 8

1.5. The Methodological Approach 9

1.6. Contribution to Academic Debates 11

1.7. The Road Map of the Book 12

Chapter II The Debates on State–Business Relations in the Literature 15

2.1. The Role of SBRs 15

2.2. Characteristics of the *Strategic SBRs* 19

2.3. Institutional Prerequisites for the Emergence of *Strategic SBRs* 25

2.4. Conclusion 33

Chapter III Theoretical Considerations and Operationalisation of SBRs 35

3.1. Theoretical Considerations on Institutions and Economic Performance 35

3.1.1. The Conceptualization of Institutions and Organizations 35

3.1.2. Institutions Matter 37

3.1.3. The Origins of Institutions and Institutional Change 38

3.2. The Institutionalist Approach to SBRs 41

3.2.1. The Game of SBRs: Play or Not Play? 41

3.2.2. The Rules of the Game of *Strategic SBRs* 41

3.2.2.1. Information Exchange 42

3.2.2.2. Reciprocity 43

3.2.2.3. Credibility and Trust 45

3.2.2.4. Feedback Mechanism 46

3.3. The Prerequisites for Emergence of *Strategic* SBRs 47

3.3.1. The Structure of the Public Sector in Relation to the Private Sector 48

3.3.2. The Structure of the Private Sector in Relation to Public Sector 49

3.3.3. Information Exchange Mechanisms 51

3.4. The Theory Applied to State–Agribusiness Relations in Georgia 52

3.4.1. The 'Ideal Typification' of the Institutions of *Strategic SBRs* ... 52
3.4.2. Operationalization of the Variables ... 55

Chapter IV Methodological Considerations for the Empirical Research ... 61
4.1. Methodological Decisions ... 62
4.2. Data Collection ... 66
4.3. Validity and Reliability ... 68
4.4. Data Analysis ... 68

Chapter V The Food and Agriculture Sector of Georgia – State Intervention and the Sector's Performance ... 73
Introduction ... 73
5.1. The First Wave of State Intervention ... 74
5.2. The Second Wave of State Intervention ... 79
5.3. The Performance of the Sector ... 86
Conclusion ... 93

Chapter VI The Nature of the Institutions of State–Agribusiness Relations in Georgia ... 95
Introduction ... 95
6.1. The Institutional Setting that Maintains *Strategic SBRs* ... 96
6. 2. The Case of Preferential Agrocredit ... 98
6.2.1. The Project Overview ... 98
6.2.2. State–Agribusiness Relations ... 99
6.2.2.1. Information Exchange ... 100
6.2.2.2. Reciprocity ... 103
6.2.2.3. Credibility and Trust ... 108
6.2.2.4. Feedback Mechanism ... 109

6.2.2.5. Conclusion 109

6.3. The Case of Plant the Future 111

6.3.1. The Project Introduction 111

6.3.2. State–Agribusiness Relations 113

6.3.2.1. Information Exchange 113

6.3.2.2. Reciprocity 115

6.3.2.3. Credibility and Trust 117

6.3.2.4. Feedback Mechanism 118

6.3.2.5. Conclusion 119

6.4. Co-Financing the Agriculture Products Processing and Storage Enterprises 119

6.4.1. Project Introduction 119

6.4.2. State-Agribusiness Relations 121

6.4.2.1. Information Exchange 121

6.4.2.2. Reciprocity 121

6.4.2.3. Credibility and Trust 125

6.4.2.4. Feedback Mechanism 125

6.4.2.5. Conclusion 126

Conclusion 126

Chapter VII The Institutional Prerequisites for the Emergence of *Strategic SBRs* 129

Introduction 129

7.1. The Structure of the State in Relation to the Private Sector 130

7.1.1. The Presence of the Pilot Agency: Agriculture Project Management Agency (APMA) 130

7.1.2. State Capacity 132

7.2. The Private Sector in Relation to Public Sector 135

7.2.1. The Presence and Length of Existence of Umbrella Organizations 135

7.2.3. The Capacity of the Agribusiness 141
7.3. Information Exchange Mechanisms 143
Conclusion 145

Chapter VIII Discussion and Conclusion 147
8.1. Main Findings 147
8.2. Research Contribution 155
8.3. Implications and Recommendations 159
8.3.1. The Recommendations to the Ministry of Environmental Protection and Agriculture (MEPA) 159
8.3.2. The Recommendations to the Pilot Agency-APMA (RDA) 161
8.3.3. The Recommendations to the Umbrella Organisations 164
8.4. Limitations and Future Research 165

Appendix 1. 167
The List of Interviewees 167

Bibliography 169

Acknowledgement

This publication is a doctoral thesis, supervised by Professor Herman W. Hoen and Professor Joachim Ahrens, and submitted to the University of Groningen to acquire Ph.D. Working on this research was a thought-provoking journey, which contributed to my professional and personal development. The process of learning to manage time, to discipline self, to cope with stress, and to defeat procrastination accompanied this journey. We, academic researchers, often remark that working on a research project is a lonely journey. I could not have reached the end of this journey without the professional and personal support of the individuals I have met on the road of my life, exchanged ideas, and shared time with during short or long breaks from the writing process.

First, I want to express my immeasurable gratitude to my supervisors Professor Herman W. Hoen and Professor Joachim Ahrens. As a Ph.D. candidate, I had the luck to have very supportive, inspiring, modest, and friendly supervisors. Undoubtedly, I could not have completed this research without the outstanding guidance, thought-provoking feedback, and constructive criticism provided by both professors. The meetings and discussions with the professors were always appealing, giving hope that it is possible to get through the tunnel and see the light at the end. Throughout this 4-year journey, Professor Herman W. Hoen and Professor Joachim Ahrens contributed much to my professional development as an academic researcher. Over time, my supervisors read the dissertation chapters and kindly provided substantive feedback that visibly improved the quality and coherence of the dissertation's argument and messages.

I also want to express immense gratitude to the Governance in Emerging Economies (GEE) Research Group, run by the University of Groningen and PFH Private University Göttingen. This research is the product of the regular meetings and discussions with colleagues from the GEE team, which unites energetic, and motivated intellectuals from Germany, South Korea, Uzbekistan, Turkey, Russia, Kazakhstan, and Georgia. The team meetings were always thought-provoking, giving the fuel for further work. Having been part of the GEE research team allowed me to receive excellent knowledge in institutional economics and industrial policy, to develop academic and policy research skills. I am very grateful to the GEE group's team leader, Christian Timm, who has always been supportive, sharing his experience regarding the various stages of the dissertation writing, reading the chapters of the dissertation, and providing constructive feedback. I want to express my gratefulness to my colleagues Axel Woelk, Cenk Sinar, Diana

Usmanova, Franziska Wehinger Misook Choi, Yana Zabanova, and Zhanat Murzakulova for the exchanged ideas and feedback.

I am very grateful to the Volkswagen Foundation, which financially supported this Ph.D. project for three years, as a part of the initiative 'Between Europe and the Orient – A Focus on Research and Higher Education in/on Central Asia and the Caucasus.'

This research could not have been completed without the respondents' support, who showed their interest in the research topic, dedicated their valuable time to the interviews, and shared their experiences. Predominantly, I want to thank Irakli Kochlamazashvili, Lasha Zivzivadze, Salome Gelashvili, and Mindia Gaphrindashvili for their generous support, without which it would have been challenging and, in the most cases, impossible to get contacts and to reach the respondents during the fieldwork in Georgia.

On a personal note, I want to thank my friends Dr. Salome Baslandze, Dr. Yauheniya Varabyova, Niccolo Fiorentino Polipo, Dr. Douglas Rugh, who expressed interest in reading the introductory chapter of the dissertation and provided valuable feedback. I am very grateful to my friend Dr. Adina Maricut-Akbik, who has always been interested in my dissertation writing progress, generously shared with me her academic expertize, which was always the source of opening new, more straightforward approaches. I am indebted to Thomas Hartkopf, whose emotional feedback was crucial. He shared his positive energy, humour, and laughter, encouraged me to move forward and made me believe that I could successfully reach the end of the tunnel. I am thankful to my friends Dr. Salome Minesashvili, Dr. Mina Sumadi, and Dr. Nikoloz Tokhvadze, who have been on their road to Ph.D in the same period, shared their progress and breakthroughs and made the Ph.D. journey a less lonely process. I also want to express my gratitude to Aleksi Aleksishvili, Dr. Elene Jibladze, Houcem Eddine Daoud, Irinka Mezurnishvili, James Joseph, Julian Kocher, Katrin Chimento, Ketevan Babiashvili, Dr. Lasha Chochua, Mariam Azarashvli, Lauren Billingsley, Maka Chitanava, Natalia Shatirishvili, Rahiela Mustafovska, Salome Gvetadze, Salome Tvaloldze, Shota Gvaramadze, Tamara Fernandez Mino, Dr. Tanja Dramac and Thea Goginashvili for their friendship, attention, shared opinions and feedback in various stages of this journey.

Finally, I want to express my gratitude to my family for providing love and encouragement. I am indebted to my aunt Ciuri and parents, Naili and Tamazi, who have, always encouraged my brothers and me to study well, making us believe that learning is our key responsibility to ourselves and to the society. I am very grateful to my brother, Levani, who is always inspiring me to be open to changes and opportunities that life offers and to explore my intellectual and personal potential fully. I am very grateful to my brother, Shalva, my sister-in-law Tamuna, my niece Barbare and nephews Giorgi, Luka, and Saba, for their unconditional love and support.

I also thank all whom I was not able to name here.

Berlin, October 8, 2020
Tamar Jugheli

Figures

Fig. 1.1. The shares (%) of agriculture, industry, and services in total value added, 2004–2016 4
Fig. 3.1. The model: the institutionalist approach to SBRs 55
Fig. 5.1. The annual growth of the budget allocation of the MoA and its share of government spending, 2008–2016 75
Fig. 5.2. Credit to Georgia's food and agricultural sector, 2008–2016 84
Fig. 5.3. Growth in productivity and value-added in the food & agricultural sector 88
Fig. 5.4. The structure of employment 90
Fig. 5.5. The structure of value added (VA) 90
Fig. 5.6. The dynamics of the export of the food and beverages, its share in total export and in world agriculture export 92

Tables

Tab. 1.1. The Research Approach: Analyticism (Jackson, 2011) 10
Tab. 3.1. The Research Approach Analyticism (Jackson, 2011) Applied to the State Agribusiness Relations in Georgia 54
Tab. 3.2. The Operationalization of Information Exchange 56
Tab. 3.3. The Operationalization of Reciprocity 57
Tab. 3.4. The Operationalization of Credibility and Trust 58
Tab. 3.5. The Operationalization of the Feedback Mechanism 58
Tab. 3.6. The Operationalization of the Prerequisites for the Emergence of *Strategic SBRs* 59
Tab. 4.1. The Characteristics of the Selected Cases, 2015-2018 63
Tab. 4.2. The Scheme of the Profile Matrix of the Interview Data from the Fieldwork in Georgia 71
Tab. 6.1. Loans Issued under Preferential Agrocredit 2013–2016 105
Tab. 7.1. Distribution of Agribusinesses by Size and Industries, 2016 141

Abbreviations and Acronyms

ADB	Asian Development Bank
AGI	Association of Ghana Industries
APMA	Agricultural Projects Management Agency [Georgia]
APRC	Agricultural Policy Research Centre [Georgia]
BAG	Business Association of Georgia
CAGR	Compound Annual Growth Rate
CAPSE	Co-financing Agro Processing and Storage Enterprises [Georgia]
CC	Chamber of Commerce
CEDAE	Committee on Economic Development Acceleration and Expansion [Indonesia]
CNFA	Cultivating New Frontiers in Agriculture
CSO	Civil Society Organisations
DC	Deliberation Councils [Korea and Japan]
DCFTA	Deep and Comprehensive Free Trade Agreement
EA	East Asia
EBRD	European Bank for Reconstruction and Development
EDA	Export Development Association [Georgia]
EFTA	European Free Trade Association
ENPARD	European Neighbourhood Programme for Agriculture and Rural Development
EPRC	Economic Policy Research Centre [Georgia]
EQuIP	Enhancing the Quality of Industrial Policies
EU	European Union
FAO	Food and Agriculture Organisation of the United Nations
FDI	Foreign Direct Investment
FGA	Flower Growers Association [Ethiopia]
FTI	Federation of Thai Industries
GBCJCF	Government and Business Community Joint Consultation Forum [Ethiopia]
GD	Georgian Dream
GDP	Gross Domestic Product
GEE	Governance in Emerging Economies [Germany]
GEOSTAT	National Statistics Office of Georgia
GFA	Georgian Farmers' Association
GSMEA	Georgian Small and Medium Enterprise Association

GWA	Georgian Wine Association
HPIE	High Performing Asian Economies
ILO	International Labour Organisation
IO	International Organisation
IPM	Integrated Pest Management
JEC	Joint Economic Council [Mauritius]
JPPCC	Joint Public and Private Consultative Committee [Thailand]
MBC	Malaysian Business Council
MEPA	Ministry of Environmental Protection and Agriculture of Georgia
MITI	Ministry of International Trade and Industry [Japan]
MoA	Ministry of Agriculture of Georgia
MoF	Ministry of Finance of Georgia
NDP	New Development Policy [Malaysia]
NDRC	National Development Reform Commission [China]
NEDLC	National Economic Development and Labour Council [South Africa]
NGO	Non-Governmental Organisation
NIE	New Institutional Economics
NPA	National Personnel Authority [Japan]
NSCICT	National Steering Committee on Information and Communication Technology [Vietnam]
ODA	Official Development Aid
PA	Preferential Agrocredit [Georgia]
PDC	Penang Development Corporation [Malaysia]
PEF	Private Enterprise Federation
PIAC	Presidential Investors Advisory Councils [Ghana, Tanzania, Senegal, Mali, Uganda, Mauritius, and Benin]
PMDU	Performance Management and Delivery Unit [Malaysia]
PTF	Plant the Future [Georgia]
SBR	State Business Relations
TBA	Thai Bankers Association
TEMA	Taiwan's Footwear Manufacturers Association
TFP	Total Factor Productivity
TMA	Turkish Manufacturer's Association
TPSEA	Taiwan Plastic Shoe Exporters Association
TT	Think Tanks
UN	United Nations
UNIDO	United Nations Industrial Development Organisation
UNM	United National Movement

UO	Umbrella Organisations
VA	Value Added
WB	World Bank
WDI	World Development Index

Abstract

State intervention in economic activities to drive development requires specific institutional prerequisites that maintain strategic collaboration between the state and businesses. Arguing that the design of institutions of state business relations (SBRs) is critical for successful state intervention in the industry, sector, or the economy as a whole, this study seeks to understand the nature of the institutions of the state-agribusiness relations in Georgia and its functional compatibilities to the institutions of *strategic SBRs*. The research analyses the nature of SBRs in Georgia through the lens of the New Institutional Economics (NIE). Consequently, the framework of the institutional characteristics of *strategic SBRs* is formed based on the institutionalist approach to *strategic SBRs*. The institutions of *strategic SBRs* can be definedwith respect to the dimensions of information exchange, reciprocity, credibility and trust between the state and private actors and feedback mechanisms on state policies and programmes. This framework is applied to analyse SBRs in three cases of state intervention in the food and agricultural sector of Georgia: Preferential Agrocredit (PA), Plant the Future (PTF), and Co-financing Agro Processing and Storage Enterprises (CAPSE). The key units of study are the formal and informal rules of interaction between the state and agribusinesses and their enforcement mechanisms. The study employs a qualitative research strategy for the systematic collection, organisation, and interpretation of the data. Data from 39 interviews, documents on relevant regulations and laws, and the reports from the international organisations are triangulated to address the research question. This publication contributes to the literature of transition studies, regional studies, institutional economics, developmental studies, and empirical studies of state-led economic activities.

Keywords: institutions, state-business relations, state-led economic activities, economic development, food and agricultural sector, transition studies, regional studies.

Chapter I Introduction

'Although only a few may originate a policy, we are all able to judge it.'
Pericles of Athens (Popper, 2011, p. 177)

1.1. State Intervention as a Driver of Development

As advanced countries' experiences show, the role of the state has been crucial to boosting productivity, regardless of whether activities are located within agriculture, manufacturing, or knowledge-based services (Buur et al., 2015). However, state intervention does not always yield growth (productivity, production, export), diversification (production, export), structural transformation, hence development. The outcomes of state intervention are diverse and depend on the coordination of activities between the state and private sectors. The state needs businesses to make investments for growth, and the private sector needs policy design and implementation to be in line with their investment plans (Sen, 2013d). State intervention requires an understanding of market constraints and coordination failures (Trubek, 2010). For state intervention to drive economic development, it requires discovering obstacles the private sector faces in the production processes (Rodrik, 2004, 2009) and addressing private sector's concerns about their ability to profit from investment decisions (Moore and Smitz, 2008). The state will not be capable of intervening effectively and cannot overcome market and coordination failures if it lacks reliable information about markets, technological bottlenecks, and local or sectoral needs. Private actors can provide this information. Therefore, while intervening in the economy, consultations with private sector are crucial (Ahrens, 2002).

However, for a long time, the prevailing argument in the literature has been that businesses should be excluded from public policy elaboration processes (Furubotn and Richter, 2005), as close state-business relations (SBRs) may drive cronyism, nepotism, and collusion (Mody, 1993; Adly, 2010; Nattrass and Seekings, 2010). The rationale beyond the argument is that state actions, such as restricting entry into certain markets or granting special privileges through subsidies or regulations, create rents (unearned profits). Availability of rents gives incentives to businesses to lobby for actions that will allow them to capture the unearned profits and direct resources away from their most optimal use (Krueger, 1974; Tullock, 1975; Bhagwati, 1982; Olson, 1982; Tollison, 1982; Mueller, 1989; Lusztig, 1998; Congleton, 2015). This argument has led to the prescription of the market-oriented reforms in the Washington Consensus (Williamson, 1990), considering that eliminating rents would allow businesses to concentrate their efforts on market competition and allocative efficiency, which in turn could drive an economy's transformation.

The Washington Consensus was grounded on the idea that businesses' contribution to economic transformation is granted if political intervention does not distract economic decisions of businesses (Evans, 1997; Marangos, 2009). Economic transformation involves exploring unknown economic territory; however, businesses as economic actors are risk-averse and search for profit. This may cause them to stay involved with activities for which the sunk costs are already covered, and successful routes are already established, rather than exploring new opportunities (Evans, 1997). Over the last three decades, it has been argued that institutions linking the state and businesses are crucial for the state intervention to drive development (Ahrens, 2002; Te Velde, 2010). In the 1990s, the institutionalist analysis of development often concluded that the strategic relations between state and businesses account for a large part of the variation in economic performance (Maxfield and Schneider, 1997). Based on this conclusion, ideas asserting that growth-enhancing relations between businesses and state elites are possible, arose.

As Ahrens (2002) states, the critical question is not whether state intervention should rely on SBRs, but how the institutions of consultation and cooperation should be designed to maintain collaboration, enhance policy experimentation and adaptation, support market functions reduce potential economic and political risks. Institutions are the set of formal and informal rules and their enforcement mechanisms, which structure and constrain interactions between various parts of society (North, 1990; Ahrens, 2002). North (1990, p. 3) defines institutions as "humanly devised constraints that shape human interactions. Constraints can be formal (written political (judicial) rules, economic rules, and contracts) and informal (sanctions, taboos, customs, traditions, norms of behaviour, codes of conduct and conventions)" (North, 1990, p. 7). These constraints are prescriptions about required, prohibited, or permitted actions, introduced to and used by a set of players in repetitive interdependent relationships (Ostrom, 1986, p. 5). Informal constraints are revealed in daily interactions, whether within the family, in external social relations, business activities, or governing structures (North, 1990, p. 36). They are part of the culture defined as the transmission of values and other factors that influence behaviours from one generation to the next (Boyd and Richerson, 1985). The institutional matrix that determines the interaction between the state and businesses is crucial for the efficiency of SBRs. The purpose of the design and enforcement of an institutional matrix is to define the way the game is played (North, 1990). The players of the game are organizations, purposeful entities composed of individuals, who act to pursue shared objectives. These organizations include political bodies (regulatory agencies, city councils), economic bodies (firms, trade unions, family farms, and cooperatives), social bodies (clubs, churches, associations), and educational bodies (education, vocational training centres) (North, 1990, p. 5). Even though there is significant diversity in the institutional settings of SBRs both within and between countries, the strategic relationships have similar features. The institutions of *strategic SBRs* can be definedwith respect to the dimensions of information exchange, reciprocity, credibility, and trust between the state and private actors (Lemma and te Velde, 2017). Also, with respect to feedback mechanisms on state policies and programmes and taking into account the provided feedback (Page and Tarp, 2017). Economic history shows that while it is essential to learn from other countries' successes and failures, each country shall build intervention and SBRs on its specificities, and it has to experiment individually and learn by doing.

1.2. Georgia as a Locus of the Study: Increased State Intervention

The empirical basis for this study is Georgia, a post-Communist, Eastern European country with a transition economy, which is an interventionist latecomer. In the 1990s, after the collapse of the Soviet Union (SU), the country experienced economic practices legated from the communist past, with oligarchs and rent-seekers managing to optimise their benefits and stop further reforms (Bauman, 2012). In 2003, after the peaceful, so-called 'Rose Revolution,' the country experienced a change of power through democratic elections. From 2004 until 2007, Georgia experienced a rapid phase of economic reforms. The state, headed by the United National Movement Party (UNM), committed to the Washington Consensus guidelines while planning its economic development agenda. The state implemented economic and institutional reforms to achieve extensive liberalization, privatization, and deregulation (Jobelius, 2011). Simplification of administrative procedures and a consistent introduction of e-governance systems were meant to diminish interactions between the public administration and businesses and to limit opportunities for corruption (Engvall, 2012, p. 7).

The reforms contributed to the improvement of the business environment and Foreign Direct Investment (FDI) flow in the economy, which was a key driver in the turnaround of Gross Domestic Product (GDP) growth (World Bank, 2012b). Therefore, Georgia attracted the international community's attention and earned the status of the top reformer for the period of 2005–2010 (World Bank, 2012a). Despite the rapid economic growth (9.4 % on average) during 2004–2008, there was only a slight change in the structure of the economy (Fig. 1.1). During the mentioned period, the share of agriculture value-added (VA) declined (3 % point), the share of industry value-added (VA) increased (1.7 % point), and the share of services increased (1.3 % point) (Fig. 1.1).

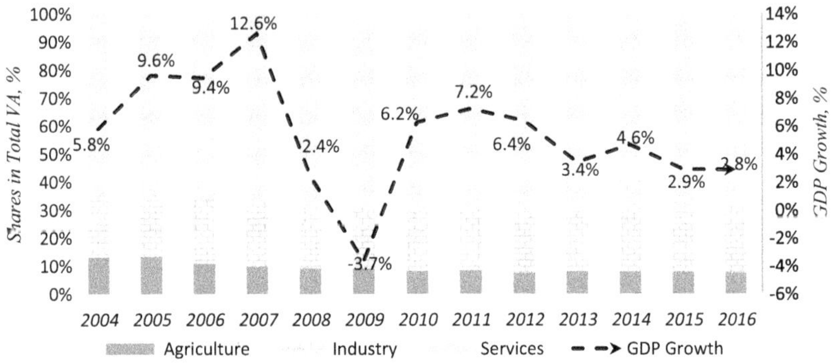

Fig. 1.1: The shares (%) of agriculture, industry, and services in total value added, 2004–2016

Source: UN statistics (2019)

Note: The graph presents the shares of agriculture, industry and services in total value added.

Despite the non-intervention dogma, the state began intervening informally in economic processes. Firstly, it initiated a process of property redistribution that benefitted the new political elites and their allies. Secondly, the state managed to regulate access to markets and resources on an informal basis (Timm, 2013). After the global financial crisis and the military conflict with Russia in 2008, which resulted in a sharp fall in FDI and GDP, Georgia shifted its official economic policy towards more formal state-led, coordinating approaches (Timm, 2014).

In 2012, a new government headed by the Georgian Dream Party (GD) came into power. With the change of power, the state initiated more interventionist approaches for economic development and combined liberal economic policy achievements with more active state led approaches. One of the critical targets of the interventionist economic policy since 2012 has been the food and agricultural sector (Shergelashvili and Tokmazashvili, 2012). The state intervenes in the country's food and agricultural sector to support its development, and more specifically, to increase and to diversify production and export capacities.

Agriculture can be a source of economic growth, in terms of providing attractive investment This graph does not belong here, it need to be set above (as it was in original file, beginng of this page , after the paragraph which ends wiyj (Fig, 1.1.) opportunities for the private sector and facilitating agriculture-related industries and boosting the rural non-farm economy (World Bank, 2008). Today's advanced economies were all able to enhance agriculture productivity during their economic take-offs (UNCTAD, 2016), which released labour and capital from this sector and shifted the resources into other more productive sectors, such as manufacturing or services (UNCTAD, 2016). Despite state intervention in the sector, the production and export dimensions of Georgia's food and agricultural sector remain moderately concentrated. The structure of the economy does not show any changes since the state intervention from 2013 (Fig. 1.1). Economic policies, even those designed according to the best available practices, can fail for a variety of reasons. Foremost among these are incomplete information in policy formulation, ineffective implementation (when private agents choose not to comply), and adverse side effects (when policies induce corruption) (Maxfield and Schneider, 1997). Arguing that *strategic SBRs* are crucial in the process of state intervention in economic activities to drive the sector's development, the dissertation seeks to understand the following: *How does the state manage the relationship with agribusinesses while intervening in the food and agricultural sector of Georgia? More specifically: 1. how are the institutions of state-business relations (SBRs) designed? 2. why strategic SBRs failed to emerge in the food and agricultural sector of Georgia? 3. which institutional prerequisites determine the emergence of strategic SBRs?*The main goal is to understand if the institutional setting of the state agribusiness relations is conductive to identify the obstacles and opportunities of Georgia's food and agricultural sector and direct resources to overcome the bottlenecks that detract its development and to realize its opportunities.

In this dissertation, SBRs refers to interactions between the state (the Ministry of Agriculture of Georgia (MoA) [currently [2020] the Ministry of Environmental Protection and Agriculture (MEPA), , the Agricultural Projects Management Agency (APMA) (,currently [2020] Rural Development Agency (RDA), policymakers and bureaucrats) and the private sector (firms/entrepreneurs/businesses, umbrella organisations, and networks) in Georgia's food and agricultural sector. Throughout this research, the institutional setting refers to the formal and informal rules that guide the interaction between the state and agribusinesses and their enforcement mechanisms. Looking through the lens of the New Institutional Economics and the institutionalist approach to SBRs, the thesis explains the nature of the institutions of SBRs in the process of state intervention in economic activities.

1.3. The Puzzling Area of the Economy: The Food and Agriculture Sector of Georgia in 2004–2016

The assets of the food and agricultural sector of Georgia include 2.4 million hectares of agricultural land, of which only 35 % is utilized (FAO, 2019). There are 22 climate zones varying from the subtropical climate along the Black Sea border to more temperate and arid climate zones in the eastern part of the country. A variety of soils is suitable for growing different kinds of high value-added (VA) agricultural products, as well as there are sufficient freshwater resources to grow crops (Lootty, 2013; Bluashvili and Sukhanskaya, 2015; Babakholov, 2018). The country's wide variety of ecological and climatic zones encourages the growth of crops such as cereals, subtropical crops, potatoes, other vegetables, melons, grapes, and other fruits. The Georgian food processing industry relies on local as well as imported resources. The products that rely on local resources include wine, other alcoholic beverages, mineral water, tea, essential oils, and canned food. These products are oriented to export. The products that rely on imported resources include milk and dairy products, meat, fish, sugar, oil, fat, and non-alcoholic drinks. These products are oriented to local markets (Bluashvili and Sukhanskaya, 2015).

As Georgia's resource situation favours agricultural production, one would expect the government to focus on developing the sector, but the sector lacked state attention until 2012 (Land, 2013). In addition, the sector faced other shortcomings, such as a lack of knowledge and technology transfer, the absence of modern machinery services, degraded rural infrastructure, and poor connectivity to markets (FAO, 2012). All these resulted in declines in cultivated areas and the production of primary agricultural products. The agricultural sector did not respond to macroeconomic reforms and an improved business environment, which had been achieved through the economic reforms implemented in 2004–2007. The sector was not able to respond to the intense competition brought about by trade reforms because of weaknesses in essential agricultural services, infrastructure, and the peasant style of production that persists (FAO, 2014). The major export goods continued to be produced by small, family-run businesses. The private sector lacked the capital required for investments and productivity increases, and did not have access to loans (Jobelius, 2011).

Until 2012, government policy had paid little direct attention to the agricultural sector, particularly after the Rose Revolution of 2003 (Bluashvili and Sukhanskaya, 2015). At the initial stage of its ruling period, the state did not prioritize any sector, considering that a discrimination against sectors undermines the functioning of markets. The policy elaboration was focused on the reforms for the facilitation of the economy and the promotion of free trade. The

United Nation's Food and Agriculture Organization (FAO), in the assessment report of Georgia's agriculture, stated that the agricultural sector of Georgia is 'the Cinderella of development assistance due to a lack of any defined state policy or strategy for the sector, other than laissez-faire, abandoned by Government' (FAO, 2012, p. 9).

1.3.1. State Intervention in the Food and Agriculture Sector in 2008–2012

In 2006, after Russia had restricted imports of Georgian wine and mineral waters into Russian markets, the Georgian government started emphasizing the importance of the country's food and agricultural sector in public rhetoric (Newnham, 2015). Until the end of 2011, the state did not have any strategy for the sector's development (Bardzik et al., 2011). The President of Georgia announced that 2011 would be the year of agricultural development and progress, to express the political will of the ruling elites to support the food and agriculture sector of Georgia. The new emphasis on the agricultural sector was reflected in the *10 Points Plan 2011–2015*, which proposed the development of business-oriented agriculture in addition to traditional household-based agriculture (FAO, 2014).

In 2011, the Government of Georgia approved an agricultural development strategy, which was the first strategy elaborated after the collapse of the Soviet Union. The strategy aimed to attract investment through a partnership with the private sector, to increase production and productivity, to increase and diversify exports and to substitute imports of agricultural products. The state, following the recipe of the Washington Consensus, aimed to achieve the targeted goals not via direct subsidies, but via increasing competitiveness and productivity of the private sector based on market principles. Therefore, the state saw its role as a supporter of the private sector in modernizing production processes and adopting modern technologies, as well as providing infrastructure and information on markets and the achievements of modern technologies.

1.3.2. State Intervention in the Food and Agriculture Sector in 2012–2016

With a change of power in 2012, the state's approach to the agricultural sector changed. In 2012, authorities began a direct intervention in terms of providing technical and financial support. The government explicitly declared agricultural development as the top priority and increased the Ministry of Agriculture (MoA) budget by 4.5 times (The Annual Report of the MoA, 2017). The MoA's budget and its share to the total budget continued to increase from 2012 to 2016 (The Annual Report of the MoA, 2017).

In 2014, after two years of formulation process, the MoA published the agriculture development strategy for 2015–2020. The new strategy's broad goals were quite similar to the ones in the previous strategy, such as aiming to achieve productivity and production growth, investment growth, export diversification and growth, technological upgrading, and building value chains. However, the instruments and state activities to reach these goals and mechanisms to interact with the private sector differed. The government activated several instruments to promote the development of agricultural production; the array of newly proposed measures included the provision of land cultivation and amelioration services for free, access to concessional loans, subsidies to producers of certain agricultural products, and supporting farmers to better access markets (Bluashvili and Sukhanskaya, 2015, p. 8). In 2013, the state elaborated instruments, such as interest rate subsidies on loans, co-financing investment, and grants, to create incentives for businesses to invest in this sector. In order to manage the investment projects initiated for agriculture development, the state established the Agriculture Project Management Agency (APMA) in 2014 (The Annual Report of the Ministry of Agriculture of Georgia, 2017).

1.4. The Research Question and Theoretical Argument

Since 2013, the state has intervened formally in Georgia's food and agricultural sector. The question is how state intervention in the food and agricultural sector identifies and addresses the obstacles that constrain the sector's development. Arguing that the institutional setting of SBRs is critical for the state intervention in the food and agricultural sector to result in successful sectoral development, this study seeks to understand the nature of the institutions of state-agribusiness interaction in Georgia and explain why *strategic SBRs* have not emerged. Explicitly, the key questions of the research interest are:

> *How does the state intervene in the food and agricultural sector of Georgia? How does the state manage relationships with agribusinesses while intervening in the food and agricultural sector of Georgia? Why did strategic state–agribusiness relations fail to emerge in Georgia?*

These questions address the knowledge gap this research aims to fill. Empirically, the research looks at the specific characteristics of the existing SBRs and how they are institutionalized in the case of a transition economy and interprets these specific characteristics in comparison with the institutional settings of *strategic SBRs*. This study examines three cases of state intervention in Georgia's food and agricultural sector: Preferential Agro Credit (PA), Plant the Future (PTF), and Co-financing Agriculture Processing and Storage Enterprises (CAPSE). These cases are state programmes intended to achieve Georgia's Agricultural Development Strategy goals, such as to create incentives for local businesses to invest in the food and agricultural sector of Georgia, to increase and diversify the production and export, and to enhance productivity, and hence to support the economic performance of the sector. The Preferential Agro Credit programme aims to stimulate primary and secondary production, processing, storage, and selling through supporting the registered agribusinesses with subsidized, preferential long-term loans. The Plant the Future programme seeks to increase primary production and export potential of fruits. Co-financing Agriculture Processing and Storage Enterprises programme supports establishing new or reconstructing old enterprises in regions of low economic activities in Georgia. The key unit of study is the rules (both formal and informal) of interaction between the state and agribusiness, and their enforcement mechanisms in each case. The study of these three selected cases aims to shed light on the nature of the institutions of state agribusiness relations in Georgia. More specifically, studying these three cases reveal how the state manages the relationship with agribusinesses while intervening in the food and agricultural sector, how the institutions of the state-agribusiness relations are designed, and help to understand why strategic SBRs failed to emerge in the food and agricultural sector of Georgia.

This study applies the analytical tools of the New Institutional Economics (NIE) to understand the nature of the institutions of the state-agribusiness relations. The justification for using the NIE approach is that SBRs are always characterised by formal and informal institutions; therefore, the NIE is the appropriate analytical frame. Based on the institutionalist approach to state intervention in economic activities, the thesis argues that the nature of formal and informal rules of SBRs and their enforcement mechanisms are crucial for success in the process of state intervention in the sector.

1.5. The Methodological Approach

The research design is a logical plan to link the research questions, the required data, and the strategies for data collection and analysis to approach the research topic (Yin, 2011, p. 75). The research conducted in this dissertation relies on analyticism (Jackson, 2011) as a research approach. Analyticism 'seeks to ground the production of knowledge in concrete, practical involvements of the researcher, and does so through a strategy involving the instrumental oversimplification of complex, actual situations; ideal-types, are then utilized to form case-specific analytical narratives that explain particular outcomes' (Jackson, 2011, p. 142). This research relies on New Institutionalism to form the framework of the characteristics of the *strategic SBRs* based on the institutionalist approach to SBRs. An ideal type arrangement of the institutions of *strategic SBRs* is formed based on the institutionalist approach to *strategic SBRs*. The ideal type arrangement of the *strategic SBRs* is used as a means for the comparison and interpretation of actuality (Weber, 1999a, in Jackson, 2011, p. 142) in the selected three state intervention cases to organize empirical observation into systematic facts.

Tab. 1.1. The Research Approach: Analyticism (Jackson, 2011)

The Weberian Procedures of Ideal Typification (Jackson, 2011)			
Step I	**Step II**	**Step III**	**Step IV**
The stand taking framework: NIE	The characteristics of the institutions of *strategic SBRs*	Application	Analysis

According to the institutionalist approach to SBRs, *strategic SBRs* are characterized by information exchange, reciprocity, credibility, and trust between the state and businesses (Maxfield and Schneider, 1997; Harriss, 2006; te Velde, 2006; Leftwich, 2009; Buur et al., 2015), and feedback mechanisms on state programmes and policies. The emergence of *strategic SBRs* depends on the structure of the state in relation to the private sector, the structure of the private sector in relation to the state, information exchange mechanisms, the capabilities of the state, and the capabilities of businesses (te Velde, 2006).

Addressing the research questions stated in this research requires in-depth information about the country-specific situation. The required information includes norms determining the interaction between the state and private actors, their capabilities, and their motivation to contribute to the sector's development in the long term. Such information is best captured in analytical narratives, which requires qualitative data (Buur et al., 2015). Qualitative data is a source of well-grounded, rich descriptions and explanations of processes occurring in local contexts. With qualitative data, one can preserve the chronological flow, assess local causality, and derive fruitful explanations (Miles and Huberman, 1984, pp. 21–22). Therefore, this study employs a qualitative research approach. From the strategies of the qualitative research approach (Creswell, 2009), this research employs a case study, aiming to explore the answers to the questions mentioned above in-depth through studying three cases. The research aims to understand if these differences in programmes result in a difference in the institutions of the state–agribusiness relations.

Yin (2011, p. 8) states that a qualitative research approach requires substantial data collection, which needs to be based on multiple sources. This thesis employs such a strategy for the systematic collection, organization, and interpretation of data. Data from 39 interviews, documents on relevant regulations and laws, and international organizations' reports are triangulated to address the research question. Data from the interviews are organized in MAXQDA, which is the statistical software for qualitative data analysis.

The research employs qualitative text analysis to analyse the data. The analysis covers three parts: (1) the state intervention in Georgia's food and agricultural sector and the sector's performance from 2004 through 2016; (2) the nature of the institutions of the state–agribusiness relations in Georgia. This includes analysis of the institutions of state-agribusiness relation in the cases of three state programs: the Plant in Future, Preferential Agrocredit, and Co-financing Agriculture Processing and Storage Enterprises, and (3) the prerequisites for the emergence of *strategicstate–agribusiness relations*.

1.6. Contribution to Academic Debates

The earlier discussions on state intervention in economic activities focused mostly on the ideological, *whether at all* questions instead of focusing on the intervention's institutional design (Lemma and Te Velde, 2017). Empirical studies on the role of SBRs in the process of state intervention and the institutional setting for the *strategic SBRs* have evolved during the last three decades. The research started in the mid-1990s, further developed in the 2000s, and gained more general acceptance in the 2010s (Sen, 2015).

One of the empirical chapters of this manuscript, Chapter V, explores the instruments of state intervention in the food and agricultural sector of Georgia. This contributes to the empirical literature of state interventions. The study puts emphasis on the role of *strategic SBRs* in the process of state-led economic activities. Existing literature on the role of SBRs faces a gap regarding the regional dimensions of empirical studies. Empirical research on the SBRs has been undertaken mostly in East Asia, Latin America, and in some Sub-Saharan African countries (Batcha, 2012; Buur et al., 2015), it has been mostly neglected from empirical studies of post-Communist countries. Hence, this research will fill the regional gap in the literature and contribute to the cutting-edge, controversial, and policy-relevant academic debate about the role of institutions of SBRs in the process of state intervention. Furthermore, by exploring the case of Georgia, a small open transition economy, the study contributes to transition studies.

The remaining two empirical chapters of this research, Chapters VI and VII, explore the institutions of SBRs and the prerequisites for the emergence of the *strategic SBRs*. The thesisoffers a comprehensive analysis of the behaviour of the actors (state and businesses), the rules behind their actions, and the enforcement mechanisms of the rules in the food and agricultural sector of Georgia. By studying institutions of state agribusiness relations in Georgia, this publication contributes to the empirical literature of institutional economics.

The research will unequivocally add a new chapter to the long-lasting discussions on state-economy relations at a theoretical level. The decreasing influence of the neoliberal paradigm opened up room for renewed academic thinking. Applying the analytical framework of New Institutional Economics to the case of a small, open, transition economy promises to identify the specifics of SBRs applicable to countries on a similar developmental path. Considering that most of the theorizing about the institutions of state-business relations refer to the experiences of the East Asian, African, and Latin American countries (Buur et al., 2015), this research will contribute to expanding the framework via expanding the geographic area of empirical observations on this topic.

1.7. The Road Map of the Book

The outline of the remaining chapters is as follows: Chapter II reviews the literature on the debates on SBRs. More specifically, it looks at the literature that explores the role of *strategic SBRs* in the process of state intervention, the necessary conditions for the emergence of *strategic SBRs*, and the institutional setting that maintains strategic relations between the state and business once they have emerged. The chapter highlights the literature's main themes and arguments, intending to identify the ones that could be relevant in explaining the emergence and the institutional design of state-agribusiness relations in Georgia. The chapter also identifies gaps in existing studies.

Chapter III consists of two parts, theoretical considerations, and their application to the food and agricultural sector of Georgia. The first part discusses the concept of the institutions, their origin, and their changes, as well as theoretical considerations on the *strategic SBRs* and the institutional settings for emergence of *strategic SBRs*. The second part discusses the application of theoretical considerations to the food and agricultural sector of Georgia. Chapter IV explains the research design; more specifically, the methodological procedure to address the research question.

Chapter V analyses state intervention in the food and agricultural sector of Georgia, and the sectoral performance, with emphasis on understanding the changes after state intervention. The key performance indicators (PI) include the capacity and growth of production and export dimensions, the diversification of domestic and export dimensions, employment, and productivity. These performance indicators are selected based on the United Nations Industrial Development Organisation's (UNIDO) Enhancing the Quality of Industrial Policies (EQuIP) toolbox, which proposes metrics of economic performance of an economic sector.

Chapter VI analyses the nature of institutions of state-agribusiness relations in the three cases of state intervention (Plant the Future, Preferential Agro Credit, and Co-financing Agriculture Processing and Storage Enterprises). The separation of these three cases is necessary for a better illustration of whether differences in characteristics of each case (number of actors, duration and size of support) influence the institutions of the SBRs. Chapter VII presents the analytical results on prerequisites for the emergence of *strategic state-agribusiness relations*. Chapter VIII offers a general discussion and conclusion.

Chapter II The Debates on State–Business Relations in the Literature

This chapter discusses empirical evidence on the role of state business relations (SBRs), the nature, prerequisites, and importance of the institutions of *strategic* SBRs and their contribution to policy elaboration processes, productivity growth, firm performance, short-term and long-term output, economic growth, and development.

2.1. The Role of SBRs

The state intervenes in Georgia's food and agricultural sector to support its development, and more specifically, to increase and diversify production and export. Diversification is not a natural process and rarely takes place without substantial state intervention in economic activities through various types of instruments (Rodrik, 2004). However, state intervention is not a simple solution for promoting economic diversification and development. Policymakers need to find a way to avoid adverse effects like rent-seeking, business capture, nepotism, or populist policies. State intervention is effective when it identifies and addresses the obstacles faced by private actors in a targeted industry, sector, or economy (Moore and Schmitz, 2008). The outcome of intervention depends on the coordination of activities between the state and the private sector. In countries with institutional frameworks that strengthen *strategic SBRs*, the opportunities for growth and development are increased (Batcha, 2012). As Ahrens (2002) states, the critical question is not whether state intervention shall rely on SBRs or not, but how these forms of consultation and cooperation should be designed institutionally to reduce potential economic and political risks. With this in mind, this chapter reviews the debates on SBRs, and more specifically, the literature that explores the role of *strategic SBRs* in the process of state intervention, institutional setting of *strategic SBRs*, and the prerequisites that maintain the emergence and sustain of strategic relations between the state and business actors. This chapter puts forward the main themes and arguments on SBRs that the literature discusses to identify those that could be relevant to understand the nature of the institutions of the state–agribusiness relations in Georgia.

Evidence from various countries shows diversity in the outcomes of state intervention, as well as in the roles of SBRs in this process. State intervention in the development process has nurtured successful cases of enterprises, such as the steel firm POSCO in South Korea (Sohal and Ferme, 1996), aircraft manufacturer Embraer in Brazil (Goldstein, 2002), the salmon industry in Chile (UNCTAD, 2016), and makers of car parts in India and China (Sutton, 2005). The top five non-traditional export commodities to the USA from Latin American economies (Brazil, Chile, and Mexico) are beneficiaries of state support programmes. In the case of Chile, success stories include industries from the food and agricultural sector, more specifically grapes and salmon. The support of Fundacion Chile contributed to the development of the salmon industry. As to the grape, in the 1960s, state-supported R&D contributed to transforming an initially local market-oriented industry into a global powerhouse (Jarvis, 1994).

Government intervention had the best outcomes when the state bureaucrats consulted with the private sector regarding the needs of the sector or industry and mediated these needs to the political interest of the ruling elites (Buur et al., 2015). Interaction with the businesses provided bureaucrats with information on obstacles that individual firms, segments of the industry, and the industry as a whole faced. Besides, it allowed them to observe business behaviour and develop a more targeted strategy to support particular industries. Moreover, the embeddedness of the bureaucrats gave an impression of credible commitments to businesses. Hence, collaborative relations refer to the alliances of the political elites, industry actors, and bureaucrats working together to solve coordination and information-related failures. The unit of analysis is the interactions between businesses and bureaucrats (Buur et al., 2015).

State intervention was successful in promoting economic transformation in East Asia (EA). The key driver of the success of the High-Performing Asian Economies (HPAEs) was the creation and maintenance of institutions, which enabled the coordination of the activities of the state and businesses. However, the institutions differed across countries. In South Korea, SBRs were drivers for the rapid economic growth that followed for the next few decades (Amsden, 1989). In South Korea, developmental SBRs had been established since the early 1960s and complemented the process of industrial policymaking. The state provided support for a technological upgrade, production, and export processes for the largest family-owned enterprises, called *chaebols*. The support provided was performance-based. When a *chaebol* was not meeting performance standards, the state withdrew support and transferred it to another family-owned enterprise (Amsden, 1989; Chang, 1990, 1993). The industrial development of Vietnam in the period 1986–2012 was determined significantly by the SBRs, as the state built close relationships with businesses to create strong reform coalitions (Vu-Thanh, 2014). Johnson (1987) states that South Korea and Taiwan's economic performances were the outcomes of institutional settings combining the autonomy of bureaucracy and administrative guidance with interaction with large-scale business groups. Amsden (1989) also credits the dynamics between two fundamental institutions—reciprocity between big businesses and the state and behaviour of diversified business groups—to improve economic performance. In Indonesia, state intervention through SBRs encouraged oil palm agribusinesses to increase employment and support economic development (Bissonnette, 2013). Since the 1980s, the Indonesian government has introduced aggressive development policies to ensure a continuous increase in palm oil production for export (Hawkes, 2006, p. 38). In 1984, palm oil's globally increased demand led state plantation companies to implement the first smallholding oil palm agribusiness programme (Zahari et al., 2006). In most cases, this programme presupposed a partnership between the state, a private oil palm company, and a financial institution. The project had unintended outcomes that have resulted both from weak planning and from insufficient mechanisms of monitoring (Bissonnette, 2013).

The limited number of quantitative studies examines SBRs through macro and micro lenses. At the macro level, the studies explore the links between SBRs and economic growth, and at the micro-level, they look for the relationship between SBRs and firm-level total factor productivity (TFP). Evidence from Asian and African countries indicates a positive relationship at both levels, meaning that SBRs lead to higher economic growth and firm productivity (te Velde, 2013). The improvement of SBRs contributes to enhancing the rate and productivity of investment and hence to economic growth (Sen, 2013d). Sen and te Velde (2009) explore the role of *strategic SBRs* in 19 Sub-Saharan African countries. The outcome of their research indicates that controlling for other determinants of economic growth, the improvement of SBRs in the period 1970–2004 led to higher economic growth (Sen and te Velde, 2009). Identical results are derived by Cali and Sen (2012), using quantitative measures of SBRs for 16 Indian states, where the improvement of SBRs in the period 1985–2006 significantly increased economic growth at the subnational level. In Zambia, state–business dialogues on the fiscal policy provided the information that enabled policymakers to devise more targeted taxes and expenditures and strengthen transparency and accountability of the state budget. The state formalized consultations by establishing a budget reform coalition with the Zambia Business Forum (Bwalya et al., 2011). In the case of Ethiopia, state–business coordination facilitated the involvement of local firms in the global cut-flower value chain (Gebreeyesus and Lizuka, 2012). The case of Mauritius is in line with this trend as well, as the quantitative research revealed the significant and positive impact of the SBRs on short-term and long-term output (Rojid and Seetanah, 2013).

SBRs supported output growth mainly through the enhancement of private investments, the openness of economies, and the quality of labour (Lemma and te Velde, 2017). Qureshi and te Velde (2012) use firm-level data from seven Sub-Saharan African countries (Benin, Ethiopia, Madagascar, Malawi, Mauritius, South Africa, and Zambia), which illustrate that *strategic SBRs* positively contribute to firm productivity. A similar impact of SBRs on firm productivity in the cases of Ghana, India, and Zambia is found by Ackah et al. (2010), Kathuria et al. (2013), and Hampwaye and Jeppesen (2014). Ackah et al. (2010), via a panel data analysis of 256 Ghanaian firms for the period 1991–2002, explore that *strategic* SBRs correlate positively with firm performance, as the collaboration between policymakers and businesses resulted in a more optimal allocation of resources in an economy, leading to better firm productivity. Also, Qureshi and te Velde (2013), studying the SBRs' impact on firm performance based on a World Bank Enterprise Survey data for 200 firms in Zambia, explored that membership in a business association enhances firm productivity between 37 % and 41 %, in cases when the umbrella organization has a high capacity to lobby. It is worth mentioning that while statistical evidence that relies on country level panels and country case studies indicate associations between *strategic SBRs* and economic growth, they have significant limitations to establish causality due to endogeneity. This is because, with economic growth, the private sector grows and diversifies as well, and is more capable of coordinating its obstacles, needs and activities with the state; hence, the effectiveness of SBRs improves too (te Velde, 2006). Therefore, the direction of causality between these two variables remains a matter of empirical debate.

Steer and Sen (2008) explore SBRs in the case of transition economies. The research outcomes show that formalized institutions of SBRs are often absent in the case of transition economies. However, informal institutions are crucial for the economic exchange to take place and for firms to invest and grow. It appears that informal institutions of SBRs are essential instruments of risk management in the case of transition economies, as firms acquire information and trust through long-term relationships, and social and business networks are essential reputation mechanisms. However, informal institutions may be less effective if personal and professional ties are not distinct, like in the case of the Pacific region (Peiffer, 2012a), as well as if there is limited institutional memory both in the state and business due to frequent changes, as in the case of Samoa (ADB, 2008).

2.2. Characteristics of the *Strategic SBRs*

The diversity in the design of institutions of SBR results in the diversity of the outcomes of state business interactions. As discussed in the literature, SBRs entailed successful state intervention in economic activities in East Asian countries. However, in some Latin American countries, they resulted in the inefficient use of rents. East Asian countries observed the presence of *strategic SBRs*, featuring the collaboration of political elites, businesses, and bureaucrats to address firm, industry, sector-specific coordination and information failures, which had distracted growth and investment flows (Doner and Schneider, 2000). Based on the evidence from emerging economies of East Asia and Latin America, Schneider and Maxfield (1997) explore the common characteristics of *strategic SBRs*, which determined the effectiveness of state interventions. These characteristics are information exchange, reciprocity, credibility and trust between state and private actors and an enacted feedback mechanism for initiated policies and programmes.

An information exchange component of SBRs contributes to elaborating more targeted state policies and private investment (Campos and Root, 1996). The evidence from *strategic SBRs* indicates that the SBRs aimed to build an institutional framework that maintains an ongoing dialogue between the state and businesses and strengthens the capability to address obstacles and economic opportunities selectively, identified through state–business dialogues (Sen, 2015). On the one hand, businesses provided information on the needs they faced and the feedback on state policies and programmes. On the other hand, the state informed the private actors regarding the policy and market conditions, which were essential while making investment decisions (Schneider and Maxfield, 1997). For information exchange between the state and business, Japan, Korea, Singapore, Malaysia, Thailand, and to a lesser extent, Hong Kong established deliberation councils. These councils promoted the flow of information, clarified the division of rents among the elites, signalled a commitment to the announced policies, and provided ways for the private sector to participate in economic policymaking. In Taiwan and Indonesia, the states undertook these activities without the establishment of formal deliberation councils. Taiwan depended on indirect mechanisms for coordinating public and private sector activities, and Indonesia relied on an informal tool (Campos and Root, 1996).

Institutional frameworks to achieve information exchange differ among countries, ranging from formal, regular meetings to informal, spontaneous ones. In some cases, formality matters, such as in Japan and Singapore. In other cases, such as the reform programme in Vietnam, informal arrangements, rules, and norms dominate (Lemma and te Velde, 2017). The major formal mechanism for information exchange in *strategic SBRs* was deliberation councils, among which Japan's deliberation councils were the most well developed and widely recognized (Campos and Root, 1996). The Japanese deliberation councils, set up by the state in the late 1940s, were linked with specific bureaus within the corresponding ministries. There are two types of deliberation councils: functional or thematic and industry/sector-specific. The councils are a forum where government officials and representatives from the private sector/industry, academia, the press, and the labour force exchange views on policy matters, discuss trends in markets and products and share other relevant information. The policy formulation process is institutionalized. At the initial stage, the Ministry of International Trade and Industry (MITI) organizes meetings with various parties to gather data. Based on these data, MITI drafts a report that goes to the appropriate research group at MITI that prepares a discussion in the appropriate council. The council considers and incorporates the views of businesses, academics, consumers, and other interested parties into a plan. The research group then makes changes to the report based on the feedback from council members. The last stage of the process resembles an advertising campaign through which MITI explains to the general public the objectives and reasons for the new policy (Campos and Root, 1996).

Deliberation councils also served as the major formal mechanism for information exchange in South Korea. Between the 1960s and 1980s, when the economy observed rapid economic growth, South Korean SBRs were characterized by monthly, weekly, and sometimes even daily meetings for information exchange, rent allocation, and business participation in policymaking (Chang, 1993b). Through these meetings, deliberation councils extracted the necessary information from exporters and producers to formulate better export promotion policies and to allocate rents—that is, credit subsidies and production licenses-in a systematic, transparent, and objective fashion (Amsden, 1989). The business elites were the principal information source on the feasibility of the economic transformation goals and the state's primary partner in the economic transformation process. In turn, the state was the information source for business elites on export opportunities, sectoral markets, labour market conditions, and other vital issues for investment planning (Maxfield and Schneider, 1997). Like in Japan, there were two categories of meetings in Korea, the functional and the sectoral. The functional meetings were centered around presenting various viewpoints from known experts on topics usually identified and chosen by the bureaucracy. The state bureaucrats usually just listened to expert opinions. Even though the bureaucracy made the final decision, the adopted policies generally attempted to incorporate various viewpoints. The sectoral meetings involved representatives from the relevant industry who discussed their perspectives on an issue with representatives from the Ministry of Trade and Industry. At this level, the outcome was gathering information rather than collaborative decision-making (Campos and Root, 1996). Through formal meetings and informal consultations, the information exchange reduced private enterprises' risks to engage in export activity. The information exchange mechanism enabled the state to ensure that the right signals were received by the right managers (Doner and Schneider, 2000). It shaped businesses' expectations regarding the state policy course and gave enhanced credibility to the state regarding the political commitments to specific courses of action.

In Thailand's case, the National Joint Public and Private Consultative Committee (NJPPCC), a formalised public and private sector collaboration mechanism, was established in 1981. The formalisation of SBRs aimed to overcome the tradition of mistrust between the state and businesses, wherein the belief was that the SBRs served only those few, who had massive financial resources or good personal connections with high-ranking officials. Through the creation of NJPPPC, under-the-table dealings were reduced by the availability of on-the-table consultation (Laothamatas, 1992, p. 82). NJPPCC discussed development policies jointly and openly with high-ranking government officials and private sector representatives from the Thai Chamber of Commerce (TCO), the Federation of Thai Industries (FTI), and the Thai Bankers Association (TBA). The Thai consultative meetings differed from the meetings in Japan and Korea. Only matters of general interest—the problems that applied to most, if not all, large firms—were discussed. Thai meetings were also open to the press, putting pressure on the Prime Minister to respond to proposed reforms from businesses. Among the innovations that occurred because of the NJPPCC dialogue was the development of graduate education in modern business management, incentives for family firms to go public by issuing equity, and establishing standards for disclosure investment by multinationals being encouraged to form joint ventures with Thai firms.

The SBRs are not formalised in the case of Vietnam (Vu-Thanh, 2014). Despite this, in the 1990s and 2000s, the state interacted with businesses and experts daily and conducted field visits at the local level to observe the economy closely. In addition to the informal meetings, regular annual meetings were organized as well. The purpose of these meetings was to understand the problems distracting private sector activities and to build trust. In China, local governments interact with individual clusters and frequently communicate with local entrepreneurs, who maintain local government-devised policies to target specific industries

(Dinh, 2017). In Malaysia, a lack of confidence between the state and business actors prevented the emergence of *strategic SBRs* until the early 1990s. In the phase of a New Development Policy (NDP) since 1986, big businesses have been given the primary role of leading the country's development. More recently, advisory groups for certain sectors were formed. Each group included representatives from industry and government. The members help to formulate policies and to develop strategies for implementation. Finally, the Malaysian Business Council (MBC) was established, facilitating direct communication between big business, labour, and the Prime Minister. The council serves as a convenient channel for collecting relevant information from and distributing it to its participants. The council also helps reduce the opportunities for and welfare losses from rent-seeking (Campos and Root, 1996; Torii, 2003).

In Mauritius, a successful case of *strategic SBRs* in Africa (Bräutigam and Diolle, 2009), the essential element of SBRs' design was the institutionalization of the Joint Economic Council (JEC) in 1970, which provided a forum for regular opportunities for meaningful consultation between the state and businesses. The meetings in the JEC allowed the private sector to express concerns about the economic policies and to normalize expectations regarding the institutionalized SBRs, rather than informal personal meetings between political and business leaders. The latter contributed to minimizing the risk of collusion and predatory engagement (Handley, 2008).

The second component of *strategic SBRs*, referred to as reciprocity by Amsden (1989), a support/performance bargain by Evans (1997) and carrots and sticks by Rodrik (2004), implies disciplining business via assigning specific performance standards, such as improvement in terms of productivity, quality and export in direct exchange for subsidies provided by the state. In practice, in many cases, the state has been unable to monitor the implementation of such performance requirements and to take appropriate actions when businesses cannot meet performance standards (Lall, 1992). In the 1960s–1990s, SBRs in East Asia typically had both elements: the state provided subsidies and disciplined businesses (Amsden, 1989; Wade, 1990). In South Korea, e.g., the state provided generous credit subsidies, and the Taiwanese state gave tax incentives for business activities, but both states also set performance standards. In South Korea, the export performance was used to allocate preferential credit and determine who would get licenses from the state to produce promoted products (Amsden, 1989). The state punished the businesses that could not meet the conditioned performance via a withdrawal of subsidies or other mechanisms. The reciprocity feature of SBRs, while allowing failures as well, incentivized many new economic activities in the cases of East Asia in the 1950s–1980s. Both South Korea and Taiwan greatly benefited from export subsidies during the 1960s–1970s. By making state support conditional on export performance, these countries set up the right incentives for firms to enhance productivity.

However, in Latin American countries, states provided too many carrots and too few sticks. As Rodrik (2009) explores, Latin American states provided significant incentives (trade protection and cheap credit) but failed to exert discipline on the beneficiaries. Providing support without disciplining business generated some successful cases, but it also kept many unproductive firms. In the 1980s–1990s, the state started disciplining businesses, but it provided too few incentives to invest in new activities. In Uruguay, the state created incentives by providing support for new economic activities in a wide variety of tradable sectors: meat, rice, soybeans, forestry, pulp and paper, ports, tourism, software, and business services. However, the created incentives did not aim to overcome existing market failures. Besides, they did not set performance indicators. The result was that existing programmes were not always well targeted and varied in effectiveness (Rodrik, 2009). In Chile's case, the state did not discipline the losers, and most of the successes of Fundacion Chile, including the salmon industry, paid for the entire budget of the many failed cases of the supporting industries (Rodrik, 2009).

The African case studies suggest that rewards are often present while rules and referees are not. Gebreeyesus and Iizuka (2012) state that even in the Ethiopian flower industry, one of the region's outstanding state intervention successes, the government made thousands of hectares of very cheap land available floriculture. However, not all investors developed the land they acquired from the government, preferring to hold it in anticipation of rising land values.

Both design features of *strategic SBRs* discussed above (information exchange and reciprocity) require mutual trust between the state and businesses (Maxfield and Schneider, 1997). As Schneider (2013) states, in the most successful cases of SBRs, trust between the state and businesses was built, not only through setting up formal institutions for SBRs but also via spontaneous meetings. In some cases, trust developed through formal mechanisms, such as regular meetings determined by deliberation councils. In others, it developed through informal mechanisms, such as networks of friends and contacts between state and private actors. In some countries, informal meetings later became coordinated through a set of institutions that upgraded over time to suit the needs and political circumstances better. For example, in India in the 1960s–1970s, the state followed a command-and-control approach to the private sector that led to collusive SBRs and negatively affected economic performance (Bhagwati, 1993). The state's strong anti-business attitude created distrust between the state and private actors (Kohli, 2007). In the 1980s, with government change, the state started the promotion of economic growth and building alliances between the political and economic elites (Kohli, 2009). The state signalled to domestic businesses its intention to commit credibly to supporting the private sector (De Long, 2003). The state puts these signals into action through slow but steady liberalization of import controls, especially on capital and intermediate goods. The credibility of commitments to verbal signals transformed distrust from mutual distrust to more collaborative and synergistic SBRs. Since 1985, the state further strengthened trust by bringing new economic elites from the emerging sectors (IT and engineering) into the relationship that the political elite had with the business sector. The latter broadened the network of business elites with the state (Mehta and Walton, 2014). Hence, the trust contributed to collaborative SBRs, which in turn resulted in a significant increase in private investment from the mid-1980s and enhanced India's economic growth (Sen, 2013d).

The literature suggests that trust between the state and the private sector is an essential factor for the state's credible commitments to policies, deals, or arrangements, crucial to *strategic SBRs* (Maxfield and Schneider, 1997). In the case of *strategic SBRs*, e.g., in East Asian economies, the state was highly committed to the coordination agenda. Senior public officials, being responsible for the coordination programmes, were publicly committed to economic development outcomes. In Japan, the powerful technocratic bureaucracy's early industrialization effort was followed by consistent pro-industry and pro-export policies (Johnson, 1982). In Indonesia, South Korea, Malaysia, and Singapore, the head of state or government credibly committed to announcements and programmes. East Asian leaders secured economic elites' support without compromising sound policy through mechanisms designed to facilitate consultation, cooperation, and coordination (Campos and Root, 1996). Once established, the country's export orientation was difficult to alter. Firms had come to expect significant rewards for success in exporting and thus had oriented their production, management, and marketing capabilities to world markets. Changing the game rules would have had severe consequences for firms' operations and, thus, on economic growth. The councils in Korea helped make export policies durable and credible to the private sector, coordinating the move from an inward-looking, protectionist trade regime to an outward-oriented one, and institutionalizing a process that made exporting virtually irreversible. Councils were especially important during the first two decades of Japanese democracy as a method for the bureaucracy to break with past credibility problems. Councils allowed the bureaucracy to claim to be representative of a constituent group (Johnson, 1982). Before 1981, in Thailand's case, the state and business relationships observed a lack of trust.

The public sector regarded the private sector as selfish entrepreneurs who focused on their profits, with little sense of social responsibility. On the other hand, the private sector suspected government officials of being extremely inefficient, corrupt, and bureaucratic. In the early 1980s, the establishment of the National Joint Public and Private Consultative Committee was partly to help overcome the tradition of mistrust by creating a mechanism for public and private sector collaboration (Laothamatas, 1992).

In the case of non-successful SBRs, e.g., in African countries, there has been a lack of credible commitment from the state (Aryeetey and Owoo, 2015). In Ghana, the political elite expresses support for the private sector in speeches, but they rarely transform that expression of support into reality. There is a lack of coherence within the government to follow up on the outcome of public-private dialogue or provided feedback and to implement the decisions. In cases when the top leadership has been engaged, e.g., in Uganda, the state regularly implemented the decisions. In cases when the top leadership has shown little engagement, inadequate implementation is observed, which is often ascribed to a lack of capability in the public administration (Aryeetey and Owoo, 2015).

Another critical feature of *strategic SBRs* is employing a feedback mechanism for state policies and programmes. In cases of *strategic SBRs*, states experimented with policies or programmes in local contexts and monitored initially defined performance indicators on implemented actions or policies and requested feedback from the private sector (Page and Tarp, 2017). The feedback mechanisms included observing economic performance regarding job creation, output, and exports (Kim, 2011). They took into account the received feedback in the policy-making process. If they failed, the policies or programmes were either modified or abandoned. If they succeeded, they were replicated in other settings.

2.3. Institutional Prerequisites for the Emergence of *Strategic SBRs*

Even though the literature widely acknowledges the role of *strategicstate–business relations* for the diversification and growth of an economy, many countries face the emergence of collusive rather than *strategic SBRs* (Chingaipe, 2013). This subsection reviews the research that seeks to understand the conditions under which *strategic SBRs* emerge and the conditions that keep them from degenerating into collusive ones. Most of this research is qualitative and theoretical. The qualitative research mostly seeks to understand the terms under which *strategic SBRs* emerged in East Asian developmental states. The literature has recently been enriched during the last three decades with case studies on Latin American, African, and South Asian countries.

Evidence from the literature shows that the continuing presence of a autonomous state agency has been a necessary prerequisite for the emergence of the *strategic SBRs*. Such an agency, on the one hand, is in charge of creating incentives for investment. On the other hand, it embeds businesses in policy or investment programme elaboration, mediates business interests and political goals of the ruling elites, and remains shielded from business or political elites' pressures. One more critical prerequisite is the bureaucrats' capability, which in turn depends on institutionalized and organizationally consistent hiring criteria and career ladders that give them the motivation to perform effectively (Evans, 1995, 2010).

As Lin (2011) states, some emerging East Asian economies had state agencies that linked the state and businesses. These are agencies like Malaysia's Performance Management and Delivery Unit (PMDU), the Committee on Economic Development Acceleration and Expansion of Indonesia (CEDAE), the National Development Reform Commission of China (NDRC), the National Steering Committee on Information and Communication Technology of Vietnam (NSCICT), and Deliberation Councils (DC) in Korea and Japan (Page, 2017). In Malaysia, the state facilitated the emergence of a synergistic relationship with businesses by establishing the Penang Development Corporation (PDC) to achieve success in export and technological upgrading. Even though PDC was a state agency, it remained independent from political elites. While creating an export hub in Penang, PDC developed links between local businesses and multinationals and addressed existing bottlenecks in skills development and infrastructure. Penang has become a significant export hub for electronics (Athukorala, 2014).

In the East Asian developmental states, the economic administrations' embedded autonomy discouraged rent-seeking, and reciprocity distinguished them from the less successful Latin American, African, and South Asian states (Evans, 1995, 2012). Specific institutional arrangements shielded the administration from pressure stemming from various sources, including organized societal interest groups, entrepreneurs and their rent-seeking efforts (Cheng et al., 1998, p. 88), and the generally short-term populist interests raised by ordinary politics (Haggard, 2004, p. 60). The bureaucrats intervened selectively, provided subsidies for technological upgrading and innovation in selected firms, and disciplined them to meet performance requirements concerning export and capability advancement (Bardhan, 2005).

In Africa, in order to create incentives for investment and to mediate business interest and political goals, Presidential Investors' Advisory Councils (PIAC) were established in Ghana, Tanzania, and Senegal in 2002, and Mali, Uganda, Mauritius, and Benin in 2004. Ethiopia launched a Public-Private Consultative Forum (PPCF) in 2010. The PIACs primarily aimed to coordinate with business leaders to understand the obstacles to investment and develop strategies to address the identified constraints (Page and Tarp, 2017). Gomez-Mera et al. (2014) find that once investors have decided to enter a specific market, PIACs appear to be a widely used and valuable resource, especially for smaller and less productive firms in Africa. Despite this, PIACs in Africa were less effective than those more successful counterparts in East Asia due to a lack of coordination within governments (Page and Tarp, 2017). In South Africa, (Page and Tarp, 2017), the new parliament established a National Economic Development and Labour Council (NEDLC), a legal, social partnership council modeled on Singapore's deliberation council, but it could not function effectively. Labour, businesses, and the state met, discussed challenges, jointly commissioned policy research, and agreed on policy recommendations. However, they had weak cooperation and trust with each other. In Ethiopia, a Government and Business Community Joint Consultation Forum (GBCJCF) was established on the government's initiative in 2002 (Gebreeyesus and Iizuka, 2012). The forum ceased in 2005 when a lack of government support and political unrest led to its complete abandonment. Though this forum collapsed, the state continued to run highly structured consultations with private investors in priority areas such as cut flowers, leather, and textiles. Meetings with investors in these subsectors were frequent and attended by senior government officials, including, many times, the Prime Minister. Actions were agreed and followed up, often on the spot.

In addition to the presence, length, and architecture of state agencies, the capability of bureaucrats involved in those agencies determines the development of *strategic SBRs*. A defining characteristic of East Asian investment promotion agencies was the bureaucrats' high capability, who was responsible for the implementation of the decisions. The bureaucrats' high capability was maintained through a strict recruitment policy and attractive, long-term career models (Evans, 1995).

In the East Asian developmental states, implementing a merit-based recruitment or promotion system was an essential step towards sustaining competent performance. Three broad types of merit-based systems can be distinguished among those countries. The first, exemplified by the Japanese and Korean systems, is more formally institutionalized. The public sector recruits staff based on a challenging civil service exam and promotes them based on proven ability.

Applicants are not required to have a college degree, but in practice, it is challenging to pass the exams without training at a well-established university. The second, which is also highly institutionalized, is exemplified by Singapore's system. They recruit according to high standards of academic performance (at undergraduate level) and rigorous personal interviews. Promotions are based on performance rather than seniority. Reaching the highest level of service, permanent secretary, can occur at a relatively young age—there are cases when individuals in their thirties got this position. Indonesia and Thailand, where exams are very perfunctory, and thus an ineffective filtering device, exemplify the third type of recruitment system. There, the filters tend to complete graduate degrees, primarily a Ph.D. from a foreign institution. Not surprisingly, these countries' bureaucracies have also been the weakest among the East Asian developmental states (Johnson, 1982; Campos and Root, 1996). The Taiwanese and Malaysian systems fall into the first category. In Taiwan, civil service exams are not as strict as in Japan and Korea. However, the constant recruitment of academics from major universities, usually for fixed periods ranging from 3–6 years, offsets the weakness of those exams. The foreign graduate degree filter, therefore, supplements the exams. In Malaysia, the results of the civil service exams are subject to affirmative action requirements. Hence, in each system, some mechanisms to identify the most competent individuals are employed to recruit the economic bureaucracy. Tough exams, academic performance, and doctoral degrees determine the selection from among a given crop of applicants (Campos and Root, 1996).

The compensation influences the potential pool of applicants for jobs for public office. Comparisons between the public sector and private sector salaries are complex. In general, however, although civil servants nearly everywhere are less well paid than their private-sector counterparts (Singapore is a notable exception), the differential between civil servants' salaries and private sector salaries is smaller in the mentioned countries than in other developing countries. Moreover, there are frequently other advantages of public sector employment in the high-performing East Asian countries, which attract competent candidates who might otherwise choose private employment. Although used mainly to establish competency in the economic bureaucracy, the merit-based recruitment and promotion system also helped secure the economic bureaucracy members the necessary independence to do their jobs. By establishing rules for appointments, the system gives bureaucrats confidence that they cannot quickly be demoted, fired, or prevented from being promoted simply because their decisions conflict with those of powerful private sector interests (Campos and Root, 1996).

In many developing countries, influential groups and even individuals can ask politicians to press a civil servant to alter a decision that they do not like. Because politicians may influence the career of a civil servant, the latter must often leave the bureaucracy. A merit-based system reduces such politically motivated interventions. In light of the established rules, politicians would have to justify exerting pressure. The system also gives politicians a convenient and valid excuse for refusing to mediate on a supporter's behalf. In Japan, an institutionalized independent agency that deals with personnel matters supplement the merit system. This is the National Personnel Authority (NPA), which is one of only two executive agencies unattached to any ministry and independent of the legislature. Its principal function is to formulate and administer personnel policies that govern recruitment and promotion in the bureaucracy. It administers the highly competitive civil service examinations and determines the pay scales and pay increases of bureaucrats. It evaluates and approves recommendations for promotion, and it hears and decides upon grievances (Campos and Root, 1996).

In addition to the structure and the capability of the state bureaucracy, the literature highlights a diversified and dynamic private sector as another necessary condition for the emergence of *strategic SBRs*. In Korea and Thailand, large corporations operated in several areas of the economy. In Mauritius and Taiwan, many small and medium-sized firms dominated the growth-oriented sectors of the economy (Maxfield and Schneider, 1997).

Another crucial element for the emergence of *strategic SBRs* is the continuing presence of umbrella organizations (UO), which link or associate businesses with similar interests at the economy, sector, or industry level, and lobby their members' interests with the state (te Velde, 2006). UOs are divided into three categories: those, which include large enterprises and lobby the interests of big businesses, those that include small businesses, including Chambers of Commerce, and those that unite the enterprises from specific sectors or industries. Empirical research shows that UOs in developing countries have multiple functions and activities. They interact with the state to address crucial issues for private sector development, including strengthening property rights, building horizontal and vertical value chains, addressing information asymmetry and coordination failures, and capacity building of members. The contributions of the UOs can be divided into two types: market supporting, which are the activities that promote property rights, infrastructure, and cleaner bureaucracies; and market complementing, which are the activities ranging from reducing inflation to setting standards for agricultural exports, promoting training, and supporting value chain building (Doner and Schneider, 2000).

In Columbia, the coffee association *Federacafe* lobbied for the right to spend the budget collected from an export tax by the state on benefits for producers, especially transportation infrastructure, port facilities, and warehouses. In Turkey, the Turkish Clothing Manufacturers' Association (TGSD) was created to manage a quota system, elaborate rules for the distribution of rents, and link them to performance. Taiwan's footwear industry offers a striking case of such functions. In 1976–1977, in response to the imposition of an Orderly Market Agreement by the USA, seven associations formed the Taiwan Footwear Manufacturers' Association (TFMA) intending to restructure the industry through upgrade-driven competition. Some umbrella organizations lead to market diversification and specialization. In Colombia, *Federacafe* used inventory management to soften international price fluctuations, reserving coffee stocks when the market price was low and selling the reserves when prices were high. The UOs have also contributed to overcoming supply, price, and quality-related coordination problems between upstream and downstream firms. In Thailand, the umbrella organizations, prompted by the state, overcame coordination problems in the sugar industry, which for years had been hamstrung by the fight of sugar millers and producers over the price of raw sugar. The associations helped to broker an arrangement acceptable to both and avoid disruptions of critical sugar exports. In other cases, the stabilization of upstream-downstream relations has helped promote dynamic efficiency by encouraging investment in new capacities and adopting new standards and technologies. In Taiwan's athletic shoe industry, the downstream footwear producers realized that the supplied inputs' quality was crucial for continued export growth. The Taiwan Plastic Shoe Exporters' Association (TPSEA) supported downstream shoe firms to coordinate their needs with upstream plastic firms. In turn, the latter gained an institutional channel to get information on the development of a downstream industry (Doner and Schneider, 2000).

One more crucial function of UOs that contributes to emergence of *strategic SBRs* is collecting and disseminating information on new markets, domestic and export, and elaborating and setting the standards for exporters, based on the requirements of the targeted export markets. In the 1950s, Thailand's Board of Trade, the major umbrella organization of agricultural exporters, organized its rice-exporting members to develop and adhere to product standards. The Thai government provided export licenses only to those producers who were members of the associations and complying with these standards. In Columbia, coffee exporters created labels to distinguish the different categories of the exported coffee. Columbia faced the issue of low-quality producers using the labels of high-quality coffee. Later, the coffee producers association *Federacafe* got the power to sanction miscreants, making the labeling standard effective (Doner and Schneider, 2000).

Quality upgrading is a related function that moves beyond providing members with information to using association incentives to change members behaviours by improving their technology and their workforces' skills. In the 1960s, the Colombian government promoted rice producers' association with the same exchange used in coffee: the government granted the rice association the proceeds of an export tax. The association was then used to promote the dissemination of required seed varieties. In the late 1960s and early 1970s, Colombian producers converted to new varieties much more quickly than other significant exporters (Doner and Schneider, 2000).

There is a literature gap on essential organizational attributes of business associations in developing countries, even in studies on their contributions. The empirical reviews suggest three essential and interrelated features: high membership density, extensive selective benefits, and effective internal interest mediation (especially for the largest members). Associations with one of these three features may be somewhat more robust than those with none, but these three attributes build the capacity. Staff and material resources seem to be a fourth factor (Doner and Schneider, 2000, p. 261).

Qureshi and te Velde (2012) reveal evidence from Africa. For example, in Zambia, becoming part of a business association allowed SMEs to participate in dialogue with the state and other businesses and bring the obstacles they faced in their activities. In Mauritius, Zambia, and Zimbabwe (Bräutigam et al., 2002), business associations had the capacity, credibility, and resources to represent a range of business interests through regular consultations. The activities of business associations contributed significantly to strengthening the effectiveness of SBRs, which in turn contributed to an increase in firms' productivity. Aryeetey and Owoo (2015) argue that the establishment of the Association of Ghana Industries (AGI) and the Private Enterprise Federation (PEF) maintained increased state business dialogue. Gebreeyesus and Iizuka (2012) point out that the private sector revealed the Ethiopian flower industry's potential. The Flower Growers' Association (FGA) was self-organized, and its aims were not merely to access rents from the state, but to address at resolving coordination problems. In contrast, in the Ethiopian metals sector with highly diversified industries, the initial idea of establishing an industry association came from the state and not from the private sector. The association's objectives were too broad, such as to develop a feasible industry action plan, and the association's activities mainly focused on lobbying the government for support (Sen, 2013).

One more crucial element for the emergence of *strategic SBRs* is the existence of an active channel for state–business dialogue and information exchange (Doner and Schneider, 2000; te Velde, 2006). The East Asian developmental states elaborated mechanisms for the interaction between state and society, allowing the private sector to contribute effectively in the policymaking process. The experience suggests that consultative committees may fail to produce similar results in other developing countries unless a reputable economic bureaucracy exists to impose discipline among private sector members of a council (Campos and Root, 1996). The literature suggests that the existence of proper channels for dialogue between the state and businesses gives businesses a voice that they would otherwise not have and provide the state with a sounding board that can improve the quality of policymaking (Herzberg and Wright, 2013). However, if this mechanism is not sufficiently transparent, SBRs might lead to rent-seeking behaviour (te Velde, 2013).

In East Asia, such channels (deliberation councils) facilitated communication between the state and businesses by offering input into the policy processes and, at the same time, providing ownership of policy outcomes. These channels were designed to reduce the high transaction costs of coordination, overcome asymmetric information and rent-seeking, stabilize the policy environment, and legitimize economic policies. More specifically, its cooperative format reduced the cost of obtaining and transmitting information about the design, implementation, and modification of existing policies. Besides, it provided the private sector with a transparent forum to bargain over the rules that determine rent allocation. Moreover, it gave the state a mechanism to build confidence among investors that the government would not change policies without appropriate consultation and support from the private sector. Thus, the councils created a channels for the government to establish the legitimacy of their policies. As discussed, these councils varied by country and sectors (Campos and Root, 1996).

Some studies find that the economic ideology of the key political actors and the intention to nurture a collaborative relationship with the private sector is critical for the emergence of *strategic SBRs* (Leftwich, 2009). The literature emphasizes that the ruling elites' long-term commitment to stable relations with economic actors is a precondition for *strategic SBRs* (Buur and Whitfield, 2013). Such long-term commitment is less likely to emerge in countries with weak governments, as in such contexts ruling elites mainly concentrate on short-term political survival and strategies, which constrains their ability to commit credibly to businesses which would be prepared and able to make long-term investments (Buur and Whitfield, 2013).

2.4. Conclusion

Much of the earlier discussions on state intervention in economic activities were focused on the ideological approaches rather than the institutional design of the intervention (te Velde and Lemma, 2017). More recently, empirical studies on the role of SBRs in the process of state intervention and the institutional settings for the *strategic SBRs* have evolved. The strand of this research started in the mid-1990s, further developed in the 2000s, and gained more general acceptance in the 2010s. The empirical evidence on SBRs has been mostly based on East Asia, Latin America, and in some Sub-Saharan African countries (Batcha, 2012). However, in the post-communist countries, role of institutions, and among them, SBRs, has mostly been neglected in empirical analyses. This thesis focuses on the case of Georgia, a small open transition economy in the post-Communist region. Hence, this thesis contributes to regional studies and transitions studies with a number of terms.

To begin with, thpublication contributes to empirical studies of state interventions in transition countries. Georgia is of particular interest, as a policy shift is observed since 2008. There have been increasing interventions in the economy. In addition to that, the state has begun to substitute its earlier commitment to neoliberal policies with active state led policies to promote economic and social development. Chapter V presents a comprehensive analysis of the policy shift in the 2004–2016 and instruments of state intervention in Georgia's food and agricultural sector. Next, by exploring the institutions of state agribusiness relations, the study contributes to the cutting-edge, controversial, and policy-relevant academic debates about the role of institutions of state-business relations in the process of state intervention in economic activities. It provides a comprehensive analysis of the actors' behaviors, state and businesses, the rules behind the behavior, and their enforcement. Also, it explores the institutional prerequisites for the emergence of *strategic SBRs*. In addition, this publication contributes to empirical studies on the nature and functions of the umbrella organisations, that associate businesses at sub-sector or sector levels. It provides a comprehensive analysis of the business associations' nature and structure at the economy, sector, and sub-sector level. The research also explores the motives of establishing the business associations at the sub-sector, sector, or economy level and their role to mediate business and state interest. Furthermore, the manuscript contributes to the empirical studies of agricultural economics in the post-Communist region. It provides a comprehensive analysis of the sector's potential for development and obstacles that distract the process of it. Moreover, the study provides an analysis of the sector's performance in 2004–2016 to observe the changes in the sector's performance since the state started active intervention.

Chapter III Theoretical Considerations and Operationalisation of SBRs

This chapter discusses the emergence of the theory of institutions, the impact of institutions on economic performance and the theoretical considerations of the institutional setting for maintaining state and business relations to support market functions and improve economic performance. The chapter consists of two parts: theoretical considerations and their operationalisation. The first part discusses the concepts of the institutions, their origin, their change and importance in the process of economic development from the New Institutional Economics viewpoint, and theoretical considerations on the nature of the institutions of *strategic SBRs* and the institutional settings for achieving them. The second part of the chapter discusses applying the theoretical considerations in Georgia's food and agricultural sector.

3.1. Theoretical Considerations on Institutions and Economic Performance

3.1.1. The Conceptualization of Institutions and Organizations

The emergence of the theory of institutions and their impact on economic performance is based on the recognition that macroeconomic stabilization, privatization, and price reforms are necessary but not sufficient conditions of policy reforms to maintain sustained economic growth and development. Besides, the existence of relevant political and economic institutions that reduce transaction-related uncertainties between actors in an economy creates incentives for new economic activities and investment and supports private sector development is essential (Ahrens, 2002).

In the social sciences, the idea that institutions matter for economic growth and development has existed for a long time (Sen, 2013b). According to the NIE analytical branch, institutions are defined as enforceable formal and informal rules that serve distinct purposes and structure social interaction (Ahrens, 2002, p. 51). New institutionalists address questions of the nature of institutions, their evolution, institutional change, and consequences for economic performance (Ahrens, 2002, p. 50). As this research aims to understand the nature of the institutional setting of state–agribusiness interactions in Georgia, theoretical considerations of the New Institutional Economics and the institutionalist approach to SBRs are applied in the case of the food and agricultural sector of Georgia.

According to the NIE, institutions are the set of formal and informal rules and their enforcement mechanisms, which structure and constrain interactions between various parts of society (North, 1990; Ahrens, 2002). North (1990, p. 3) defines institutions as 'humanly devised constraints that shape human interactions. Constraints can be formal (written political (judicial) rules, economic rules, and contracts) and informal (sanctions, taboos, customs, traditions, norms of behaviour, codes of conduct and conventions)' (North, 1990, p. 7). These constraints are prescriptions about required, prohibited, or permitted actions, introduced to and used by a set of players in repetitive interdependent relationships (Ostrom, 1986, p. 5). Informal constraints are revealed in daily interactions, whether within the family, in external social relations, business activities, or governing structures (North, 1990, p. 36). They are part of the culture defined as the transmission of values and other factors that influence behaviours from one generation to the next (Boyd and Richerson, 1985). The purpose of the design and enforcement of an institutional matrix is to define the way the game is played (North, 1990). The players of the game are organizations, purposeful entities composed of individuals, who act to pursue shared objectives. These organizations include political bodies (regulatory agencies, city councils), economic bodies (firms, trade unions, family farms, and cooperatives), social bodies (clubs, churches, associations), and educational bodies (education, vocational training centers) (North, 1990, p. 5). Each player's objective is to win the game, with a combination of skills, strategy, coordination, fear, and sometimes foul means (North, 1990, p. 5).

An essential part of enacting institutions is the costliness of ascertaining violations and the severity of punishment (North, 1990, p. 4). For the formal and informal rules to serve as an institution, they have to constitute internal subjective beliefs shared by players. Wittgenstein (1953, p. 201) argued that creating and knowing the rules of the game is insufficient to play the game. The way of grasping the rules and following the rules enables the players to have meaningful discussions about what is required to play the game successfully. Even when the objective existence of statutory law in the law book is unquestionable, if nobody believes it is implementable or enforceable, it will not prevail as an institution (Aoki, 2006, p. 9). Therefore, it is necessary for the players to believe that the introduced rules are implementable (Aumann, 1976), whether voluntarily, through customs or traditions, or policed through an external authority and a coercive incentive system (Nabli and Nugent, 1989, p. 1335). Besides, a rule needs to be predictable and applicable in repeated and future situations (Ahrens, 2002, p. 51).

3.1.2. Institutions Matter

In the social sciences, the idea that institutions matter for economic development has existed for a long time. The role of institutions on economic development has been stressed in not only classic works such as Adam Smith's *Wealth of Nations*, and in the works of the institutionalists of the 20th century, but also the literature of modern development economics (Nabli and Nugent, 1989; Aoki, 2005; Acemoglu and Robinson, 2012). The central message of NIE is in line with the idea that factor accumulation and innovation are proximate causes of growth; the fundamental explanation in differences of growth is in differences in institutions (North and Thomas, 1973). Economic, political, and social institutions provide incentives for policy makers, bureaucrats, economic actors, and citizens (North, 1990). Acemoglu and Robinson (2012, p. 88) state that institutions that influence individuals' incentive structure and the way the economy works are the primary factors for the differences in the economic success of countries.

A consensus seems to have emerged among social scientists that institutions matter for understanding the differences in economic performances among various economies over time and space (Aoki, 2005, p. 1). When functioning effectively, institutions matter because they can be understood as devices for reducing uncertainty, simplifying decision-making processes, and promoting cooperation among players of the game so that the costs of coordinating economic and other activities are lowered (Furubotn and Richter, 2005, p. 7). Economic growth is contingent on the existence of stable but adjustable political and economic institutions (Ahrens, 2002). Economic institutions matter for economic growth, as they shape key economic players' incentive structure by influencing investment and the organization of production. Economic institutions determine not only the potential for aggregate economic growth but also a pattern of economic outcomes (Acemoglu et al., 2005). Hence, economic institutions influence not only the size of the aggregate production, but also how it is distributed among different groups of society (Acemoglu et al., 2005). Most economic institutions are made in the polity; therefore, economic institutions reflect the relative bargaining strength of political parties, individual policymakers, trade unions, business associations, and other vested interests in the political markets. Major changes in formal institutions will occur if they coincide with the interests of those who have sufficient bargaining power (Ahrens, 2002, p. 101). Consequently, institutional change, which may be in general welfare enhancing, is not necessarily feasible if this change would either presuppose a reduction of or imply a threat to existing political power or challenge the power or wealth of well-organized interest groups (Ahrens and Hoen, 2013). Hence, the emergence of organizations that support political and economic institutions favorable to sustained development is crucial (Ahrens and Hoen, 2013). As institutions influence behaviours and incentives, they forge the success or failure of nations (Acemoglu and Robinson, 2012, p. 93).

While economic institutions are critical for determining countries' economic performance, political institutions are critical to determining the country's economic institutions (Acemoglu and Robinson, 2012). A politico-institutional structure matters to make the government more effective in accomplishing its tasks. Such institutionalization, however, cannot be taken for granted (Ahrens, 2002). Secure politico-institutional foundations matter as well to limit the state's ability to mistreat the rights of businesses, which in turn is essential for the emergence of a functioning market economy and its preservation. Otherwise, if the state has coercive force, those who run the state will use that force in their interest (North, 1990, p. 59). 'As Weingast (1993) states, the absence of a political foundation of policy reform can lead […] to reform failure despite the choice of adequate economic policies' (Ahrens, 2010, p. 22).

The lack of effective institution building in the economic and political realms represents one of the critical bottlenecks of transition and requires looking at the importance of crafting market institutions in the years ahead. Ahrens and Hoen (2013) state that institutions matter for the transition towards a market-oriented economy. In this process, old, market-impeding institutions need to be eliminated, and new, market-enhancing institutions need to come into existence. Since institutions do not only exhibit economizing but also redistributive functions, the process of institutional change, especially in times of systemic transformation, is frequently driven by the interests of those who are in power. Therefore, political institutions and actors' impact on economic reform and performance need to be explicitly addressed. In particular, institution-building needs to be driven by political actors, and hence it must be in the interest of these actors to craft those market institutions (Ahrens and Hoen, 2013).

3.1.3. The Origins of Institutions and Institutional Change

Institutions may be created (such as constitutions) or may evolve over time (like common law) (North, 1990, p. 4). Informal constraints come from socially transmitted information and are part of the heritage we call culture. Informal institutions may be sufficient to permit economic exchange within a small distance, like in a village. However, with the growth of long-distance exchange between the village residents and those located elsewhere, informal institutions would not be sufficient to maintain an economic exchange. Hence, to grow in size and scope, the economy would need to develop formal institutions (North, 1991). Formal institutions might be the product of deliberate design (introduced by the parliament, an entrepreneur, a team) (North, 1990, p. 111) or evolve spontaneously from the self-interest of individuals (Lewis, 1969). Initially, the rules are elaborated based on ideologies, understood as a comprehensive system of cognitive and moral beliefs (North, 1978, p. 973) referred to as the 'institutional environment' (Davis and North, 1971, p. 133). These ideologies are the shared framework of players' mental models as a result of genetic evolution, cultural heritage, progress in scientific knowledge, and recent experience, such as local learning (Denzau and North, 1994, p. 4). The mental models (North, 1995, p. 7) are the internal representations that individual cognitive systems create, based on the information minds receive about the institutional environment (Denzau and North, 1994). The mental models of the individuals in charge of creating institutions become external (Denzau and North, 1994), with the fundamental political, social, and legal rules that govern economic and political activity (Richter, 2015, p. 16). The created institutional matrix defines the set of available opportunities, which stimulates the development of interest groups and organizations (Ahrens, 2002). A design of behavioural rules of an institution and its enforcement rules may face problems because of the inevitability of institutional incompleteness due to a lack of knowledge about the future and the limitations of the human cognitive system (Wiggins, 1991). Therefore, one more fundamental feature of the rules is their adaptability (Ahrens, 2002). It is necessary to change both formal and informal institutions (enforce formal institutions and legitimize a new set of formal rules) in order to induce a coherent and consistent institutional matrix. However, changing informal institutions is time-consuming, so that successful policy reform can usually only be achieved through a long process (Ahrens, 2002, p. 101).

The institutional matrix might change over time through interaction between private and public actors (Eggertsson, 1998). Even if a new institution increases the private net benefit of some players, it does not mean that it increases social net benefit as well (Ahrens, 2002, p. 17). In this regard, the state might play a crucial role in the supply of institutions that benefits the economy as a whole (Ahrens, 2002). The ability of the state to promote institutional change that benefits the economy as a whole crucially depends on the institutional structure of the polity, and hence the incentives faced by policymakers (Ahrens, 2002, p. 17). Acemoglu and Robinson (2012) argue that conflict will arise between the beneficiaries and the non-beneficiaries of existing institutional settings, and different societies will resolve them in different ways. When they are resolved in favour of those who have power, extractive economic institutions will emerge. Extractive economic institutions force people to work on behalf of elites on low wages and enable them to capture all the spoils of economic activities. They are supported by extractive political institutions that concentrate power in the hands of the few without any checks. Conversely, when conflicts are resolved for the benefit of those who do not have power, inclusive institutions will emerge. Inclusive economic institutions try to include more people, secure property rights, allow people to trade so that a large part of society can participate in a market, and introduce court and justice systems to write contracts. Inclusive economic institutions need to be supported by inclusive political institutions, which creates an equal distribution of power and does not let anybody have absolute political power (Acemoglu and Robinson, 2012, p. 166).

The degree to which the rules of the game can be changed in a given time is always limited. Throughout history, dysfunctional institutions have tended to survive. The survival of dysfunctional institutions relates to collective action problems, path dependency on ideas, ideologies, and imperfect information due to players' bounded rationality (Fernandez and Rodrik, 1991; North, 1992) or high transaction costs (Lin and Nugent, 1995). North (1991) states that institutional change is a complicated process, as even a small change in institutions requires changes in rules and enforcement mechanisms, which are not effective. North (1990, p. 6) argues that while 'formal rules may change overnight as a result of political or judicial decisions, informal constraints embodied in customs, traditions, and codes of conduct are much more impervious to deliberative policies.'

Institutional change needs learning and understanding, and time is the dimension in which players learn. The players of the game are informed imperfectly on all issues, so not only is knowledge imperfect, but the information is imperfect as well. Therefore, the existence of a feedback mechanism, which maintains feedback on the beliefs, rules, and norms of behaviours, is crucial. Feedback mechanisms help actors learn from failures and correct organizational errors, and help policymakers enhance policy adaptability (Pelikan, 1986). Therefore, North (1990) introduces the concept of adaptive efficiency, which rests on the assumptions that a sufficiently flexible institutional framework will suitably adjust to a changing demographic, technological, and political environments, and will smoothly absorb exogenous shocks, is crucial for sustained economic performance.

3.2. The Institutionalist Approach to SBRs

3.2.1. The Game of SBRs: Play or Not Play?

This section aims to discuss the theoretical considerations of the institutionalist approach to SBRs. It seeks to understand the theoretical considerations on the nature of *strategic SBRs* (game) and the institutions (rules of the game), which underpin the collaboration between the state and businesses (players) to maintain sharing and utilizing information and, at the same time reduce potential economic and political risks. Institutions of SBRs are the underlying formal and informal rules and their enforcement mechanisms that govern the interaction between states and businesses (Beck and Laeven, 2005). In this context, the state includes ministries, state agencies, politicians, and bureaucrats (Batcha, 2012), and businesses refer to firms, umbrella organizations, and networks operating in an economy (Maxfield and Schneider, 1997). On the economic side, an institutional setting of SBRs refers to a set of enforced formal and informal rules to address information-related externalities and coordination failures to promote the effective allocation of resources. On the political side, it implies formal and informal rules for the state and businesses interaction and their enforcement mechanisms (Batcha, 2012, p. 382). The scope of interaction may include the whole economy or target specific sectors, types of firms, or policy processes (Leftwich, 2009). The *strategic SBRs* are supposed to contribute in overcoming two bottlenecks for successful economic performance: market failures (Stiglitz, 1996a), and government failures, due to the lack of perfect information and lack of coordination, or due to being captured by elites (Hausmann and Rodrik, 2002). *Strategic SBRs* can address mentioned bottlenecks through strategic consultations between the players, information exchange, and information utilization (te Velde, 2010).

3.2.2. The Rules of the Game of *Strategic SBRs*

Evans (1995) emphasizes the necessity for strategic cooperation between the state and business actors in the process of policy formulation and implementation. He termed the nature of the required state business interaction 'embedded autonomy' (Evans, 1995, p. 344). It indicates that, on the one hand, the state should collaborate with the private sector while elaborating and implementing policies, but on the other hand, it should have proper mechanisms to avoid capture by business interests and to serve the whole society. Ahrens (2002) also states that the close links between state and businesses may lead to nepotism, cronyism, and collusion. However, independent public administration will not be capable of overcoming coordination and market failures and effectively intervening in economic activities, if it lacks reliable information about markets, technological bottlenecks, and sectoral needs that can only be provided by businesses. Rodrik (2004), emphasizing the prominence of SBRs for state intervention to tackle the constraints the private sector faces, is in line with the concept of 'embedded autonomy.' He argues that the state has less information than private actors regarding the locations and nature of market failures that block diversification; therefore, to identify the most significant obstacles faced by the private sector, a strategic collaboration between the state and businesses is critical. Rodrik (2004) states that achieving cooperation between state and businesses requires a proper institutional setting. On the one hand, an institutional setting with too much autonomy for the bureaucrats minimizes corruption but fails to provide incentives targeted to the businesses' needs. On the other hand, too much embeddedness will result in the bureaucrats ending up in the pockets of business interests. Therefore, creating an institutional setting that enables state agents to interact with businesses to provide information regarding the created incentives, to get information on existing constraints, and at the same time, maintain an intermediate position between the full autonomy and full embeddedness of the state, is the most critical element in designing an intervention. As Rodrik (2004, p. 17) states,"once the 'right' institutional setting is in place, there is less need to worry about proper policy choices." To develop a proper institutional setting, "experimentation, willingness to depart from orthodoxy, and attention to local conditions" (Rodrik, 2003, p. 12) is required. *Strategic SBRs* depend on the interactions between business and state actors, with mechanisms that enable information exchange, ensure reciprocity, increase credibility, and establish high trust levels (Maxfield and Schneider, 1997). Besides, mechanisms that maintain feedback on intervention and follow up of provided feedback are crucial (Sen, 2013).

3.2.2.1. Information Exchange

Exchange of comprehensive information matters, as the causes of market and coordination failures are information externalities and coordination problems related to the costs of collecting and processing information about new investment opportunities (Lin and Chang, 2009; Sen, 2013c). Getting timely information from businesses gives the state an opportunity to understand the needs and intentions of private actors, elaborate more targeted policies fitting to economic reality, and predict the response of private actors to implemented policies (Maxfield and Schneider, 1997; te Velde, 2013). Policies that fit economic reality are more credible. On the other hand, the timely flow of information from the state to businesses can enhance the performance of private actors. If the state provides timely information on sectoral markets, export opportunities, labour market conditions, planned amendments in law or policies, or other issues that affect investment planning, this will give an opportunity for private actors to shape expectations and to reduce investment risks (Maxfield and Schneider, 1997). Such information can be disseminated despite close relations between the state and business; however, close relations allow officials to target recipients to ensure that the right information gets to the right managers.

Information flow from the private sector on the obstacles and needs they face in production and export processes can help elaborate policies that lower investment risks, hence creating incentives for new investment opportunities (Sen, 2015). The more comprehensive the information exchange is, the more accurately the response of businesses to the intended policy changes can be predicted, and the more likely the policies suitable to achieve the desired effects can be elaborated (Evans, 1997, 2013). Information exchange depends on state capacity to collect data from businesses and analyse it, and businesses' willingness to provide data to the state. For more focused activities, an exchange of information between the state and business is desirable at all levels of decision-making, from large as well as small and medium-sized businesses, and economy-wide as well as sector-specific or issue-specific (Herzberg and Wright, 2013). Formal rules about information exchange can be an essential help in some political and economic contexts, but mandates are never sufficient to establish a good dialogue between the state and business actors. Wherever hosted and whenever possible, the dialogue should maximize the potential of information exchange from both sides, and having a facilitator can improve the prospects of getting information (Herzberg and Wright, 2013).

The flow of comprehensive information, both formally and informally, shapes expectations about government intentions and enhances credibility of state policies by giving investors signals about political commitments to particular courses of action. By investing in data collection and processing, and by making information about new industries freely available to firms, the state can facilitate the production of new products, as well as structural change and technological upgrading in the economy (Lin and Monga, 2010).

3.2.2.2. Reciprocity

Another feature of *strategic SBRs* is reciprocity, which refers to a state's capacity to discipline business via exacting performance standards for the direct exchange of subsidies (Amsden, 1989). As North states (1984), when the game is played only once, like in a prisoner's dilemma game, it is a dominant strategy for the players to deviate (Nash, 1953; Shubik, 1970b) and, therefore, not to achieve what would have been the best possible outcome concerning the aggregate wellbeing of the players. However, when the game is repeated between the same players, the deviation from the rules is not necessarily the dominant strategy. In a continuously repeated game, players respond in kind to the action of the other players. This lead to Axelrod's celebrated evolution of cooperation (1984), an ability to devise cooperative solutions to problems. The resources need to be devoted to monitoring and applying rewards and punishment based on performance to acquire maximum returns from provided subsidies (North, 1990, p. 32). Enforcement of agreements is crucial. Due to the high value of reputation as an asset for future agreements, self-enforcement of agreements on the exchange is essential in repeated dealings. However, in economic exchange, the cost of discovering a cheater and punishing when free riding occurs—hence the cost of measurement and enforcement—make self-enforcement ineffective in many cases (North, 1990, p. 52). Hence, one cannot take enforcement for granted. It can come from internally enforced codes of conduct, societal sanctions, or a coercive third party (North, 1990, pp. 32–33). Without institutional constraints, self-interested behaviour will foreclose a complex exchange because of the uncertainty about the deviation from other players (North, 1990, p. 33). A similar approach is reflected in the reciprocity feature of state-business relations.

Economic theory states that when subsidies are available, investors will respond to get them, but the hard part is to ensure their strategic usage (Mueller, 1989). Therefore, the state needs the capacity and commitment to discipline businesses, which implies that the state provides subsidies or venture capital to encourage investments for specific activities with performance requirements and ensures that the businesses meet the performance standards in return for subsidies (Evans, 1998, p. 67). Hence, rents are based on clear performance standards, and private actors are aware of the criteria by which programme achievements are judged in advance (Amsden, 1989; Maxfield and Schneider, 1997; Rodrik, 2004). If subsidies are contingent on performance, firms have incentives to distort performance information. Performance standards that are clear and measurable reduce the opportunities to manipulate information. Export performance is easier to measure, harder to distort, and more transparent than policy goals such as technological development or increases in productivities (Maxfield and Schneider, 1997). The state may give subsidies with the requirement of specific performance to contribute to promoting development, but may not have the capacity to monitor this (Biddle and Milor, 1995). The state should monitor the subsidy recipient's activities and ensure that destructive projects are phased out

(Rodrik, 2004). Disciplining should not be too costly, because punishing only a few firms signals government intentions and establishes credibility. If the state does not enforce punishment mechanisms for the businesses that misuse subsidies, its demand for reciprocity loses credibility (Maxfield and Schneider, 1997). Reciprocity depends on state capacity to monitor firms and punish non-compliance as well as business willingness to provide information and abide by sanctions. Amsden (1989) links the reciprocity feature of SBRs to economic performance, stating that the more reciprocity that characterizes state–firm relations, the higher the speed of economic growth.

3.2.2.3. Credibility and Trust

Reciprocity cannot work well without credibility and trust between the state actors and the private actors (Maxfield and Schneider, 1997). A strategic collaboration between the state and businesses implies mutual dependence and vulnerability. Bureaucrats depend on businesses to implement planned policies, and businesses depend on bureaucrats to ensure the profitability of the investment. Credibility and trust are both crucial in managing this dependence. Credibility applies to particular policies, while trust characterizes repeated relationships. Policies can be credible without the existence of a trust, depending on the political support of the government or policy design, but trust makes all policies more credible (Rodrik, 1989). Trust in the context of SBRs depends on contacts and common sense and is sensitive to changes in personnel. Trust between the state and business actors depends on the length of the relationship as well (Schneider, 1993a).

A credible commitment of the state to policies, deals, or arrangements is an essential attribute of *strategic SBRs*. Investment decisions may have substantial sunk costs; that is, the costs of certain investments cannot be recovered in full if the investment decision turns out to be less profitable than anticipated (Pindyck, 1991). The state needs to commit not to change policies or deviate from the deals and arrangements to incentivize entrepreneurs to make investment and production decisions (Rodrik, 1991). If the state does not keep its announcements and promises, it is very likely that investors will not believe the state in the future, and investment will suffer (Bardhan, 2005). Economic growth requires the creation of a favourable environment for private investment, in which business has confidence that the state actions will not discourage their activities, while at the same time the state can evade rent-seeking (Harriss, 2006).

While organizations and individuals have numerous incentives to strike bargains, compliance with agreements ex-post is often a critical problem (North and

Weingast, 1989). This type of problem can be overcome principally by building up a good reputation and repeated play on the part of the players involved in the game. However, there are many circumstances in which these mechanisms alone are insufficient to prevent non-compliance. The problem mostly comes down to how credible commitments on the part of policymakers can be realized to help overcome time-inconsistent behaviour and, hence, the potentially harmful effects of political discretion, opportunism, and arbitrariness (North and Weingast, 1989). A commitment is credible either motivationally or imperatively (Shepsle, 1991). A commitment is motivationally credible if it is self-enforcing in the sense that the respective party still wants to honour its commitment at the point in time when it is to be performed. However, more important in the realm of policymaking is an imperatively credible commitment (Shepsle, 1991, p. 247), which means that despite a wish to deviate from the agreement, the respective party is unable to do so (Ahrens, 2002). In this sense, the commitment is credible because performance is coerced or discretion to do otherwise is restricted. The necessity for policymakers credibly to commit themselves to policy reforms in the imperative sense underlies the importance of political institutions (Ahrens, 2002, p. 107). Hence, credible commitment can be obtained through an institutional setting (North, 1990).

Credibility in commitments matters, as it builds trust. Trust is essential to make transaction costs low, and to do this, trust and reliance are necessary features. In the absence of trust, monitoring, arranging sanctions, and guarantees will be more costly. Banfield (1958) has argued that lack of trust is indeed one of the causes of economic underdevelopment (Furubotn and Richter, 2005). Enabling communication and understanding of a shared vision through developing a common language is essential for building trust among the players (Sen, 2015). The more reciprocal relationships we have, the more cooperative behavior tends to develop, and a better system for the development of trust will evolve (North and Weingast, 1989). Trust reduces transaction and monitoring costs, diminishes uncertainty, and creates incentives for businesses to move from 'buying cheap and sell dear' to a more developmentally desirable strategy of making a long-term investment (Maxfield and Schneider, 1997; Rodrik, 2004).

3.2.2.4. Feedback Mechanism

One more essential feature of *strategic SBRs* is the enacted feedback mechanism on proposed policies and programmes. The cumulative consequences of many political and economic decisions in the short run, directly and indirectly, shape economic performance in the long run. Political decisions reflect the decision-makers' subjective modelling of reality. The outcomes of specific policies are, to a substantial degree, unpredictable because policies are based on decision-makers' ideas, ideologies, beliefs, and perceptions. The degree to which policy outcomes are consistent with intentions reflects the degree to which the models are the right models. The models can be partially refined and improved by informational feedback on specific policies' actual consequences (North, 1990, p. 104). Future payoffs of alternative political choices are uncertain ex-ante (Ahrens, 2002, p. 103). Therefore, one more essential aspect of *strategic SBRs* is a feedback provision. This should aim to acquire knowledge regarding which interventions work and which do not. Feedback needs to be followed by the required adaptation (Sen, 2013). Hence, adaptive efficiency (North, 1990, p. 80) is another required feature of *strategic SBRs*. This concept refers to encouraging trials, experiments, and innovations with the willingness to learn and provides incentives to encourage decision-making processes that allow the maximization of efforts required to explore alternative ways of solving problems (North, 1990, p. 80). The government, its apparatus as well as businesses should learn from failures. The challenge consists of generating trials and eliminating errors, which may be only accidental and permanent due to ideologies that may give people preferences for the kinds of solutions that are not oriented to adaptive efficiency (North, 1990, p. 81). Over time, institutions, policies, and programmes that do not work are weeded out, and the ones producing economic growth survive. Thus, there is a gradual evolution of better economic, political, and social institutions (North, 1990, p. 92).

3.3. The Prerequisites for Emergence of *Strategic* SBRs

The theories on SBRs acknowledge that *strategic SBRs* are a determinant of economic success, but also admit the neoliberal view that close SBRs might result in rent-seeking and unproductive use of rents (Buur et al., 2015). Therefore, it is essential to identify the prerequisites under which *strategic SBRs* emerge and what keeps them from degenerating into collusive relations.

A set of principles to restrain collusive behaviour include the structures of the private sector and the public sector, their interrelations, and especially the existence of information exchange mechanisms (te Velde, 2006). Scholars argue that the capability of the state and the capability of the private sector, as well as their organization and existence of mutual interest, are among the necessary prerequisites for the emergence of *strategic SBRs*.

3.3.1. The Structure of the Public Sector in Relation to the Private Sector

The structure of the public sector in relation to the private sector is understood by the presence and length of the existence of state agencies to promote investment and interact with businesses as well as to be the bridge between the government and business in terms of information provision (te Velde, 2006). Existence of such state agencies requires the institutionalization of a complex set of political machinery (Evans, 1992, p. 141) because the polity specifies, implements, and enforces the formal rules of economic exchange. However, present knowledge of how to create such political institutions is limited (Ahrens, 2002, p. 13).

Strategic SBRs require a bureaucracy that knows how industries work and share a vision with businesses, as well as a bureaucracy that is free from the pressure of political and business elites to direct resources to productive sectors, firms, or industries and to discipline them (Amsden, 1989; Rodrik, 2009). When the state lacks the capability to monitor and discipline individual businesses, each interaction between a state official and business is another opportunity to generate rent for the individuals involved at the expense of society at large (Evans, 1997, p. 66).

Success of policy reform crucially depends on the administrative capability of the state. In order to satisfy the capability condition, specific institutions are required to ensure technical capability for implementing reforms and programmes and to ensure the effectiveness of legislative and enforcement coalitions (Ahrens, 2002). The traditional argument is that a collusive relationship between the state and businesses is less likely to occur when bureaucracies are more Weberian (Evans, 1995), characterized by meritocracy, a career ladder, reasonable salaries, and prestige (Maxfield and Schneider, 1997). Technical capability for implementing reforms depends on the existence of a competent and meritocratic bureaucracy, which implies promotion by merit-based criteria, insulates bureaucrats from lobbying and prevents rent-seeking as well as enhances their ability to collect and process data and monitor firms' behaviour (Tollison and Congletion, 1995). Such bureaucracy is the foundation for coherent state action (Evans, 1997). Then, close ties with the business community can become vehicles in pursuit of economic transformation. Promotion by merit criteria is a key feature that insulates bureaucrats from pressures and allows them to exact reciprocity and make credible long-term commitments. If meritocratic procedures for promotion insulate bureaucrats from lobbying, the probability that investing in lobbying will be successful declines, and rent-seeking ceases to be a profitable alternative to productive investment (Tollison and Congletion, 1995).

Evans emphasizes that key for collaboration is insulation, not isolation (1995). Such embeddedness enhances trust and reciprocity (Uzzi, 1996, p. 677). An internal organization of the state bureaucracy, based on meritocratic principles, is necessary for bureaucratic autonomy (Evans, 1995) as well as for professional decision-making (Weber, 1922). The bureaucratic autonomy allows the state to intervene selectively in favour of particular firms, sectors, and industries and provide both incentives to business and discipline them (Amsden, 1989; Wade, 1990). Long tenure in Weberian bureaucracy permits extended interaction with businesses and allows personal trust and networks to develop. As to the second criteria of the capability condition, a legislative and enforcement coalition's effectiveness implies an appropriate agenda control mechanism, and institutional arrangements for creating ministerial positions and committees (Ahrens, 2002).

3.3.2. The Structure of the Private Sector in Relation to Public Sector

One more prerequisite for collaborative SBRs is the structure of a private sector in relation to a public one, and more specifically, the existence of umbrella organizations (te Velde, 2006), which encompass diverse business representatives, aiming to maintain a 2-way flow of information between state and businesses to enhance policy design and subsequent adjustments (Maxfield and Schneider, 1997). It also suggests the existence of a dynamic private sector, which implies the presence of large companies or a large number of small and medium-sized (SMEs) firms operating in growth-oriented sectors of the economy (Maxfield and Schneider, 1997).

Umbrella organizations provide the means to construct dense networks between businesses and state officials. Moreover, they may serve as reliable and official sources of information for state officials (Maxfield and Schneider, 1997). They can aggregate data on private sector performance, obstacles, and opportunities and, at the same time, reduce the firms' incentive to bias information regarding their performance. The data collection functions of umbrella organizations can help reduce transaction and coordination costs and help members gain higher returns on investment (te Velde, 2006). Umbrella organizations may provide market-supporting and market-complementing activities, and with this, they can contribute to increasing the productivity of member firms. Market-supporting activities include lobbying to provide those public goods (roads, infrastructure, electricity), which are critical for businesses to invest in certain sectors or regions (Doner and Schneider, 2000). Hence, an umbrella organization can strengthen the overall functioning of markets. Market-complementing activities refer to coordination among businesses to address various market imperfections and adjust production and investment decisions accordingly (Doner and Schneider, 2000, p. 264).

The characteristics of umbrella organizations that drive development include a representativeness of the business sector, member entrepreneurs' capabilities, and the ability to aggregate interests across firms and act together. The idea is that more extensive and more diverse membership makes umbrella organizations more representative and enhances the lobbying and negotiating power vis-à-vis the state (Page and Tarp, 2017). Proponents of this approach focus on formal institutionalized relations through business associations, especially encompassing (multi-sectoral) business associations. However, some authors note that the industry-specific associations play an essential role in informal institutionalized relations (or networks) between businesses and bureaucrats. High barriers to exit increase the cost of defection for the members and increase the incentive to amplify their voices, especially in agriculture-related umbrella organizations (Frieden, 1991). One more fact that keeps driving the development of the business associations is the 'bad apple' syndrome that gives members the incentive to monitor and apply a severe punishment in case of deviation. This is especially visible in the case of small producers who export to international markets and cannot compete without a good sectoral reputation and a common marketing infrastructure (Maxfield and Schneider, 1997).

Umbrella organizations that can play an active role in promoting the private sector's interests are usually well organized, well resourced, and staffed by professionals (Sen, 2015). The promotion of the needs of a significant share of businesses, rather than those of a few large, politically connected companies, is one of the critical functions of umbrella organizations (Bräutigam et al., 2002; Handley, 2008). The range of information that umbrella organizations can provide to their members includes information on investment opportunities and potential problems. They can invest in the training of member firms' workers, help in enforcing industry quality standards, and voice the demands of their members to the industry- or sector-related ministries and state investment agencies (Cammett, 2007). Reducing information costs for the state as well as for consumers (via setting standards) is one of the simplest and most straightforward cases where the existence of umbrella organizations is Pareto optimal; all members gain from the provision of the information, yet the cost is frequently beyond the capacity of any one member. Quality upgrading of members by improving their technology and the skills of their workforces is a related function of umberella organisations (Doner and Schneider, 2000).

The capabilities of state and private sector are crucial for the emergence of *strategic SBRs*. In the case of SBRs, as in any game, the critical factor is the players' capabilities and the knowledge they possess (North, 1990). Even with a constant set of rules, the games will differ if they are played between amateurs and professionals or by a team in its first game and the same team in its one-hundredth game together. The contrast comes from the differences between communicable and tacit knowledge in the case of amateurs and professionals and learning by doing in the case of repeated games with the same players (North, 1990, p. 74). Communicable knowledge can be transmitted from one individual to the other, and tacit knowledge is the knowledge acquired in part by practice and can only partially be communicated. The innate ability to acquire tacit knowledge differs among individuals (Polanyi, 1967), as it implies acquiring coordination skills and developing a routine that works as a consequence of repeated interaction (Nelson and Winter, 1982). The acquired knowledge and capacities will reflect in the payoffs—i.e., the incentives—embedded in the institutional constraints (North, 1990, p. 77).

3.3.3. Information Exchange Mechanisms

The emergence of *strategic SBRs* requires the existence of a mechanism through which the state and businesses get together and discuss the relevant issues to overcome market and coordination failures. This body should be open to all and be autonomous of state intervention in decision-making. It can be a formal body or an informal one with no entrenched power, and can be broad or focused on specific issues (Herzberg and Wright, 2013). The structure should be manageable while flexible, should enable participants to be both balanced and effective, and should reflect the local private sector context (Sen, 2015).

Transparency provides another mechanism for information exchange. It is a passive form of information exchange, but distinct, as transparency of government decision-making can reduce political uncertainty for investors through the dissemination of decisions, rules, or criteria. In the private sector, business operations transparency can reduce the cost of monitoring (Maxfield and Schneider, 1997).

3.4. The Theory Applied to State–Agribusiness Relations in Georgia

3.4.1. The 'Ideal Typification' of the Institutions of *Strategic SBRs*

This study seeks to understand how the institutions of state agribusinesses relations are designed and why *strategic SBRs* failed to emerge in Georgia's food and agricultural sector. Thereby, three cases of state intervention in the food and agricultural sector of Georgia are explored. They include the state programmes Preferential Agro Credit, Plant the Future, and Co-financing Agro Processing and Storage Enterprises, which create incentives for local businesses to invest in the country's food and agricultural sector. The programmes aim to support agribusinesses, increase and diversify the primary and secondary production and export, and enhance productivity, hence the sector's economic performance.

Understanding the situation in a specific case begins with theories (Gorton, 2006, pp. 26–27). This research relies on New Institutional Economics as a perspective to understand the nature of the institutions of the state–agribusiness relations in Georgia. This study argues that the nature of the institutions of SBRs is crucial for state intervention to result in the improved economic performance of the sector. As Popper (1959, p. 59) states, theories are netcast, universal statements, to catch, rationalize, explain, and master what we call the world. Based on the theories, expectations, and singular statements that apply to the specific events in question are deducted (Popper, 1959, p. 60). Deductivism aims to discover the regularities that make natural phenomena understandable (Corvi, 1997). Popper claims that expectations that precede observations are necessary to illuminate the investigation (Gorton, 2006). Based on the theoretical considerations of the institutionalist approach to SBRs, the following expectations are deducted:

- State intervention to drive industry, sector or economic development, requires discovering and addressing obstacles, the private sector faces in the production processes (Rodrik, 2004, 2009; Moore and Smitz, 2008);
- The outcomes of state interventions in economic activities are diverse (Sen, 2013d) and depend on the consultations and coordination of activities between the state and businesses (Ahrens, 2002);
- The institutions linking the state and businesses are crucial for the state intervention to drive improved economic performance (Ahrens, 2002; Te Velde, 2010);

- Institutional matrix that determines the interaction between the state and businesses is crucial for SBRs to maintain collaboration, enhance policy experimentation and adaptation, support market functions, and reduce potential economic and political risks (Ahrens, 2002);
- *Strategic SBRs* refer to the alliances of the political elites, industry actors and bureaucrats working together to solve coordination and information-related failures (Buur et al., 2015);
- The institutional setting of *strategic SBRs* is characterisedwith information exchange, reciprocity, credibility and trust between the state and private actors (Lemma and te Velde, 2017) and enacted feedback mechanisms on state policies and programmes (Page and Tarp, 2017)
- The *institutions of strategic SBRs* maintain an ongoing dialogue between the state and businesses and strengthen the capability to address selectively economic opportunities and obstacles identified through state–business dialogue (Sen, 2015);
- The institutions that shape interactions between the state and businesses can be formal and informal (North, 1990, p. 7).
- Informal institutions may be sufficient to permit economic exchange within a small distance, however, to grow in size and scope, the economy would need to develop formal institutions (North, 1991);
- Informal institutions are less effective if personal and professional ties are not distinct (Peiffer, 2012a) and if there is limited institutional memory both in the state and business due to frequent changes (ADB, 2008);
- The nature of the state agribusiness relations in Georgia varies based on the size of the businesses, status of the businesses (the individual or association) and the size of the subsidised projects (preliminary interviews);
- In order for *strategic SBRs* to emerge existence of information exchange mechanisms, the willingness of state and agribusiness to collaborate, meritocratic bureaucratic system, capabilities of the state, agribusinesses and umbrella organisations are crucial prerequisites;

Based on a theory, a model and a framework for analysis are developed. It is possible to understand and explain the specific case when this framework is applied to the case of research interest (Gorton, 2006, pp. 26–27). This research relies on analyticism (Jackson, 2011) as a research approach. Analyticism 'seeks to ground the production of knowledge in concrete, practical involvements of the researcher, and does so through the strategy involving the instrumental oversimplification of complex, actual situations; ideal-types are then utilized to form case-specific analytical narratives that explain particular outcomes' (Jackson, 2011, p. 142). Popper argues that in order for social sciences to produce an explanation of a typical event, the best way is to construct models of typical situations (Gorton, 2006). Tab. 3.1 uses the New Institutionalism as a perspective. The frameworks that can be considered as an ideal-type arrangement of the institutions of *strategic SBRs* and their characteristics are formed based on the institutionalist approach of the SBRs. The developed analyitical framework will be used as a means for the comparison and interpretation of actuality (Weber, 1999a, in Jackson, 2011, p. 142) in the three selected cases of state intervention in the food and agriculture sector of Georgia to organize empirical observation into systematic facts.

Tab. 3.1. The Research Approach Analyticism (Jackson, 2011) Applied to the State Agribusiness Relations in Georgia

The Weberian Procedures of Ideal Typification (Jackson, 2011)			
Step I	**Step II**	**Step III**	**Step IV**
The stand taking framework: NIE	The characteristics of the institutions of the *strategic SBRs*	Application	Analysis
The formal and informal rules & their enforcement mechanisms;	Information exchange; Reciprocity; Credibility & trust; Feedback mechanisms;	The state programmes: Preferential Agrocredit; Plant the future; Co-financing Agriculture processing and storage enterprises;	Explaining facts; Interpretations;

According to the institutionalist approach to SBRs, *strategic SBRs* are characterized by information exchange, reciprocity and credibility and trust between the state and private actors (Maxfield and Schneider, 1997; Buur et al., 2005; Harris, 2006; te Velde, 2006; Leftwich, 2009). In addition, the feedback mechanisms of the institutions are crucial. Fig. 3.1 presents the institutionalist approach to SBRs and the prerequisites for their emergence.

Fig. 3.1. The model: the institutionalist approach to SBRs

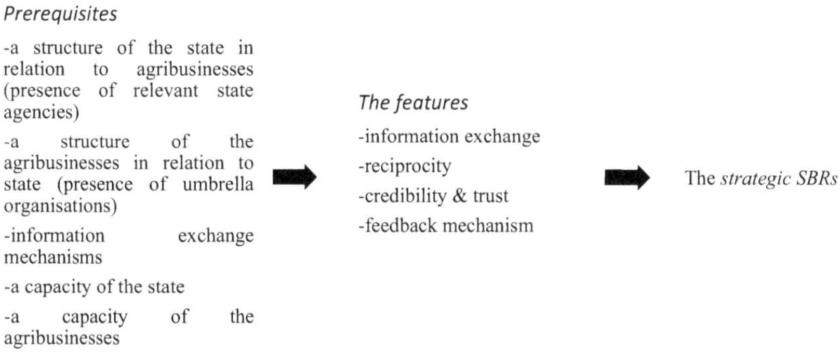

3.4.2. Operationalization of the Variables

This subsection addresses the operationalization of the variables. Tabs. 3.2 through 3.6 present the operationalization of the information exchange between the state and businesses, the reciprocity of SBRs, the variable credibility and trust in the SBRs, the adaptive efficiency of the institutions of SBRs, and the prerequisites for the emergence of the *strategic SBRs*, respectively. All cases offer insights into characteristics, evaluation criteria, and indicators.

Tab. 3.2. The Operationalization of Information Exchange

Characteristics	Evaluation criteria	Indicators
Information from state: Sectoral markets Labour market Export opportunities Customs procedures State programmes Planned amendments in policy or law Information from business: Obstacles Needs in supply chain Supply and demand matching Storage facilities Labour skills Access to local and international markets	Density Comprehensiveness	Frequency Regularity Type/context
	Formality	Regulatory framework: laws/rules that formalize state-business information exchange, and oversee transparency; Formal reporting scheme: open access reports on activities, performance and finances via online portals or periodic issues; Open to public: the existence of public networks (webpage, forums, discussions) to which all actors (civil society, labour activists, etc.) participate; Information dissemination: public discussions, emails, online publications, media sources, social media

Tab. 3.3. The Operationalization of Reciprocity

Characteristics	Evaluation criteria	Indicators
In return for the provided subsidies/support, the state sets clear and measurable performance standards for agribusiness, and in case of not meeting the performance standards, the state withdraws support from agribusiness and enforce punishment;	Sophistication of an incentive regime	A variety of support (support mechanisms employed by the state); Selection processes of state programmes to support agribusinesses; Duration of support (the period of support, one-time/repeated); The size and type of the financial support; The conditionality of support: what conditions the support is tied to; The selection procedures: transparent selection procedures for beneficiaries of the programmes; Withdrawal clause: set of conditions when the state withdraws its support; Reinvestment incentives: re-investment incentives from the state to keep agribusiness interested in projects in the long term;
	Quality of monitoring	Clear performance criteria: the existence of project-specific performance indicators, which are tied to the agribusiness; Continuous and regular assessment: The presence of well-developed monitoring schemes; The existence of evaluation units in charge of collecting performance results; The regularity of the evaluations of meeting the performance indicators; The criteria for assessing the success or the failure of the investment activity of the specific agribusiness;
	Discipline	Punishment clause: the rules according to which the state punishes programme beneficiary agribusinesses that have deviated from obligations; Enforcement mechanisms of punishment: the enforcement rules, enforcement body, required time and resources.

Tab. 3.4. The Operationalization of Credibility and Trust

Characteristics	Evaluation criteria	Indicators
Credibility means that state actors will fulfil particular policies and agreements, as well as promises to the businesses to address specific obstacles or needs, or to follow up on the feedback provided by the private sector regarding the specific programmes or policies;	Policy predictability	Compliance with the duration of the programme/policies: whether the policies last for the initially designated time; The frequency of the changes in policy/programmes after the investment decision is made; Consistency in policy implementation: state-initiated policies/projects complement or contradict each other;
Trust refers to a shared vision, expectation, between the state and businesses, ensuring that the actors will not deviate from the agreements;	Level of political support and accessibility of the actors;	The dominant ideology of the ruling party: whether it is supportive of SBRs or not; The mechanisms to access the bureaucrats designated to the specific programmes or processes; The frequency of changing bureaucrats designated to the specific programmes; Expectations of businesses regarding the addressing of obstacles businesses face for the production export process; The possibility of meetings with relevant state actors when required;

Tab. 3.5. The Operationalization of the Feedback Mechanism

Characteristics	Evaluation criteria	Indicators
Institutional matrix, which encourages trials and experiments and maintains elimination or adjustment of the programmes, policies, rules of the game, which fail to be successful in achieving defined goals;	Openness and intention to consider feedback;	A mechanism for checks and balances on the programmes or the rules; The frequency of the provided feedback; The practice of following up on the feedback; The practice of adapting the rules, programmes and policies based on the feedback

Tab. 3.6. The Operationalization of the Prerequisites for the Emergence of *Strategic SBRs*

Characteristics	**Evaluation criteria**	**Indicators**
The structure of the state in relation to private sector;	Organization, activities, capacity, achievements;	The presence of the pilot agencies/units established by the state to interact with the agribusinesses, to promote state programmes targeted at direct investment in the food and agriculture sector of Georgia, to collect data on foreign markets, investment and export opportunities, production opportunities; The length of the existence of pilot agencies; Selection criteria of officials employed in the state agencies; The capacity of state bureaucrats employed in the agencies; The activities of the pilot agencies; Mechanisms to interact with the private sector; Comprehensiveness of data collection and management capacity to collect detailed information (units/departments/employees in charge of data collection, channels for collecting sources of information, methodology of data collection); Channels of information dissemination;
The structure of the private sector in relation to the state	Organization, activities, capacity, achievements;	The presence of umbrella organizations: the existence of umbrella organizations, representatives of the sector, their capacity to gather and transfer data to/from the state, to initiate meetings and to facilitate policy/legislative changes; The length of existence of the umbrella organizations; The structure of the umbrella organizations; Funding sources and sustainability of the umbrella organizations; The activities & achievements in advocacy of agribusiness need with the state; The mechanisms of data collection; The comprehensiveness of collected data (channels for collecting, sources of information, the methodology of data collection); The management of the collected data; The channels of information dissemination;
The information exchange mechanisms	Forums/platforms for state-business dialogue;	The existence, format and frequency

Chapter IV Methodological Considerations for the Empirical Research

Gerring (2001b) divides the research methodology into three parts: concepts, propositions, and research design. While Chapter III discussed the concepts and propositions of this study, this chapter explores the rationale behind the methodological decisions taken to find the answer to the research question.

This study employs a qualitative research approach as inquiring the answers to the research interest requires in-depth information about the country-specific situation: information on the institutions determining the interaction between the state and business actors, as well as on the capabilities of the state and business actors, and their motivation to contribute to the sector's development in the long run. Such information is best captured in analytical narratives, which requires qualitative data (Buur et al., 2015). Qualitative data is a source of well-grounded, rich descriptions and explanations of processes occurring in local contexts. With qualitative data, one can preserve the chronological flow and derive fruitful explanations (Miles and Huberman, 1984, pp. 21–22). From the qualitative research approach (Creswell, 2009), the dissertation employs a case study, aiming to explore in-depth the answers to the questions mentioned above by studying three cases: the Preferential Agrocredit, Plant the Future, and Co-financing Agro Processing and Storage Enterprises programmes. These programmes are initiated and implemented by the state to create incentives for local businesses to invest in Georgia's food and agricultural sector to diversify and increase production and export and enhance productivity, hence supporting the sector's economic performance. These cases are typical cases of state intervention in economic activities in Georgia since 2013 to support economic development by facilitating production growth in specific sectors or industries. These three cases differ in terms of the duration, activities, and volume of the support, as well as in terms of the number of players involved and the categories of support (one time or repeated). The research aims to understand if these differences in programmes result in a difference in the institutions of the state–agribusiness relations. The qualitative research approach requires substantial data collection, which needs to be based on multiple sources (Yin, 2011, p. 8). The study employs a qualitative research strategy for the systematic collection, organization, and interpretation of the data. The data from interviews, documents on relevant regulations and laws, and the reports from international organizations, if available, are triangulated in order to analyse the questions of the research interest. The data from the interviews are organized in MAXQDA. To analyse the data, qualitative text analysis and explaining the outcome process tracing methods are applied.

4.1. Methodological Decisions

The research relies on several methodological decisions regarding the intersection of philosophy, inquiry strategies, and specific methods (Creswell, 2009). This subsection discusses the methodological decisions taken in the dissertation against the background of the chosen research questions. The first methodological decision refers to selecting the research approach (Guba, 1990, p. 17). As discussed in Section 3.2.2, the study relies on analyticism (Jackson, 2011) as a research approach. This approach postulates 'an ideal-typical account of a process or setting and then [utilizes] that ideal type to organize empirical observations into systematic facts' (Jackson, 2011, p. 151). It is reductionist in the sense that it is reduced to a discrete set of ideas, which comprise hypothesis and research question (Crenwell, 2009). The ideal type of institutional setting of state–agribusiness relations was deducted based on the New Institutional Economics and the institutionalist approach to SBRs.

The second methodological decision relates to the research strategy. The study explores in-depth the nature of the institutions of the state–agribusiness relations in three programmes of state intervention in the food and agricultural sector of Georgia and intends to understand why strategic state–agribusiness relations have not emerged in Georgia. Therefore, the chosen strategy of inquiry is a case study, a method used to investigate a phenomenon in depth (Yin, 1981). A case study is an "intensive study of a single case where the purpose of that study is to shed light on a broader class of cases" (Gerring, 2007, pp. 19-20). Gerring states that to refer to a work as a case study means: "(a) that its method is qualitative, small-N; (b) that the research is holistic, thick (a more or less comprehensive) examination of a phenomenon; (c) that it utilizes a particular type of evidence; (d) that its method of evidence gathering is naturalistic (a 'real-life context'); (e) that the topic is diffuse; (f) that it employs triangulation; (g) that the research investigates the properties of a single observation or (h) that the research investigates the properties of a single phenomenon, instance, or example"

(Gerring, 2007, p. 18). In order for a case study to provide insight into a broader phenomenon, it must be representative of a broader set of cases. A "typical-case" (Gerring, 2007, p. 91) approach of case selection exemplifies what is considered a typical set of values, given some general understanding of a phenomenon. Some typical cases serve as an exploratory role (Gerring, 2007, p. 91). The criteria for selecting these cases are their relevance to the research objectives (George and Bennett, 2005, p. 82). The cases selected for this study are the representative cases of the state instruments for direct intervention in economic activities in Georgia. The key unit (Gerring, 2007) of study is the formal and informal rules of interaction between the state and agribusinesses and their enforcement mechanisms in each case. These cases satisfy the conditions of being bounded by location, activities, and time (Stake, 1995). The selected three cases aim to shed light on the nature of the institutions of the state–agribusiness relations in Georgia. Tab. 4.1 presents the key features of the selected cases.

Tab. 4.1. The Characteristics of the Selected Cases, 2015-2018

	Case 1:Plant the Future	**Case 2: Preferential Agrocredit**	**Case 3:Agriculture Products Processing and Storage Enterprises**
Initiator	The MoA	The MoA	The MoA
Duration	2015-current	2013-current	2014–2017
Imple-menter	APMA	APMA	APMA
Financial support	The state budget	The state budget	The state budget
The aim of the programme	To stimulate the fruit-growing sector through planting new gardens, increasing primary production, export potential and substitute import;	To support the legal entities with cheap, affordable, long-term and preferential funds to stimulate primary and secondary production, processing, storage and sale of agricultural products	To establish new processing enterprises in the regions of low economic activity and diversify (geographically) the food processing industry; To assist facility storage enterprises to develop as future service providers;
Support type	Financial & technical	Financial	Financial & technical

Tab. 4.1. Continued

	Case 1:Plant the Future	Case 2: Preferential Agrocredit	Case 3:Agriculture Products Processing and Storage Enterprises
Instruments for financial support	Co-financing perennial gardens; Co-financing nursery gardens;	For turnover assets: co-finance interest payments on loans; For fixed assets: provide the secondary collateral and co-finance the interest rate-payments on loans;	Providing grants and co-financing interest rate payments on loans;
Financial support scheme	The state finances 70 % of the cost of saplings, and 50 % of the cost of installation of the drip irrigation system.	Loan varies between 20,000 and 1.5 million. GEL. The state co-finances the interest rate on the loan (11 %)	40 % (no more than 600,000 GEL) of the total value of the project is financed via a state grant, 50 % (but not more than
	The maximum amount of support for each project is 100,000 GEL (38,461 USD), and the area ceiling 20 hectares;	for 66 months and provides a secondary warranty (collateral) of no more than 50 % of the total principal amount of each new, non-refinanced loan;	1.5 million. GEL) of the total value of the project is supported through preferential credit and 10 % should be covered by the beneficiary in the form of a cash contribution to the enterprise capital;
	The state co-finances 50 % of the total project cost, not more than 150,000 GEL (57,692 USD);	Loan varies between 20,000 and15 million GEL. The state co-finances, interest rate on loans (8 %) for 12–24 months;	
		Leasing: the state cofinances 12 % of annual investments of the leasing issuer for 66 months; sum total of leasing(s) and loan(s) must not exceed 1.5 million GEL;	
Game	Repeated	One time	One time
Beneficiaries	572	29,981	46

Source: APMA, MoA, 2017

The third methodological decision refers to the analytical apparatus guiding the research. Most researchers begin their inquiry with theory (George and Bennett, 2005). For this dissertation, the researcher developed the analytical apparatus based on the theory of the New Institutional Economics (NIE) and the institutionalist approach to SBRs. This analytical apparatus provided the basis for the construction of the interview guide for the fieldwork. The interview guide contains a framework of questions, which were asked to the respondents during the interviews (Patton, 2002). The interview guide is organized into three parts. The opening section refers to the respondent's education and professional experience in relation to the food and agricultural sector. The second part relates to the broad picture of the sector in the period 2004–2017, with its dynamics, actors, major changes, and prerequisites for the emergence of the SBRs. The last section relates to the nature of the state–agribusiness relations. A suitable version of the interview guide was prepared for the interviews with the representatives of agribusinesses, umbrella organizations, state agencies and the Ministry of Environment Protection and Agriculture, international organizations, NGOs, academia, and former and current public officials/bureaucrats and experts. The guide was updated around issues in which the targeted respondent was involved.

The fourth methodological decision refers to the specific research methods for data collection, analysis and interpretation (Creswell, 2009). This study relies on a triangulation of sources (Jick, 1979), such as relevant documents on regulations, laws, policies, programmes, reports of international organizations and interview material from fieldwork. George and Bennett (2005) state that in order for the case study research to be more effective, the research design should include the specification of the data to be obtained during the fieldwork. The specification of the required data refers to the specification of the general questions, which are derived based on the theoretical framework and are asked for each selected case (George and Bennett, 2005, p. 86). As the method of primary data collection, qualitative methods, with semi-structured, face-to-face interviews are employed. This is considered a relevant method where the depth of meaning is important and the research is primarily focused on gaining insight and understanding (Gillham, 2000, p. 11; Ritchie and Lewis, 2003, p. 138). As to the methods for the data analysis, qualitative text analysis (Kuckartz, 2014) is employed as the primary method.

The fifth methodological decision refers to the structure of presenting empirical evidence. The analysis part covers three chapters. Firstly, Chapter V provides the analysis of the state interventions in the food and agricultural sector of Georgia and its performance during the last decade. Secondly, Chapter VI discusses the nature of the institutions of the state–agribusiness relations in Georgia. It covers three subsections related to each case (the Plant in Future, Preferential Agrocredit and Agricultural Food Processing and Storage Enterprises), and presents the facts regarding the nature of the institutions of the state–agribusiness relations in each case. The separation of these three cases is necessary for a better illustration of whether a difference in the characteristics of each case (number of actors, duration, and size of support) make the differences in the institutions of state–agribusiness relations. Finally, Chapter VII discusses the prerequisites for the emergence of the strategic state–agribusiness relations in Georgia.

4.2. Data Collection

Data collection refers to gathering organized information and serves as the foundation for a research study (Yin, 2011, p. 130). Collecting relevant data means dealing directly with a primary data source, such as field observations or interviews (Yin, 2011, p. 49). In qualitative research, the relevant data sources can be the following field-based activities: interviewing, observing, collecting and examining (materials) (Yin, 2011, p. 129). "Interviewing" relies on a questionnaire with specific interview protocols. "Collecting" could occur through a formal search and retrieval procedures that use electronic bibliographic searches as a tool (Yin, 2011, p. 130). For this research, the collection of primary data in the form of semi-standardized interviews is seen as a necessary tool for obtaining in-depth, reliable information and enabling valid research results (Yin, 2011, p. 89).

To collect the information through interviews, the qualitative interviewing method, which is a flexible and powerful tool to capture respondents' experiences, was applied (Rabionet, 2011). Gathering the data through the semi-structured interviews required establishing ethical guidelines, designing the interview protocol, conducting and recording the interview, and reporting the findings in the data analysis software (MAXQDA). The semi-structured interview was selected as the data collection method because it allows the questions to be narrowed down to the themes, derived from the theory, I aimed to cover during the interviews (Rabionet, 2011).

The respondents were selected purposefully, in order to provide the information to answer the questions of research interest (Creswell, 2009). In order to collect the required data, I interviewed representatives of the state, agribusiness, beneficiaries of the programmes of research interest, international donor organizations (EBRD, EU, FAO, USAID), research organizations, independent experts, and umbrella organizations. The sampling goal was to identify key informants: individuals who have knowledge regarding and experience in the food and agricultural sector of Georgia. For the sampling, I combined two techniques: criteria sampling and snowball sampling. At the initial stage, I defined the criteria which the selected respondents should meet. Based on these criteria, I identified a list of the potential respondents and acquired their contact details through personal ties and networking. The list was extended based on the recommendation of the initially selected participants. The meetings were organized face to face, in most cases, at the respondent's office or via Skype. Following the methodology of conducting the semi-structured interviews (DiCicco-Bloom and Crabtree, 2006), I contacted the targeted respondent at least one week in advance via email to schedule the interview and to agree on the meeting date and location. The email introduced the research project and stated the purpose of conducting the interview, and highlighted that the research was of an academic nature. If the respondent was not available on the suggested date for the meeting, I gave flexibility to the respondent to offer a possible alternative date for the meeting. If I did not get a reply to the request via email, I tried to reach the targeted respondent via phone. First of all, I introduced myself and referred to the individual who provided me with the targeted respondent's phone number, and then I requested the meeting for an interview. If the individual agreed to the interview, the date and location for the meeting were agreed.

The average duration of conducted interviews was 60 minutes. I started the interview with a brief introduction of myself and the purpose of the research and provided an information template regarding the project. Then, I requested permission to record the interview. Most of the respondents gave their permission for the interview to be recorded. When I was not permitted to record the interview, I took notes. At the end of the interview, I asked about other relevant information, which was not referred to in the questions, but the respondent considered essential to sharing. I also asked if the respondent could recommend relevant individuals to interview on the same research. If the recommended individual met the criteria, I reached out to them; hence, I employed the snowball method for sampling (Boehnke et al., 2011).

Thirty-nine interviews were conducted from April 2017 through January 2018. The sample size was determined based on theoretical saturation, which is the point at which no more concepts emerge from the data. In addition to the primary data, I collected secondary data from the literature and the reports of the relevant organizations. These organizations include the Food and Agriculture Organization of United Nations (FAO), the United Nations Industrial Development Organization (UNIDO), UN statistics, the International Trade Statistics Database (UN Comtrade), the International Labor Organization (ILO), the World Bank (WB), the World Development Indicators (WDI), the European Bank for Reconstruction and Development (EBRD), the National Statistics Office of Georgia (Geostat), the Ministry of Finance of Georgia, the Ministry of Economy and Sustainable Development of Georgia, the Ministry of Environmental Protection and Agriculture of Georgia, and the Government of Georgia. I employed the principle of triangulation, which aims to seek at least three ways of verifying a particular event or fact reported by a study. Such corroboration serves as another way of strengthening the validity of a study.

4.3. Validity and Reliability

Validity in qualitative research refers to checking the accuracy of the findings by employing specific procedures, while qualitative reliability relates to the fact that the research approach is across different researchers and different projects (Gibbs, 2007). A valid study is one that has adequately collected and interpreted the data so that the conclusions accurately reflect and represent the situation that was studied (Yin, 2011, p. 79). This implies that the qualitative research procedures are described so that those who are interested can scrutinize the study and the evidence used to support the findings and conclusions (Yardley, 2009, pp. 243–250). A study's conclusions should be drawn based on the collected data (Yin, 2011). Maxwell states that validity is referred to as 'the correctness or credibility of a description, conclusion, explanation, interpretation' (1996, p. 87). One of the methods for validity is triangulation—to collect converging evidence from different sources (Maxwell, 2009, pp. 244–245), which is addressed in the present research.

To ensure the validity and reliability of the obtained results, various strategies are employed. The data collection and analysis methods are described in detail. The transcripts are checked several times to make sure that they do not contain any mistakes. Besides, triangulation is applied, which means that the facts are examined from various sources, and various sources are used to build a coherent justification for themes. If themes are established based on converging several sources of data or perspectives from participants, then this process can be claimed as adding to the validity of the study (Creswell, 2007).

4.4. Data Analysis

The qualitative data analysis refers to preparing the data for analysis, moving deeper into understanding it, representing the data and making the interpretation of the broader meaning of the data (Creswell, 2007). According to Yin (2011), the analysis of the qualitative data usually involves five phases. The first phase refers to organizing the data, compiling it into a formal database. The second phase is disassembling the data in the database, which involves a formal coding procedure. The coding procedure is followed by identifying themes to reorganize the disassembled fragments into sequences that might have been in the original notes. The third phase, i.e. reassembling, requires insightfulness to observe the emerging patterns. The fourth phase, which can be considered as interpreting the reassembled data, involves using observed patterns to provide a narrative, with accompanying tables and graphs, which might become the key analytic portion of the draft manuscript. The fifth and final phase may be considered the conclusion of the entire study (Yin, 2011, p. 176). This study applies the following procedures of data analysis (Creswell, 2007):

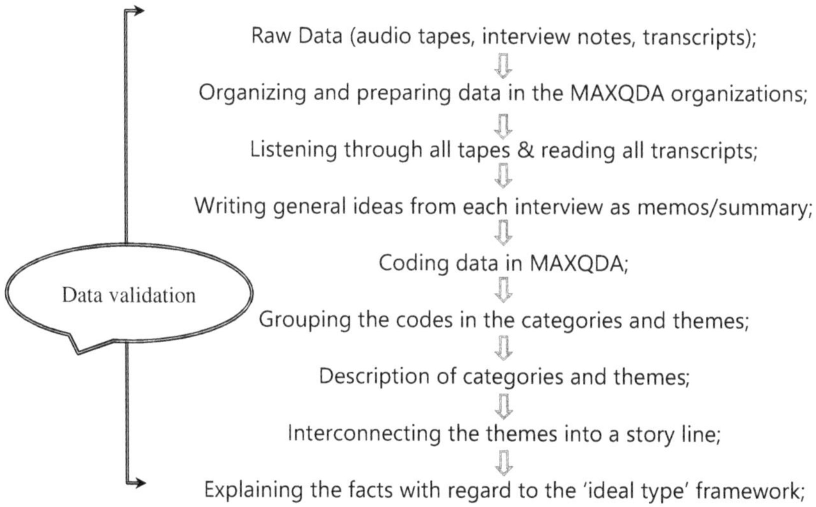

After the fieldwork, the data was transferred to MAXQDA. The data were sorted according to the information sources: public officials, agribusiness, experts, umbrella organizations, and international donor organization. Codes, which refer to a short phrase representing the coded segments' key attributes, were defined. Codes allow all the segments relating to a particular question, hypothesis, concept, or theme to be spotted quickly, pulled out, and clustered (Miles and Huberman, 1984). For coding, the start list method is applied (Kuckartz, 2014); hence, the deductive approach, as the codes are based on the preliminary defined framework, following the theory. The data's codebook is derived from the operationalisation of the variables (Tabes. 3.2, 3.3, 3.4, 3.5, and 3.6). The codes are applied to the audio types saved in MAXQDA, and only the parts that the researcher uses in the dissertation are transcribed. A multi-stage process of categorizing and coding is applied (Kuckartz, 2014). In the first stage of the analysis, the data is coded into major categories. In the next phase, the categories are further developed and differentiated based on the data. The entire data set is then coded again (Kuckartz, 2014).

Qualitative text analysis is employed as the method of systematic data analysis (Kuckartz, 2014). Qualitative text analysis is the most frequently applied method of display of qualitative research (Miles and Huberman, 1984), where results are presented in a narrative, descriptive way. The descriptive analysis includes what is out there and what we call it (Gerring, 2001a). The key advantage of this qualitative text analysis method is that it forces the researcher to focus only on the selected and relevant aspects of the interview material (Schreier, 2012). In this research the qualitative text analysis is used to build the profile matrix of the themes derived from the data (Kuckartz, 2014). As Kuckartz (2014) states, the profile matrix's idea is fundamental to qualitative text analysis. A profile matrix includes topics (themes) as structuring elements in the columns; hence it is a thematic matrix. It creates a clear and comprehensible interpretation of the information that is included in such a profile matrix. The matrix's cells do not contain numbers, but text from each observation on the relevant theme. Summarizing one column creates thematic summaries of all information provided by the respondents during the interview. Moreover, the rows and columns can be summarized in a vertical as well as horizontal fashion. This means that individuals can be assigned to groups according to specific characteristics, and topics can be grouped under broader or more abstract, overarching categories (Kuckartz, 2014). Tab. 4.2 represents the profile matrix, the structure of the fact/themes from the primary data from the fieldwork conducted in Georgia for the present dissertation:

Tab. 4.2. The Scheme of the Profile Matrix of the Interview Data from the Fieldwork in Georgia

	The Profile Matrix									
	Dynamics	**The nature of the institutions of SBRs**				**The prerequisites for emergence of *strategic SBRs***				
	State intervention & sector's performance	**Information exchange**	**Reciprocity**	**Credibility & trust**	**Feedback mechanism**	**APMA**	**State capacity**	**Umbrella organizations**	**Agribusiness capacity**	**Information exchange mechanisms**
Obs.1	Text	Text	Text	Text	Text	Text	Text	Text	Text	Text
Obs. 2	Text	Text	Text	Text	Text	Text	Text	Text	Text	Text
Obs.39	Text	Text	Text	Text	Text	Text	Text	Text	Text	Text
	Text	Text	Text	Text	Text	Text	Text	Text	Text	Text
Total 39 obs.	Summary	Summary	Summary	Summary	Summary	Summary	Summary	Summary	Summary	Summary

The qualitative text analysis is applied to understand the facts regarding the state intervention in the sector, the sector's performance, the nature of the institutions of state–agribusiness relations, and the prerequisites for the emergence of strategic state–agribusiness relations. The analysis methods implicitly apply explaining the outcome process tracing method (Beach and Pedersen, 2013), while attempting to explain why *strategic SBRs* have failed to emerge in the food and agricultural sector of Georgia. The ambition is not to build or to test the theory, but to craft an explanation of the outcome, such as the nature of the existing institutions of the state–agribusiness relations in Georgia. The question asked is as follows:

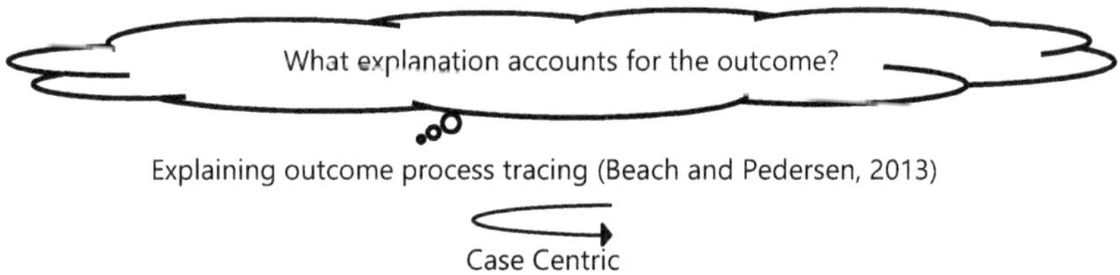

The aim of the explaining outcome process tracing is to craft a minimally sufficient explanation of a particular outcome, in this case the nature of state–agribusiness relations, where sufficiency is defined as an explanation that accounts for all of the important aspects of an outcome with no redundant parts being present (Mackie, 1965).

Chapter V The Food and Agriculture Sector of Georgia – State Intervention and the Sector's Performance

Introduction

As indicated in Chapter I, the structural transformation comprises several separate but interrelated processes, among them upgrading agricultural processes and raising agricultural productivity, diversifying production, and export capacities (Buur et al., 2015). During their economic take-offs, today's advanced economies managed to enhance productivity in agriculture (UNCTAD, 2016). Evidence shows that the highest productivity in agriculture characterizes countries in the top 10 % of the world income distribution, producing 50.1 times as much agricultural output per agricultural worker as countries in the bottom 10 % (Gollin et al., 2014). Boosting productivity in agriculture appears to be a key underline mechanism for development and structural transformation (Timmer, 2007). As increasing productivity in agriculture is essential for structural transformation, it is attention-grabbing to explore how state intervention in the food and agricultural sector of Georgia contributes in sector's performance. Has state intervention already spurred productivity growth? Have the volume of production and export of food and agricultural products undergone noteworthy changes? Have production and export diversified?

Today, as in the past, governments play a significant role in facilitating transformation, regardless of whether activities are located within agriculture, manufacturing, or knowledge-based services (Buur et al., 2015). State intervention to achieve development requires discovering and addressing obstacles the private sector faces in the production and product realization processes (Rodrik, 2004, 2009). It also requires the existence of a long-term development strategy targeting the sectors with export, job, and knowledge creation potentials (Reich, 1982; UNCTAD, 2016). This chapter analyses the state activities in the food and agricultural sector since the Rose Revolution of 2003, covering two periods—2004–2012 governed by the United National Movement (UNM) party, and 2012–2016 governed by the Georgian Dream (GD). Furthermore, the chapter assesses the changes in the sector's performance since the state's formal intervention in 2013. This chapter answers the question: *how has the state been intervening in Georgia's food and agricultural sector during the last decade, and how has the sector's performance changed since the state's active intervention from 2013?*

This chapter comprises four sections. Section 5.1 discusses the first wave of interventions, which relates to the period of United National Movement (UNM) party being in power. Section 5.2 discusses the second wave of intervention related to the state-led activities since the Georgian Dream (GD) has been in power. Section 5.3 discusses the sector's performance in terms of productivity, production, and export capacity of primary and processed agricultural products. The final section offers a conclusion.

5.1. The First Wave of State Intervention

The Georgian agricultural sector has several valuable assets to boost and to diversify its production. These assets include 2.4 million hectares of agricultural land, of which only 35 % is utilized (FAO, 2019). Also, 22 climate zones varying from the subtropical climate along the Black Sea border to more temperate and arid climate zones in the eastern part of the country. The country is rich with various soils suitable for growing different kinds of high value-added eriences illustrate (see Chapter II), state i (VA) agricultural products. Furthermore, the country is rich with freshwater resources (Bluashvili and Sukhanskaya, 2015). However, only a small part of the productive potential is being absorbed (Silagadze, 2013).

Georgia's resource situation favours agriculture production, so one would expect the government to focus on facilitation of developing the agricultural sector (Jobelius, 2011). Nevertheless, the sector lacked attention from the state (Land, 2013), particularly between the Rose Revolution of 2003 and 2012 (Bluashvili and Sukhanskaya, 2015). The Food and Agriculture Organisation of United Nation (FAO) in its agriculture assessment report (2012) states that the food and agricultural sector of Georgia is 'the cinderella of development assistance due to a lack of any defined state policy or strategy for the sector, other than laissez-faire, abandoned by Government' (FAO, 2012, p. 9).

One of the explanations for the neglect of agriculture policy during the Saakashvili administration (2004–2012) was the ruling party's political ideology, representing the liberal economic school. In 2004–2005, the government was against subsidizing the sector (interview with a beneficiary of the Preferential Agrocredit programme, 16 November 2017). The attitude was that the sector should survive independently in the process of "swimming," meaning to win the competition (interview with the local expert, Transparency International, 22 November 2017). In a similar vein, a local investor operating in agribusiness at that time stated that:

> During the UNM period, the state ignored the sector. The outcome was that on the one hand, through agribusiness, one could not earn much, but still enough to keep the

> family well. On the other hand, it gave an opportunity to be away from everyday political life, as the state involved everyone in its politics (Interview with the beneficiary of the Preferential Agrocredit programme, 23 November 2017).

The other reason behind the sector's neglect was that a large part of the labour force (50 %) was stuck in this sector. The Saakashvili administration believed that in order for the economy to grow, Georgia should undergo a rapid process of urbanization, as no developed country has more than 3–4 % of its labour force in agriculture (ISET Policy Institute, 2016).

The state's attitude to the sector was reflected in reducing the budget of the Ministry of Agriculture of Georgia (MoA). The policy was to spend as little as possible in the agricultural sector. Consequently, the budget was directed only to administrative expenses (interview with the former Deputy Head of the Department of the Agriculture Development, the Ministry of Agriculture of Georgia (MoA), 14 November 2017). In 2004–2007, government spending on agriculture was 2 % of total spending. In 2008, the indicator started declining. The budget of the MoA declined by 42 % compared to 2007; its share of total spending was 0.9 %. The indicator further decreased until 2011. From 2008 through 2010, the indicator declined by 40 %, and its share of the total spending went down to 0.6 % (Fig. 5.1).

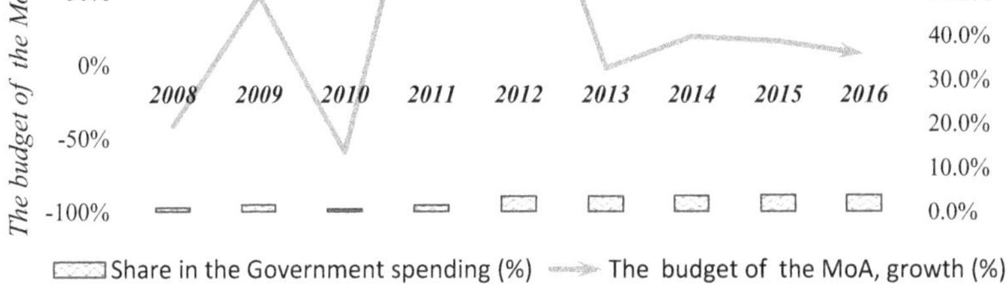

Fig. 5.1. The annual growth of the budget allocation of the MoA and its share of government spending, 2008–2016

Source: Ministry of Finance of Georgia (MoF), the State Budget, 2017

Notes: The Budget of the MoA is the MoA's available financial resources from the state budget for spending during the budget year;

The graph indicates that the budget assignments of the MoA declined from 2008 through 2010. It has increased since 2011 with the state prioritizing the sector, but the share in the total government budget remains low (1 %).

The government started emphasizing the importance of Georgia's food and agricultural sector in public rhetoric in 2006. This happened after the import restrictions on Georgian wine and mineral waters from the Russian markets, which was the destination of 80 %–90 % of wine exported from Georgia. 'Although alternate outlets were found—for example, Ukraine became the leading purchaser—in 2012 the overall volume of exported wine stood at only 33 % of pre-embargo levels' (Newnham, 2015, p. 166). Hence, the full substitution of that market was impossible, and the government started subsidizing the wine sector, although this was 'a tribute' paid for political reasons (interview with the Former Minister of Finance of Georgia, MoF, 18 January 2018). As clarified by a foreign expert, who had been actively providing advice on economic policy development issues to the various state agencies since 2007:

> Closing the Russian market was the result of political decisions made by Mikheil Saakashvili (the former President of Georgia), so he had to 'pay' for this action; hence, the state intervened in the wine sector and bought the grapes for five times the market price (Interview with a foreign expert, 24 November 2017).

During the UNM period, the subsidies were purely for political reasons (ISET Policy Institute, 2016), not targeting development. The only state action targeting developing that sector during this period was policies to encourage foreigners to invest in agriculture and bring modern technology and management. The state started the privatization of agricultural land. Incomplete land registration remained an obstacle to the sector (ISET Policy Institute, 2016). However, despite the obstacles concerning land registration, as well as lack of infrastructure and social capital, there were several successful investment projects at the time (Bluashvili and Sukhanskaya, 2015). Among these projects are investments by global food industry companies such as Ferrero and Hipps, as well as investments from joint ventures of the foreign and local investors in agriculture production and food processing (ISET Policy Institute, 2016). However, these activities were small in terms of scale. Between 2007 and 2011, the volume of FDI in the sector increased by 10 %; nevertheless, the volume and its share in total investment were still low (1 %) (Source Geostat, author's calculations).

The government did not favour the sector with development-oriented subsidies from the state budget, but it used its political power to force local investors—successful businesses in other sectors—to invest in the food and agricultural sector. There were cases of intervention in the sector when the state used its political power to informally force investors to buy grapes. There were also cases when businesses procured grapes to upgrade their status, earning a good relationship with the state (Interview with a local investor, agribusiness, 16 November 2017). According to the former public official:

> The rationale from the business side to invest was either the fear of the state reaction in case of not investing, an informal obligation to the state or/and expectations that the state would do a favour in the future in exchange for investment in the sector. These investments were unsuccessful and a waste of money (Interview with the former Deputy Head of the Department of Agriculture Development at MoA, 14 November 2017).

This type of informal intervention did not contribute to the development of the sector. The food and agricultural sector has returned to a development priority of the state since 2011 (FAO, 2012). At the end of 2011, the President of Georgia announced 'the year of agricultural development and progress' to express the ruling elites' political will to support the food and agricultural sector of Georgia. The new emphasis on the agriculture sector was reflected in the '10 Point Plan 2011–2015,' which proposed the development of business-oriented agriculture and traditional household-based agriculture (FAO, 2014). On the one hand, this was because the sector itself did not respond to macro-economic reforms in 2004–2007 and an improved business environment (FAO, 2012). 'The government worried that while all other sectors were developing, agriculture stayed at the same level. That was the fact, and no one changes this fact' (interview with the Local Expert, FAO/ENPARD, 27 December 2017). On the other hand, growing hardships experienced by the rural population, which comprised almost 50 % of the population, may have motivated the decision to allow state intervention in the primary sector (Jobelius, 2011) in order to please voters (interview with the Executive Director of BAG, 4 December 2017). This motivation might have been stronger in 2011, as the election was approaching the following year, in 2012.

Until the end of 2011, the government did not have any strategy for the sector's development. 'The MoA does not currently [2011] have a strategy in place for the sector. It has made progress towards developing the draft strategy for 2012–2020' (Bardzik et al., 2011). In 2011, the state elaborated on the agriculture development strategy through the active consultation process with the FAO (Bardzik et al., 2011). The elaborated strategy was the first agriculture development strategy since the collapse of the Soviet Union. 'This was a small but necessary document. There was no strategy before that, although there were some trials, starting from 2002, from USAID or different independent experts' (interview with a local expert, FAO/ENPARD, 27 December 2017). However, the strategy was not based on the analysis of the existing situation and risks, and there were no accompanying action plan or performance indicators (Shergelashvili and Tokmazashvili,

2012). In the process of strategy elaboration, the priority was to develop the sector based on the principles of a market economy (interview with the former Deputy Head of the Department of Agricultural Development at MoA, 14 November 2017). Though the strategy elaborated by the UNM is not publicly accessible, as stated in th=e '10 Points Plan 2011–2015,' the incentives were to attract investment through a partnership with the private sector, increase production and productivity, increase and diversify exports, and substitute imports of agricultural products. Following the Washington Consensus recipe, the state aimed to achieve the targeted goals not via direct subsidies, but via increasing competitiveness and productivity based on the market principles. Therefore, the state saw its role as a supporter of the private sector in the modernization of the production, as well as a provider of infrastructure and information regarding the markets and modern technological achievements.

To support the modernization of production processes and adopt modern technologies, the state started providing technological support and services to the sector. A former public official explained that the rationale behind this was a market failure, meaning that there was a demand for technologies, but the sector faced a lack of supply. However, there have been concerns about the quality of the imported technologies (interview with the former Head of the Department of the Agriculture Development, MoA, 14 November 2017).

To achieve the target of export promotion, the state established a small department under the agency Invest in Georgia at the end of 2010, under the Ministry of the Economy and Sustainable Development of Georgia. The department comprised four individuals: two employees and two interns (interview with the Head of the Export Development Association, 1 February 2018). Through this unit, the state tried to facilitate export and to implement specific activities. As the Head of the Export Development Association, who was the Head of the Export Development Department at Invest in Georgia during the referred period, emphasized at the initial stage, export was not a priority for the state; no one mentioned it, and one could only come across the term in small strategy documents. The first cases of state intervention for export facilitation started actively in 2011. The unit, which could manage and implement events and activities in this direction, was not in place before (interview with the Head of the Export Development Association, 1 February 2018).

The key focus was the popularisation of Georgian products through the participation of agribusinesses in exhibitions (interview with the former Head of the Department of Agriculture Development, MoA, 14 November 2017). In 2011–2012, the state-organized exhibitions and invited international traders and distributors to introduce Georgian products. Concerning the state activities to support export, the local investor stated: 'we had a push from the export development unit under the Ministry of the Economy and Sustainable Development of Georgia to participate in exhibitions, and it was essential to motivate us to participate in the exhibition' (interview with a local investor, agribusiness, 24 January 2018).

To sum up, from 2008 through 2012, part of the state interventions in Georgia's food and agricultural sector were for political reasons rather than aiming to achieve any significant changes in terms of the sector's performance. Although one might criticize the state for politically motivated initiatives; nevertheless, this is the reality of governments in power in most democratic countries (Land, 2013). The state saw its role as a supporter of the private sector in the modernization of production, as well as a provider of infrastructure and information regarding the markets and modern technological achievements. The government used its power to force private investment in the sector; however, its motivation was more political rather than developmental. The state encouraged FDI flows through the policies, which improved the country's business environment; however, the volume of FDI in the sector remained low due to the unsolved core obstacles in the sector, which included incomplete land registration.

5.2. The Second Wave of State Intervention

With a change in power at the end of 2012, the government explicitly declared agricultural development as its top priority. With this, a new phase of state intervention in the sector started, as the state took the course of direct intervention in terms of providing technical and financial support. There are some explanations as to why the state started an active course of intervention in the sector. There was the argument that the state ignored the sector, and if it had continued that way, it would have finished very poorly (interview with a local expert, APRC, 9 November 2017). As the local expert from the local office of the FAO put it, the prioritization of the sector was a political decision:

> The prioritization of the sector made it possible to start the European Neighbourhood Program for Agriculture and Rural Development (ENPARD) in Georgia. The initial condition for starting this programme was to announce the sector as a priority. Subsequently, this action was followed by other donors entering, which would not have happened without the state's prioritization of agriculture (Interview with a local expert, FAO/ENPARD, 27 December 2018).

Following this line of thought, a local expert working at a local think tank stated that the prioritization of the sector was somewhat political, to fulfil pre-election promises on social programmes. Particularly the programmes such as the small farmer programme, or the free sowing programme, which were introduced at the start of the Georgian Dream's (GD) term in office, were implemented for political reasons (Interview with the Project Manager at the EPRC, 20 November 2017) rather than being development-oriented. 'What the state did in 2013 was wasteful because it was political, quick, but they scaled it down in the following years. They kept some of the programmes smarter than the way Saakashvili's administration was intervening' (interview with a foreign expert, 24 November 2017). Hence, the idea that the driver of the prioritization of the sector was political prevails among the different economic actors.

In 2012, the shifts in the state's priorities were followed by an increase in the Ministry of Agriculture (MoA) budget by 2.6 times in comparison to 2011. Even if the UNM had remained in power after the election in 2012, they would have increased the budget for the sector, as the election programmes of the UNM as well as GD both contained significant increases in budget allocations for agriculture (Interview with a local expert, FAO-ENPARD, 27 December 2018). The budget of MoA, as well as its share of the total budget, continued to increase from 2012 through 2016 (Fig. 5.1). At the initial stage, the intention was to increase state allocations in 2015–2020, but during the next years, they are expected to either stay the same or decline and be replaced by private investment (interview with a local expert, FAO-ENPARD, 27 December 2017).

Development-oriented state interventions require the existence of a long-term development strategy. In Georgia's case, the state reorganized the MoA and established the Department of Policy and Analysis in 2013, which has been in charge of the elaboration of the agricultural development strategy. The term of the strategy elaborated by the UNM was not over, but the current government nevertheless rewrote it. In 2014, after two years of elaboration, the MoA presented a renewed agriculture development strategy for 2015–2020 to the public (interview with the Head of the Division of Statistics and Analysis, MoA, 4 December 2017). As a local expert stated:

> Working on the strategy is always followed by some issues related to state bureaucracy, such as 'I will accept today, I will accept tomorrow.' In 2014, the MoA presented the draft strategy publicly. That minister resigned soon afterward, and a new minister was appointed. The new minister made some amendments, corrections in the elaborated strategy, nothing crucial; however, it still took some time. That version of the strategy was approved in 2015, and we use that version of the strategy as a guide (Interview with the Local Expert, FAO/ENPARD, 27 December 2017).

Hence, some directions of the strategy might change not only due to the change of the government but also due to the change of the minister within the same government. These changes were not radical. Although key directions remained the same due to the bureaucratic procedures, even small changes in the strategy slowed down activities. The process of strategy elaboration was followed by developing a detailed annual action plan updated every year. The strategy elaboration was a very open process; however, the action plan was not accessible publicly quite long. It was not public during the term of the previous minister. Now it is public (interview with the Deputy Director of the GFA, 14 December 2017).

The broad goals highlighted in the new strategy are quite similar to the ones in the strategy, which was elaborated by the UNM party, aiming to achieve investment growth, productivity and production growth, export diversification, and growth. Nevertheless, the instruments and state activities to reach these goals differ. The instruments elaborated since 2013 by the GD include interest rate subsidies on bank loans, co-financing investment, and providing grants. They aim to create incentives for businesses to invest in the food and agricultural sector. The goals set in the strategy are favorable for everyone. However, it remains vague about how the state will achieve these goals. The strategy does not contain measurable performance indicators (interview with the Local Investor, agribusiness, 7 December 2017). 'It is evident that everyone is working; though, the outcome of the conducted work requires an assessment at the end of the fiscal year. The existence of indicators would have been good for assessing the performances; however, I have not heard about the existence of such indicators.' (interview with the Agribusiness Project Coordinator at EBRD, 30 January 2018). As the former Minister of Agriculture of Georgia, during whose term in office the strategy was elaborated, emphasized:

> The strategy targets the period of 2015–2020; however, we should not have an illusion that we will achieve all goals defined in the strategy by 2020. After 2020, some directions might be added, and some might be changed somehow or excluded; however, the key direction will remain the same in the strategy (Interview with the Former Minister of Agriculture of Georgia, MoA, 11 December 2017).

With the increased budget, the state started elaborating on the new projects, which target the goals defined in the strategy (interview with the Public Officer, MoA, 5 December 2019). Since 2013 through these state programs, 30599 investment projects were supported. To manage the projects initiated for agriculture development, in 2014, the state established the Agriculture Project Management Agency (APMA) (in 2019 APMA became the part of the Rural Development Agency) as a subordinate body to the Ministry of Agriculture of

Georgia. 'The state has defined the priority projects, and APMA is implementing them. Of course, the projects were refined through active participation of APMA' (Interview with the Former Minister of Agriculture of Georgia, MoA, 11 December 2017).

One of the strategic priorities for the development of the sector is to facilitate export. However, the state does not have an agriculture-export growth and diversification facilitation strategy, except the small part in Georgia's Social Economic Development Strategy 'Georgia 2020,' which does not have feasible performance indicators. Therefore no one is aware of long term targets (interview with the Head of the Export Development Association, 1 February 2018). The information shared by the former minister of agriculture conveys a similar message (interview with the Former Minister of Agriculture of Georgia, MoA, 11 December 2017). The state's first economically significant intervention to support export was to open access for Georgian exports to the Russian market in eight months after the election. 'It was a purposeful effort; the state deserves all the credits for that' (interview with the Foreign Expert, 24 November 2017). The other mechanism of the intervention to support export promotion is to give an incentive to businesses to participate in the exhibitions. As a public official, who currently [2018] works at the MoA, clarified, when the state gets information about approaching international exhibitions, the state decides on the pavilion's size to buy at the exhibition. Afterward, the state decides how many companies can participate in the selected exhibition. The next steps are to distribute information among the relevant agribusinesses regarding the exhibition and recommend participation. An agribusiness, which expresses interest in participating in the exhibition, is supported to participate (interview with the Head of the Division of the Statistics and Analysis at MoA, 4 December 2017).

The other state intervention target in the food and agricultural sector is diversifying export products and markets. Therefore, the state selects countries to initiate free trade agreements. The department of International Relations and International Trade at the Ministry of Economy and Sustainable Development is in charge of studying the practices of signing free trade agreements with the identified countries. Based on the research, the mentioned department prepares statistical analyses for the leadership of the Ministry of the Economy and Sustainable Development and the Government Administration. Afterward, the preparation for the negotiation and discussion process with the targeted country starts (interview with the Chief Specialist at the Department of the International Relations and International Trade, the Ministry of Economics and Sustainable Development of Georgia, 28 November 2017). Since 2013, the state signed free trade agreements with European Free Trade Associations (EFTA) states, with the EU Deep and Comprehensive Free Trade Area (DCFTA), China, and Hong-Kong. The state renewed negotiations with Turkey to add more services and to liberalize further tariffs (interview with the Chief Specialist at the Department of the International Relations and International Trade, the Ministry of Economy and Sustainable Development, 28 November 2017).

Another target of state intervention is to increase production and export capacity. Therefore, the state provides financial assistance to local investors through the projects Plant the Future, the Preferential Agro Credit, Co-Financing Food Processing, and Storage Enterprises. The Agriculture Project Management Agency [2018] manages these projects. Only local businesses are eligible to apply, as the initial condition is that the land is to be registered and owned by the investor. 'As foreign investors are not allowed to buy agricultural land anymore, foreign investors who do not have local partners cannot apply for the projects; therefore we recommend them to find a local investor and to apply through them' (interview with a public official, MoA, 4 December 2017). Through these projects, the state subsidizes interest rates on bank loans, co-finances investment, and provides grants for investors who meet the project criteria. According to the local investor:

> The state programmes gave the perception to the local investors that the capital would flow to the sector; however, it was unclear how the state would manage this fiscally [...] I as an investor need to have a guarantee that these conditions will be respected despite possible changes in government or other circumstances. The loan is for ten years, but what if the state tells me that it is not creditworthy and cannot pay? (interview with a local investor, agribusiness, 16 November 2017).

Investing in Georgian agriculture does not have a long history. For financial organizations, there was a lack of experience in giving agro credits. From the farmers' side, there was a lack of knowledge and skills. It was hard for the financial organizations to see how the system was developing, so interest rates on bank loans for agriculture were high (interview with a project manager, APMA, 15 December 2017). The message conveyed by the former Minister of Agriculture is in line with this as well:

> As agriculture faced high risks, the commercial banks could not assess those risks and were offering short-term and expensive money to the private sector while the sector needed cheap and long-term money. Therefore, the micro-financial organizations got interested in the sector, but the problem was that the money of the microfinance organizations was more expensive than that from the banks. Consequently, the portfolio of loans in the sector was meagre a few years ago (Interview with a former Minister of Agriculture, MoA, 11 December 2017).

Due to the obstacles accessing credit and the need for investment in the sector, the state has been providing support to the private sector since 2013. As a result, the credit to agriculture in 2013 increased 4.5 times compared to 2012 and accounted for 16.5 million USD, which is 3 % of the total loan portfolio (FAO Statistics, see Fig. 5.2).

Fig. 5.2. Credit to Georgia's food and agricultural sector, 2008–2016

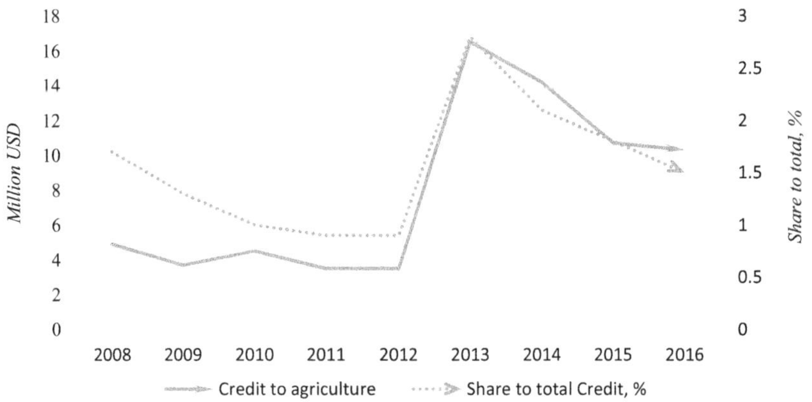

Source: FAO, 2019

Notes: Credit to agriculture is the bank loans provided to the agriculture sector, and total credit is the bank loans provided to the whole economy.

The graph indicates that in 2013 there was a drastic increase in the loans to the agriculture sector in Georgia, which reflected in an increase of its share to total credits to the economy.

Hence, the state programme favoured local investment in the food and agricultural sector by providing interest rate subsidies for bank loans. However, although Georgia's agriculture is in dire need of investment in physical capital and technology, state policies since 2013 have not favoured FDI in agriculture (ISET Policy Institute, 2016, p. 9). 'In June 2013, foreign investment in Georgia's agriculture was put on hold with introducing a temporary one-year moratorium on the acquisition of agricultural land by foreigners. The moratorium was lifted a year later, following a legal challenge by Transparency International. However, transactions involving agriculture land are not registered by the Public Registry pending new legislation' (ISET Policy Institute, 2016, p. 9). 'We do not know who pushed the initiation of this law, but this is a political issue, and we cannot change anything' (interview with the Executive Director of BAG, 4 December 2017). The determinant of this decision was sentiments rather than expected economic effects. The idea was initiated by politicians, as they were putting emphasis on nationalities and phobias (interview with a former Deputy Head of the Department of the Agriculture Development at MoA, 14 November 2011). The representative of agribusiness conveys a similar message in his interview:

> It was the speech delivered like if you ask in any country: "do you want our holy land to be bought by foreigners?" well, in any country, they will say no. However, if you ask: "what is the single most important concern your family has now?" and get the answer "work," those two questions are linked. Therefore, if you highlight that, asking,"do you want the investment, which gives jobs to you and your family?" you can get a different outcome. It is the task of the political elite to highlight specific important aspects in the questions (interview with a beneficiary of the Preferential Agrocredit programme, 15 December 2017).

In terms of economic outcomes, this law was not appropriate, as a large part of the agricultural land is not cultivated, but the current government tried to avoid the dissatisfaction of radical social groups, either very religious or very traditional ones (interview with Local Expert in Monitoring and Evaluation of the Economic Development Projects at APRC, 24 November 2017). On the one hand, this law distracts FDI flows in the sector and, on the other hand, restricts issuing agricultural loans from the financial organizations under foreign ownership. For example, Pro-Credit bank, which used to be one of the largest lenders of agriculture loans, has to cease providing agriculture loans. The same concerns to the microfinance organizations (interview with the International Expert, CNFA, 9 November 2017). The idea that the economic outcomes of the policy was not a priority while adopting this law is confirmed by the message conveyed by the public official, stating that: 'The national interest was determinant of the decision. This is the capital, on which Georgians want to have access always. Some issues have a national interest, and this interest is more important than economic benefit in this case' (interview with the Public Official, MoA, 4 December 2017).

So far, this chapter explored state activism in the Georgian food and agricultural sector from 2004 through 2016. The sector had been back to the country's development priorities since the end of 2012. The government has started active intervention in the sector since 2013 in order to boost productivity, facilitate the production and export growth, and diversify production and export patterns. The next section aims to assess the changes in the sector's key performance indicators to understand if state intervention leads to the improved performance of the sector and the change of the economy's structure. These indicators include the capacity and growth of the production and export dimensions, the sector's competitive performance, the diversification of the domestic and export dimensions, employment, and productivity. These performance indicators are selected following the United Nations Industrial Development Organisation's (UNIDO) Enhancing the Quality of Industrial Policies (EQuIP) toolbox, which proposes these indicators to measure a sector's economic performance.

5.3. The Performance of the Sector

The state provides financial assistance to the food and agricultural sector of Georgia. Provision of financial assistance created incentives for businesses to invest in the sector. In addition to public resources, private resources were directed to the sector (interview with a beneficiary of the Preferential Agrocredit programme, 16 November 2017). However, 'there are no documents, empirical evidence on the impact assessment of any interventions in Georgia, and no one makes the state accountable for the existence of those empirics. Therefore, the fact that the processes going on in the sector are not properly analysed is an issue' (interview with a local expert, FAO-ENPARD, 27 December 2017).

This section aims to understand how the sector's performance has changed since the state started intervening actively. It looks at the dynamics of economic indicators, which measure the productivity and capacity of domestic production and export dimensions. The aim is to understand whether the increased support to the sector has proved to be developmental, i.e., that it induced a sustained increase of productivity, production, and export and contributed to a change of the employment structure and diversification of production and export. It should be noted that the projects which have been initiated by the state to support the sector's development are long-term, and approximately half of them have not started operating fully yet (interview with a local expert, Transparency International, 22 November 2017).

One of the targets of state intervention is to increase productivity and production levels, including primary production, agriculture, as well as secondary production, i.e., food processing. Currently, Georgia cultivates a wide variety of crops, such as cereals, early and late vegetables, potatoes, nuts, subtropical crops, grapes, melons, and a variety of other fruits. In economically advanced countries, the underlying mechanism was productivity growth in agriculture, followed by a change in the structure of employment as well as a change in the structure of the economy. In Georgia's case, in 2013, productivity in agriculture increased by 7 % compared to 2012. The indicator continued to grow in the next years, but at a lower rate. In 2016, the productivity in agriculture exceeded the corresponding indicator in 2012 by 23 %, though its growth rate slowed down by 5 % points compared to 2013 (Fig. 5.3). Overall, from 2013 through 2016, the productivity growth of primary production in agriculture showed a positive trend, yet the growth rates were not sustained at a high level, and the average annual growth (3.5 %) rate is not high enough to drive development. Value Added (VA) in agriculture grew from 2012 through 2016 by 3.5 % annually on average (Fig. 5.3); however, with volatile rates. In 2013, this indicator showed a considerable increase (11.3 %) compared to 2012, yet in 2014 it dropped down to 1.3 %, and in 2016 slowed down to 0.3 %, meaning that in 2016 the value-added of agriculture grew very slightly in comparison to 2015. Overall, the indicator of VA of agriculture in 2016 exceeds the corresponding indicator in 2012 by 12 %; however, its growth rate slowed down compared to 2013 by 11 % point (Fig. 5.3). Despite the positive trends in the numbers, the local food processor emphasized:

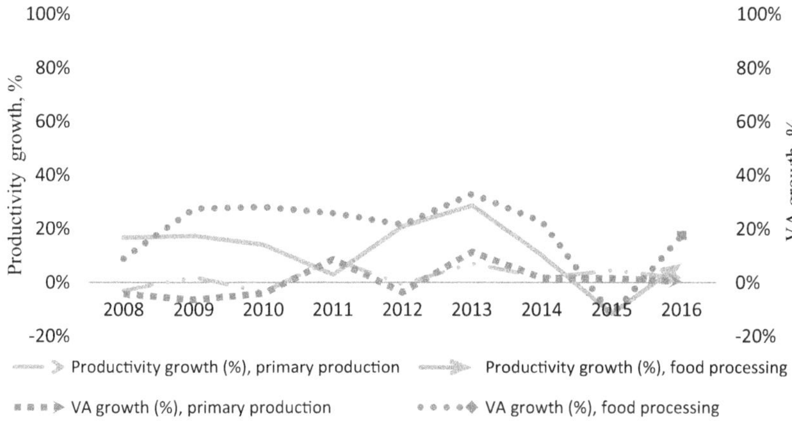

Fig. 5.3. Growth in productivity and value-added in the food & agricultural sector

Source: UN statistics, 2019 and the National Statistics Office of Georgia, 2019;

Notes: Productivity growth of primary production measures the growth of VA of agriculture per worker in comparison to the previous year; productivity growth in food processing measures a growth of food industry value added per worker compared to the previous year; VA growth of primary production is the growth of the volume of VA of agriculture in comparison to the previous year; VA growth of food processing is the growth of VA of food processing in comparison to the previous year.

The graph indicates that overall, from 2012 through 2016, productivity in agriculture increased by 23 %, VA in agriculture increased 13 %, productivity in food processing increased 34 % and the VA of food processing increased 68 %. At the beginning of the active intervention, in 2013, these indicators boost, however, the growth has not been stable and sustained at a high rate and is characterized by volatility in this period.

> There is a lack of supply of primary production [...] Getting loans is not a remedy, as long as knowledge and skills are not increased in the sector. The loans are not automatically followed by an increased knowledge for production of high quality products. We need to increase productivity, but nothing has changed in this direction. That is why we are not moving forward and standing in one place and going around in circles (Interview with local investor, agribusiness, 7 December 2018).

The information provided by the public official confirms the message that the food processors have obstacles in the production processes in terms of the supply of local primary production. Therefore, they have to import primary products, e.g., even the processors producing juice have to import primary products, or fruit concentrates (interview with the Head of the Rural Development Coordination Division, MoA, 4 December 2017).

There is a problem regarding the volume of supply of primary products and their quality (interview with the Agribusiness Project Coordinator, EBRD, 30 January 2018). Due to insufficient primary production volume, some successful food processors produce at a lower level than their maximum potential. They cannot entirely meet local market demands and lack capability for exports (interview with a project manager, EPRC, 20 November 2017). Moreover, there are many broken value chains between comparatively larger food processors, participants of the forward linkages, and suppliers, due to deviation from supply or payment requirements. To make more value from the state activities that support primary production, a value chain needs to be developed. There are some cases of supported primary production, creating new industries in the sector, yet the scaling and replicating of this process are not establishing a sustainable trend (interview with Local Expert at APRC, 9 November 2017).

The food processing industry in Georgia relies on local as well as imported resources. The products that rely on local resources include wine, other alcohol, mineral water, tea, essential oil, and canned food. These are the products that are oriented at export as well. The products that rely on imported resources include milk and dairy, meat and ham, fish, sugar, oil, fat, and non-alcoholic drinks. These products are oriented at local markets. From 2012 through 2016, the food industry's productivity and its VA grew (Fig. 5.3). These indicators were growing even before the state intervention with a higher average annual rate. The average annual growth rate of the productivity in the food processing from 2008 through 2012 (before active state intervention) was 14 % and VA 22 %, and from 2013 to

2016, the average annual growth rate of the productivity in the food processing was 8 % and VA 15 %, hence lower than before the intervention. In 2013 we saw a 29 % boost in productivity compared to 2012. In the next years, the growth rates dropped down significantly, yet remained positive except in 2015, where we saw a 12 % decline compared to 2014. In 2016, the indicator of productivity in food processing exceeded the corresponding indicator in 2012 by 34 %. As to the VA of the food industry, the indicator of 2016 exceeds the indicator of 2012 by 68 %; however, its growth rate declined by 15 % point compared to the corresponding indicator in 2013 (Fig. 5.3).

One of the targets of state interventions is the diversification of production. The diversity of climatic zones allows the country to produce diverse crops, though only on small scales, due to the small size of the land. An investor who has been successfully operating in the sector since 2009 emphasized that:

> Georgia's agriculture is unique, as there is a combination of diverse climatic zones [...]there is everything that California has, in some regions totally different products grow next to each other in totally different ways. On the one hand, this makes Georgia have significant agricultural opportunities; on the other hand, due to the lack of scale, it makes it incredibly hard for a single developmental strategy for the country (Interview with a beneficiary of the Preferential Agrocredit programme, 15 December 2017).

Regarding diversification of production, significant changes were not observed from 2012 through 2016. There were neither new crops nor a significant increase in the volumes of crop production except wheat (1.5 times), barley (2.3 times) and parsley (2 times). The domestic dimensions of production are moderately concentrated. The products with the highest value in gross production were milk (19 %), beef (11 %), chicken (8 %), pork (7 %), potatoes (7 %), maize (7 %), eggs (6 %), grapes (5 %), hazelnuts (3 %), wheat (3 %), apples (3 %), peaches (2 %) and tomatoes (2 %), which covers 84 % of total gross production value. Most of these products are for local markets, and hence not exported (Source Geostat, the author's calculation).

The positive dynamics in the productivity and value added of agriculture have not been followed with relevant changes in the structure of employment or changes in the shares of the agriculture, industry and services value added in total value added (Figs. 5.4 and 5.5).

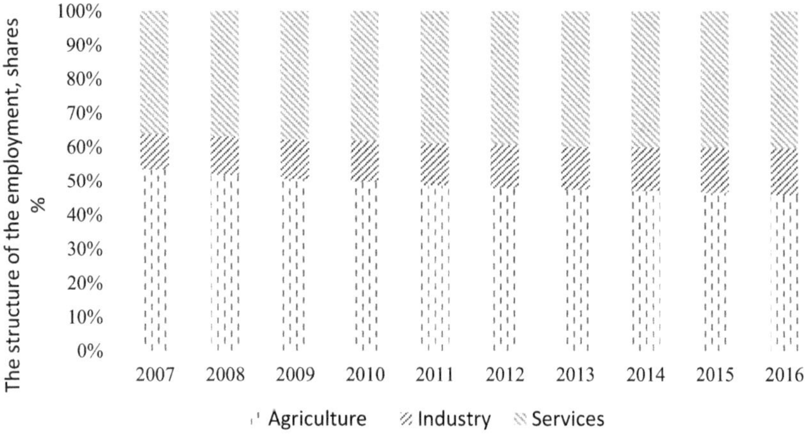

Fig. 5.4. The structure of employment

Source: ILO 2019

Notes: The graph shows the shares of employment in agriculture, industry and the service sector as part of total employment.

The structure of employment does not show much change from 2012 through 2016. In terms of total employment the share of the labour force employed in agriculture is 46 %, the share in industry is 14 %, and in services is 40 %.

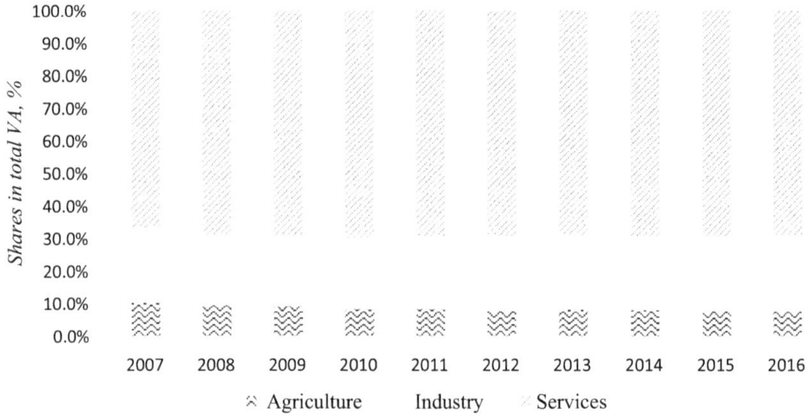

Fig. 5.5. The structure of value added (VA)

Source: UN statistics, 2019

Note: The graph presents the value added in agriculture, industry, and services as a share of the total value added. From 2012 through 2016, the structure does not show any noteworthy changes. In 2016 the share of agriculture VA in total value added is 7.6 %, the share of industry VA 23.4 % and the share of services VA 69 %. In 2012, the corresponding indicators were 7.6 %, 23.2 %, and 69.2 %, respectively.

The structure of employment and the shares of VA of the sector compared to the total economy are indicators to measure structural transformation (UNCTAD, 2016). In 2016, the share of employment in agriculture was 46 % of total employment, and the share of the sector in GDP was 9 %. Typically, in the early stages of a lagging-behind country's structural transformation, there is a substantial gap between the share of the labour force employed in agriculture and the GDP share generated by that workforce. This gap narrows with advances in growth and development. This convergence is part and consequence of the structural transformation, reflecting better-integrated labour and financial markets (Gardner, 2002; Johnson, 1997). In the case of Georgia, such convergence has not been observed yet. From 2012 through 2016, the active labour force in agriculture declined by 2 % points, and the share to GDP increased by 0.4 % points. In East and South East Asia, the reduction of agriculture employment ranging between 4 % and 26 % points was associated with output growth rates around 6 %. By contrast, in Sub Saharan Africa and Northern Africa, countries reduced their agriculture employment by less than 5 % point, and their economic growth rates accounted for 3.6 % and 4.4 %, respectively (UNCTAD, 2016).

One more target of state intervention in the food and agricultural sector is to facilitate export growth. Agriculture has not responded to the intense competition brought by trade reforms after the Rose Revolution in 2003, because of weaknesses in essential agricultural services, infrastructure, and operating peasant-style production (FAO, 2012). The state started activities to facilitate export at the end of 2010. From 2010 through 2016, the volume of exports increased by 95 % (Fig. 5.6). In 2013, the volume of exports increased drastically, by 50 %, compared to 2012. The boost of exports in 2013 was due to regaining access to the Russian markets for Georgian food and beverage exporters (Fig. 5.6.). The volume of exports continued to grow in 2014 as well. However, it was not sustained for the next year due to the currency crisis in 2014. Despite the subsequent currency devaluation, exports declined because the currencies of the neighboring countries, which are major trading partners of Georgia, also devalued. In 2015, exports declined by 26 % compared to 2014 (Fig. 5.6).

Fig. 5.6. The dynamics of the export of the food and beverages, its share in total export and in world agriculture export

Sources: WDI, UN comtrade

Note: The graph presents the dynamics of the exports of food and beverages, and their share in Georgia's total exports as well as in world agriculture exports. The volume of the exports, as well as their share of the total exports increased from 2012 through 2016, and its share of the world export changed by only 0.01 % during the mentioned period, and remains low, at 0.05 %.

In 2016, the export of agricultural products accounted for 33 % of total exports. To strengthen the sector's resilience to external shocks, diversification of export markets and products is crucial. To measure the diversification of the export products and markets, the Hirschman-Herfindahl Index (HHI), which is a measure of market concentration, is applied to Georgia's food and agricultural sector. The country's export structure and its markets are moderately concentrated, with HHI 0.11 (own calculations). The export basket is dominated by a few products, including hazelnuts (26 %), wine (16 %), other alcoholic beverages (13 %), mineral and freshwater produce (12 %), beef (5 %), sparkling water (2 %) and citrus fruits (2 %). The share of the top three exported products in total agricultural export is 55 %. Exports are concentrated in a few markets: the EU (32 %), Russia (20 %), Ukraine (8 %), Armenia (6 %), Iraq (6 %), Kazakhstan (5 %), Azerbaijan (4 %) and Turkey (4 %). The dominant export markets are the EU, Russia, and Ukraine, accounting for 67 % of food and beverage export. In 2016, the country had 88 trade partners in export, which is higher than the number of trading partners in 2012. The types of export goods do not show much change compared to 2012. The new products in the export structure include lettuce, grapes, citrus fruit peel, cinnamon, and soya bean oil, but their scale is very low. 'The country used to have and still has a small choice of products ready for export. For Georgia, the key issue is to find a qualified exporter who has a qualified product ready for export' (interview with the Head of the Export Development Association, 1 February 2018). As a local expert emphasized, there is no diversity of export products, even though there is much talk about exports. There are some individual success cases of production of high-quality products, but at a low quantity, so they can only meet meagre demand in terms of scale. There are cases when the state invites businesses to an exhibition of food and agricultural products. However, when these businesses start negotiations with potential importers, it appears that they cannot meet minimum requirements for export in terms of quantity (interview with a local expert, APRC, 9 November 2017). Due to its limited agricultural land area, Georgia cannot compete in international markets by utilizing economies of scale.I Instead, it has to find its niche as a producer of high-quality produce. In this context, the development of organic production methods could become a key factor in the agricultural development strategy. However, little attention has been paid to promoting organic production by the state (Bluashvili and Sukhanskayia, 2015).

To sum up, since the active intervention of the state in the food and agricultural sector, productivity and production and export growth have shown positive trends, but the growth rates have not been sustained at high levels. The growth of productivity and production has not been followed by transforming the structure of employment and value-added, and hence structural transformation and development. The diversification of domestic and export dimensions does not follow production and export growth, meaning that we do not see more diversified markets and exported products since the state intervention in Georgia's food and agricultural sector.

Conclusion

This chapter examined the effects of state interventions in Georgia's food and agricultural sector from 2004 through 2016. From 2008 through 2012, state activities were purely driven by political reasons rather than aiming to achieve a significant improvement in the sector's performance. Until 2012, the government saw its role as a supporter of the private sector in the modernization of the production and a provider of infrastructure and information regarding the markets and modern technological achievements. The state used its power to force private investment in the sector; however, the motivation was more political than developmental. Authorities encouraged FDI flows through policies that improved the country's business environment; however, the volume of FDI in the sector remained low due to unresolved obstacles in the sector, which included incomplete land registration.

Since the end of 2012, the agricultural sector has been back as the country's developmental priorities. A new phase of state intervention in the sector started, as the state took the course of direct intervention in terms of providing technical and financial support. The government renewed the agriculture development strategy and started active intervention from 2013 to boost productivity, facilitate the growth of production and export, and diversify production and export dimensions. The state elaborated instruments to reach these goals, including interest rate subsidies on bank loans, co-financing investment, and grants. These instruments aim to create incentives for businesses to invest in the agriculture or food processing industry.

Since the state's active intervention, productivity and production and export growth have had a positive trend. However, growth rates have not remained high. There was growth, but it has not been accompanied by the transformation of employment structure and value-added, and hence structural transformation and development. The diversification of domestic and export dimensions has not followed the growth of production and export. Export products and markets remain moderately concentrated, and the domestic dimensions of production remain moderately concentrated. Hence, since state intervention we do not observe significant changes in terms of creating new production and export opportunities in the sector.The Food and Agricultural Sector of Georgia

Chapter VI The Nature of the Institutions of State–Agribusiness Relations in Georgia

Introduction

As various countries' experiences illustrate (see Chapter II), state intervention, which drives development, requires specific institutional prerequisites (Ahrens, 2002). As discussed in Chapters II and III, among the specific prerequisites for effective intervention, the institutions of state–business relations (SBRs) that maintain collaboration between the state and businesses, enhance policy experimentation and adaptation, and support market functions are crucial (Trubek, 2010). Institutions of SBRs, when functioning strategically, can be devices for lowering the cost of coordinating economic and other activities, reducing uncertainty, simplifying decision making, and promoting coordination and cooperation among actors within the economy (Furubotn and Richter, 2005, p. 7).

Arguing that the nature of SBRs is critical for successful state interventions, this chapter seeks to understand how the state interacts with agribusinesses in the process of the state intervention in the food and agricultural sector of Georgia. Therefore, this chapter addresses the research question: *How does the state manage its relationship with agribusinesses in the process of state intervention in the food and agricultural sector of Georgia?* With this in mind, this chapter intends to explore the nature of the institutions of the state–agribusiness relations in Georgia's food and agricultural sector. The analysis is presented through three cases of state intervention. These cases are specific state programmes entitled *Preferential Agro Credit, Plant the Future,* and *Co-financing Agriculture Processing and Storage Enterprises.* They are intended to create incentives for local businesses to invest in the food and agricultural sector with the goals of diversifying and increasing production and export dimensions, as well as enhancing productivity, thereby supporting the economic performance of the sector. The programmes are typical cases of state instruments for direct interventions in economic activities in Georgia. In each selected case, the research seeks to understand the nature of the SBRs and the interactions between the actors (state and agribusinesses). The number of actors involved, the amount of provided support, and this support's duration differ among these cases. Thus, it is to be explored if differences in these state programmes result in differences in the nature of the state–agribusiness relations.

Large parts of this chapter draw on the analysis of interviews of public officials in the food and agricultural sector, agribusinesses (including beneficiaries of the state food and agricultural support programmes), local and foreign experts from key developmental/donor organizations, think tanks, and organizations specialized in food and agricultural development research or policy advising. Interviews were essential to understanding state agribusiness relations in the process of state interventions from 2013-through 2017, as secondary data on this issue are not available

This chapter consists of six sections. Section 6.1 presents the main argument, which is also the critical argument of this study. Section 6.2 outlines the characteristics of the institutional setting of *strategic SBRs*. Section 6.3 presents the 'Preferential Agrocredit' case and the nature of SBRs within this state programme. In Section 6.4, the support programme, 'Plant the Future,' is reviewed, along with its SBRs. Section 6.5 presents the SBRs underlying the third programme 'Co-financing Agriculture Processing and Storage Enterprises.' Section 6.6 provides a concluding summary of the nature of the state agribusiness relations in Georgia.

6.1. The Institutional Setting that Maintains *Strategic SBRs*

There is significant diversity in the design of SBRs, however, as discussed in Chapters II and III, *strategic SBRs* that maintain fruitful consultations between the state and private sector, and strengthen the capacity to selectively address existing economic opportunities and obstacles (Sen, 2015) show similar features. These features relate to information exchange, reciprocity, credibility, and trust between state and private actors (Schneider and Maxfield, 1997), as well as the existence of a feedback mechanisms (Pelikan, 1986), which is linked to the concept of Northian adaptive efficiency (North, 1990).

As Chapter III illustrates, information exchange between the state and businesses depends on the capability of the state to collect information and data from private sector, and analyse it, and the willingness of businesses to provide information/data to the state (Maxfield and Schneider, 1997; te Velde, 2013). The dialogue, whenever possible and wherever hosted, shall maximize the potential of comprehensive information exchange from both sides (Herzberg and Wright, 2013).

The second feature of *strategic SBRs*, reciprocity, refers to the capability of a state to discipline businesses by requiring them to comply with state performance standards to qualify for direct subsidies (Amsden, 1989). Economic theory states that when subsidies are available, investors' demand for them will be high, but ensuring their effective usage will be difficult (Mueller, 1989). Therefore, the state needs the capability and commitment to discipline businesses. This implies that the state provides subsidies or venture capital to encourage investments for specific activities, with performance requirements; and ensures that the business meets the performance standards in return for subsidies (Evans, 1998, p. 67). The resources need to be devoted to monitoring and applying rewards or punishment, based on performance, in order to acquire maximum returns from the subsidies (North, 1990, p. 32). The state shall also ensure that substandard, unprofitable projects are phased out (Rodrik, 2004).

One more critical feature for *strategic SBRs* is credibility and trust. Credibility of the state refers to a commitment to detailed policies, deals, and arrangements designed to encourage entrepreneurs to make the desired investment and production decisions (Rodrik, 1991). If the state does not keep its commitments and promises, investors will lose confidence in future credibility of the state, and investment will suffer (Bardhan, 2005). Credibility in commitments matters, as it builds trust, which is essential to lowering transaction costs. To do this, trust and reliance are necessary features. In the absence of trust, monitoring and arranging sanctions and guarantees will be more costly. Banfield (1958) has argued that lack of trust is indeed one of the critical causes of economic underdevelopment (Furubotn and Richter, 2005).

In addition, it is crucial for *strategic SBRs* to have mechanisms in place that provide feedback on the institutions, policies and performances of the actors (Pelikan, 1986). Feedback mechanisms help economic actors learn from failures in order to correct organizational errors, and policy makers to enhance policy adaptability. The adaptability of interventionist policies and programmes (North, 1990), on its turn, encourages trials and experiments and provides for elimination or adjustment of the programmes, policies, or rules of the game that fail to reach targeted goals. In cases of *strategic SBRs*, states tested policies/programmes in local contexts, defined, then monitored the performance indicators of their degrees of success, requested feedback from the private sector, and applied the feedback to the process of adapting policies/programmes (Page and Tarp, 2017). Enacting a feedback mechanism provided the opportunity to understand which interventions worked and which did not. These feedback mechanisms employed economic performance monitoring of the rate of job growth, output, and exports (Kim, 2015). In cases of failure to meet expectations, the policies/programmes were either modified or abandoned. In cases of success, they were replicated in other settings; hence, the feedback was followed by required adaptations (Sen, 2013).

6. 2. The Case of Preferential Agrocredit

6.2.1. The Project Overview

In 2013, the Ministry of Agriculture of Georgia (MoA) - curently [2020] refered as the Ministry of Environmental Protection and Agricultura (MEPA)- initiated the Preferential Agrocredit project. The project's goal is to simplify access to finance for investors to create new, or extend pre-existing, primary agricultural production, processing, or food storage enterprises. As the research findings in Chapter V illustrate, lack of access to long-term, cheap financial resources was one of the critical obstacles of the food and agricultural sector of Georgia before 2013. The reason behind that was that this sector was considered to be high-risk. Therefore, the interest rates on agricultural loans were significantly higher in comparison to interest rates on loans to other sectors (Moistsraphishvili, 2017). In line with this, the former Minister of Agriculture, who was in office while launching of Preferential Agrocredit, stated that:

> For financial organizations, the food and agricultural sector had been always less appealing compared to alternative sectors, where financial institutions could invest. The sector needed cheap and long-term money, yet financial institutions were providing short-term and expensive money (Interview with the former Minister of Agriculture of Georgia, MoA, 11 December 2017).

The focal objectives of the programme are to facilitate local, high-quality primary and secondary production, to create infrastructure for food processing and storage, to increase production for local and export markets and to create jobs (ENPARD, 2016). The programme does not set limitations on investment in terms of specific industry/products as long as the project belongs to the food and agricultural sector.

The eligibility criteria for investment projects within the Preferential Agrocredit framework are defined in the Government of Georgia's Decree N139 attachment N1 (2014). Conditions for investment require that beneficiaries employ local labour, and in the case of food processing, as an input usage of primary products produced in Georgia. Conditions for investment through Preferential Agroleasing are the import of new or second hand machinery, or the purchase of foreign or local technology in Georgia (The Government of Georgia Decree N139, 2014).

In 2013, the state started implementing the Preferential Agrocredit project via the Agriculture Project Management Agency (APMA)-currently [2020] restructured as a Rural Development Agency (RDA). APMA offers a co-financing interest rate on loans, and leasing for producing primary agricultural products, for enhancing the food processing industry, for building food storage-facilities, and for technological upgrades(The Government of Georgia Decree N 139, 2014). The APMA runs the programme in partnership with thirteen financial organizations (commercial banks) and two agroleasing organisations, which are in charge of issuing and monitoring loans and leasing for investment projects that match the goals and conditions defined by the Government of Georgia Decree N139 attachment N1.

In the process of issuing a loan, a financial organisation is responsible for assessing, independently from APMA, an investor's credibility for repaying the loan. In this process, the financial organisation must take into account the list of project goals and specific conditions for investment projects, as defined by the APMA (interview with the Manager of Preferential Agrocredit, APMA, 15 December 2017). For the applicant, it is crucial to know which financial organisation and which credit officer to approach to avoid the delays in issuing loans. A beneficiary of a Preferential Agrocredit programme mentioned that he had delay for three months because the credit officer in charge of the Preferential Agrocredit loan lacked the relevant experience and capability to deal with the issue:

> Finally, I addressed a financial organisation where I knew credit officer, whose capability I trusted. The credit officer analysed the volume of credit I was eligible to access, and the loan was issued in a month (Interview with a beneficiary of the Preferential Agrocredit programme, 24 January 2018).

After determining credit eligibility, the financial organisation informs APMA that a new loan has been issued. If the issued loan meets the targets of the Preferential Agrocredit programme, the state starts subsidizing interest rates on the loan (Interview with Manager of Preferential Agrocredit, APMA, 15 December 2017). The conditions of support are based on the Government of Georgia Decree N139 Appendix 1 (2014). The interest rate ceiling is 16 %, meaning that a financial organisation cannot set a higher interest rate payment on agroloan. From 2013 through 2016, within the framework of the programme, 39151 loans were issued. The beneficiaries of this programme include all size of agribusinesses (small, medium, and large). Thus, the case of the Preferential Agrocredit programme sheds light on the general picture of state agribusiness relations in Georgia.

6.2.2. State–Agribusiness Relations

This section aims to illustrate research outcomes regarding the nature of the institutions of the state–agribusiness relations in the case of the Preferential Agrocredit programme. In four subsections, this section discusses, in turn, the information exchange, reciprocity, credibility and trust, and feedback mechanism for programme. The results rely on the data gathered from the interviews of the relevant actors and government laws and regulations.

6.2.2.1. Information Exchange

The manager of Preferential Agrocredit, as well as respondents from the private sector, revealed during the interviews that there are no formal rules that oblige the state and businesses to meet regularly or exchange information within the framework of Preferential Agrocredit. However, in case of need, it is easy to reach the programme manager of Preferential Agrocredit, who is open to meeting or giving consultations. During the project design period, which lasted for four months, the state did not organise consultations with the umbrella organisations in the sector (interview with the Deputy Executive Director of the Business Association of Georgia, 4 December 2012) or with leading agribusinesses (interview with a beneficiary of Preferential Agrocredit, 16 January 2016). However, the state consulted with financial organizations and input suppliers, which are partners of the state in the programme implementation processes (interview with a former Minister of Agriculture, MoA, 11 December 2017). The local expert, who by the time the programme was initiated was employed by Agro Group in the TBC Bank (one of the partner commercial organizations of the programme), confirmed that the APMA had periodical meetings, which were informal and arranged as needed, with financial organizations. During the meetings, the discussions related to procedural obstacles, as it was difficult to modify directly the products of the financial organizations in a way to meet the requirements of both the state projects and the clients (interview with local expert, USAID-REAP, 29 November 2017).

Despite the fact that there are no formal rules that oblige the state and agribusinesses to meet, if there are issues to discuss, arranging a meeting is easily manageable. The Ministry of Agriculture of Georgia is a very open body; even the Minister is reachable for a meeting (interview with the Agribusiness Project Coordinator, EBRD, 30 January 2018). However, there are some informal criteria that determine the level of access to the state, depending on the size of the agribusiness, network and the rank of public official involved. According to a public official:

> The information exchange between the state and business happens via a physical meeting or via email. When a meeting is requested from a private actor, a public official to meet with the investor is determined based on the size of the investment project. The larger business is, the higher the rank of the public official who attends the meeting. If

> the investor is too small, the information requested is provided via email (interview with a Public Official, MoA, 4 December 2017).

Professional and personal networks matter in establishing communications with the representatives of state (interview with Local Expert, OXFAM, 6 November 2017). APMA is open to all sizes of agribusiness, and it is easy to meet or reach a programme manager via phone. Large agribusiness and successful players in the sector can easily reach the state, up to through the Ministerial level. Small and medium-size enterprises (SMEs) communicate their concerns with the state through industry-specific umbrella organizations (interview with local expert, APRC, 9 November 2017), or through personal networks (interview with a beneficiary of Preferential Agrocredit programme, 23 November 2017).

At the programme level, there are no public networks (webpage, forums, and regular meetings) dedicated to the information exchange between agribusiness, state and other interested actors from the civil society organizations, developmental organizations, think tanks and independent experts in the sector. These networks do not exist at either an industry or sector level. As a beneficiary of the programme emphasized:

> Formally, there is no strategy for regular meetings or information exchange. However, the state is entirely accessible: "You can talk, and you can say that, hey, there is this going on, or even phone the Minister. I mean I do not call, but my partners do. And that is a big deal [...] because a lot of the things evolve relatively quickly." (interview with the beneficiary of the Preferential Agrocredit, 15 December 2017).

Even without formal public networks or formal rules for information exchange between the actors in the food and agricultural sector, to 'make a noise' regarding concerns and convey these concerns to the state is not hard, because of the small size of the country. The question is whether these concerns are and can be addressed. It is easy to access the state through a personal or professional networks and to share the concerns at all levels if needed, however this is not followed by relevant changes, as the decision-making process is very slow and trapped in time (interview with the Beneficiary of Preferential Agrocredit, 16 January 2018). Another interviewee confirmed that there are the problems of follow-up after sharing concerns (interview with foreign expert, 24 November 2017).

In addition to individual meetings initiated by agribusinesses, there are various types of events organized by civil society organisations (CSOs), think tanks, developmental organisations, or by the state. However, it is said that many of these meetings are pointless, as they do not yield any operational information or advice (interview with the Beneficiary of Preferential Agrocredit, 15 December 2017). The beneficiary of the programme explained that:

> There have been quarterly meetings at the MoA just for the sake of meeting [...]no decisions have been made during these meetings,. The culture of organising meetings 'to hear the voice of agribusiness' does not exist yet (interview with the beneficiary of Preferential Agrocredit, 24 January 2018).

The local expert revealed, on the one hand, that the state's response to shared concerns or recommendations starts with scepticism regarding the likelihood of making relevant changes. On the other hand, the state maintains a 'we know better' attitude (interview with the Local Expert at the Private Sector Development Research Centre, ISET, 14 November 2017). Moreover, the local expert, who is invited frequently to such meetings once they are organized, stated that the impression is that at the meetings, which are organized by the state to get feedback on initated ammandements in policy or programme , the state invites experts from whom they expect accaptence /agreement rather than opposition to the presented initiative. Concequently, in those meetings, it often happens that most participants support the initiative or prefer not to oppose it (interview with the Local Expert, 9 November 2017). In line with this, the expert highlighted:

> [...] does it make any sense to express an opinion? You do not want to be a "Guinea Pig," I had experience with this. If you express an opinion which opposes the project/ programme in question, the initiators take the opposition personally, and it becomes hard to communicate with them in the future (interview with the Local Expert, 9 November 2017).

Regarding the sharing of opinions, the representative of agribusiness conveys a similar message, stating that it is not their task to be "guinea pigs" (interview with the Beneficiary of Preferential Agrocredit, 15 December 2017). Besides, the private sector expects that even in case of sharing information, nothing will be changed.

The state's 'we know better' attitude and agribusinesses' expectation that sharing feedback will not bring about relevant actions might explain the fact that during the meetings of the Trade Advisor Group at the Ministry of Economy and Sustainable Development, the represented businesses did not actively share information about the export obstacles they faced. A public official who participated in these meetings revealed:

> Georgia could not export wine in Turkey, and we were wondering what the obstacles the exporters faced were. However, neither large nor SMEs expressed any interest in sharing information regarding the obstacles they faced (interview with the Senior Specialist at the Department of the International Relations and International Trade at the Ministry of Economy and Sustainable Development, 28 November 2017).

Interview results reveal that there is neither a regulatory framework nor formal rules that require businesses to regularly report their activities and performance to the state. A local investor, who is a beneficiary of this programme, emphasized in the framework of the Preferential Agrocredit programme that businesses do not have any obligations to supply information to the state regarding their production or realization of the products. "The only data I submit on basic operations are quarterly statistics to the Business Statistics Department of the National Statistics Office of Georgia"(interview with the Beneficiary of Preferential Agrocredit, 24 January 2018). On the one hand, the state does not express interest in collecting the data necessary to assess the economic performance of the beneficiaries of the programme, unless the information is from successful cases in the sector. "Evaluation is used to create a good story," said the beneficiary (interview with the Beneficiary of Preferential Agrocredit, 15 December 2017). On the other hand, business lacks the willingness to share such information:

> We would not give banks (the implementing partners of this programme and contacts for the beneficiary) the Excel spreadsheets on how our operations work [...], nor the operations manual, nor internal calculations (interview with the Beneficiary of Preferential Agrocredit, 15 December 2017).

As the head of the Export Development Association (EDA) emphasized, none of the members of the associations are willing to share the financial statements of their businesses even with EDA, which lobbies with the state in the interest of its members. One explanation for this attitude from business is that there is no culture for sharing such information outside the business community (interview with the Head of the Export Development Association, 2 February 2018).

The state disseminates information regarding programme-related issues via email, online publications, and other media sources, including social media. According to the local investor, "It is essential to know a person in that agency, with whom you have constant communication, in order for updates from the state to reach you consistently" (interview with the beneficiary of Preferential Agrocredit, 24 January 2018).

6.2.2.2. Reciprocity

The Preferential Agrocredit programme creates incentives for the private sector to invest in the food and agricultural sector of Georgia. The support mechanisms employed in the framework of this programme are co-financing interest rate for turnover assets, providing secondary collateral for fixed assets, and co-financing the lease payments. For each of these components, the amount of available loan funding, as well as the subsidy level of the interest rate vary. The range of the plan for fixed assets is between 20 thousand GEL (minimum) and 1.5 million GEL (maximum). The state co-finances the interest at the rate of 11 % of the loan for 66 months, and 10 % for 24 months, as well as provides a secondary warranty (collateral) of not more than 50 % of the total principal amount of each new, non-refinanced loan. It is possible to issue parallel loans if the total amount of the parallel loans does not exceed the ceiling of the loan for the project component (1.5 million GEL) and each of the loans is not lower than the minimum amount (20 thousand GEL). The loan amount for turnover assets varies between 20 thousand and 15 million GEL; the state co-finances the interest rate payment at 8 % for 12–24 months, depending on the goal of the investment project. In the case of the agroleasing, the volume ranges between 20 thousands and 1.5 million GEL, and the state subsidizes 12 % of the interest rate on leases for 66 months. A business is eligible to get both agroleasing and loans simultaneously, as well as several agroleasing. However, the sum of the leases must not exceed 1.5 million, and the sum of the loan(s) must not exceed 15 million GEL (The Annual Report of MoA, 2017). Hence, in the framework of the Preferential Agrocredit programme, the state subsidizes interest payments for loans and leases. The duration of the support ranges from 12 months to 66 months, and the beneficiaries can apply for support several times, as long as the sum of the loans and leases does not exceed the ceiling set by the programme.

The incentives created by the state through the Preferential Agrocredit programme result in an increase of agroloans for investment in the food and agricultural sector. From 2013 through 2016, the programme issued 27,573 loans for fixed assets. Of these, 25,313 are denominated in GEL and 2,260 are denominated in USD. In the corresponding period, in the framework of this project, 11,578 loans were issued for turnover assets, among them, 11,508 denominated in GEL and 70 in USD (Tab. 6.1). Regarding the simplification of the access to credit, one of the beneficiaries of the programme, a local investor in agribusiness, stressed that once the loan is issued and the beneficiaries receive the money, in most cases, they think that the business is done […] however, difficulties start after getting the money, because building agribusiness is a complicated process (interview with the Beneficiary of Preferential Agrocredit, 24 January 2017). The example mentioned during the interview confirms that building agribusiness is not an easy process and is accompanied with many risks not perceived before getting the state support:

> "One of my friends, who is a beneficiary of Preferential Agrocredit, invested the preferential agro loan in the poultry industry. At the initial stage, he did not have any idea how this business works, therefore, he made many mistakes, and his business had higher costs. He did not give up, however, and through these mistakes, he gained experience

and learned how to manage the business by the fourth year. Now it is going well." (Interview with the Public Official, MoA, 4 December 2017).

Tab. 6.1. Loans Issued under Preferential Agrocredit 2013–2016

	The loans issued from 2013 through 2016	
	Number of Loans	**Amount**
Fixed assets (GEL)	25,313	760.8 million GEL
Fixed assets (USD)	2 260	240 million USD
Turnover assets (GEL)	11,508	392 million GEL
Turnover assets (USD)	70	25 million USD

Source: The Ministry of Environment Protection and Agriculture of Georgia, Annual Report of 2017

The programme contributed not only in the growth of the investment in the sector, but fastened the investing process. According to one of the successful dairy agribusinesses, the availability of the subsidy allowed them to expand the business. As the investor mentioned, they would have made that investment without state support, but for less, and more cautiously at a later date (Interview with a Preferential Agrocredit beneficiary, 16 November 2017).

The selection procedures for beneficiaries of Preferential Agrocredit are made by the financial organizations that are implementing partners of the programme. The potential investor goes directly to the credit officer at any of the commercial (partner) organisations. The bank requires the client to present cost estimation of the project for which the loan is requested. One beneficiary said, "A business plan is not on the list of mandatory documents for issuing the loan, as all investors might not know how to prepare one" (interview with a beneficiary of Preferential Agrocredit, 23 November 2017). The commercial bank asks about the project's long-term goals, but only to check the creditworthiness of investor (interview with a beneficiary of the Preferential Agrocredit, 15 December 2017). Another beneficiary of the same programme confirms that the credit officer analysed neither the feasibility nor the sustainability of the plan while deciding on the loan issuance; the officer conducted only a financial analysis to determine whether the client met the bank's creditworthiness standards. If so, the credit officer issued the loan (interview with a beneficiary of the Preferential Agrocredit programme, 24 January 2018). In line with this, as explained by another beneficiary of the programme:

"The bank kind of looks at you trying to figure it out straightaway how this story ends up: yes or no. In our case, we showed that this is a Georgian product that has already been exported. They saw it as a sign of being serious" (Interview with a beneficiary of Preferential Agrocredit, 15 December 2017).

There was concern that the programme could quickly become nepotistic, considering that the small size of the country, makes it possible for one to find contacts anywhere through personal or professional networks. However, the state found a sensible way to implement this programme, which implies that itis easy to access for everyone and its administration is fear (Interview with a beneficiary of Preferential Agrocredit, 15 December 2017).

Performance targets are crucial to monitor the success of the programme. In the case of Preferential Agrocredit, the state provides support to agribusiness. However, this support is not tied to specific performance standards. The only required conditions are the ability to repay the loan, to employ local labour, and to use local primary agricultural production as inputs. If the borrower meets the conditions set by the financial organisation, and the project qualifies as a direct investment in primary agricultural production, processing, or storage, then the applicant gets the loan. There are no any additional conditions regarding the number of job positions, volume of production, selling, or exporting (interview with a beneficiary of Preferential Agrocredit, 24 January 2018). ""'the only indicator for the state to assess the programme's success at initial stage was the growth of the agrocredit portfolio" (Moiswrafishvili, 2017, p. 36). As the research findings in Chapter V illustrate, an increase of the agrocredit portfolio was taken as a sign of the success of the programme by the the representatives of the state (interview with a former Minister of Agriculture, MoA, 11 December 2017).

The support through Preferential Agrocredit is withdrawn if a beneficiary repays the loan or if the beneficiary violates the contract conditions. Preferential Agrocredit support is suspended if the beneficiary's payments are overdue, and it is terminated if the beneficiary receives an enforcement sheet (Government Decree N139, 2014).

To ensure the reciprocity function of *strategic SBRs*, a well-defined monitoring scheme of the programme outcomes is required. As defined in Government Decree N139, the APMA is obliged to monitor whether the partner banks and leasing companies fulfil their contract requirements. The APMA is further obliged to monitor whether the usage of the financial support by the recipient follows the goals of the programme. To this end, the enterprise must maintain its profile for which the support was provided for two years (Government of Georgia Decree N139 Article 11, 2014). However, APMA does not have a formal obligation to monitor the economic performance of the beneficiary agribusinesses. As emphasized by the programme manager of Preferential Agrocredit, APMA has three phases of monitoring: document monitoring, operational monitoring, and field monitoring at the initial stage of the supported project. The goal of document monitoring is the control of the process of issuing loans by the financial organisations, to determine whether they meet the purpose defined in the contract with the APMA. For document monitoring, three staff members are involved from the APMA, who assess the contracts provided from the financial organizations. If all is technically correct, then document monitoring is complete (interview with Manager of the Preferential Agrocredit programme, APMA, 15 December 2017). The second phase is operational monitoring, which controls the money transfers from the account. As for field monitoring, it seeks to ensure purposeful usage of the funds by the beneficiary (Moistraphishvili, 2017). Due to the lack of resources and capability to monitor all beneficiaries, the APMA randomly selects those that are to be monitored (interview with a former Minister of Agriculture, MoA, 11 December 2017). In line with this, the local investor emphasized that representatives of the state made monitoring visits; however, they did not strictly count the number of animals purchased within the framework of the project. "Maybe it should be controlled more strictly; however, the state does not have sufficient control instruments within the existing legal system, as there are no document issuances in the market of live animals" (Interview with a beneficiary of Preferential Agrocredit, 23 November 2017).

The state employs punishment mechanisms for partner financial organizations as well as for agribusiness in breach of contract cases (Government of Georgia Decree N 139). For financial institutions that issue loans that do not meet the criteria set by the APMA, the financial institutions have to pay a fine defined according to the contract. As local expert highlighted APMA strictly enforces this. "For example," she said," when I was working at Agro Group in TBC Bank there were several cases when we, TBC bank, were fined due to mismatching the financed project to programme goals" (Interview with a local expert, USAID-REAP, 29 November 2017). There is also a punishment scheme in case of default by the beneficiary. If the beneficiary does not use the subsidized loan for its intended purpose, the investor has to return the subsidized interest rate. In case the agribusiness uses the subsidized loan for its intended purpose; however, the beneficiary could not continue operating, or has changed the profile of the enterprise within two years from startup, the state terminates support; and the bank shifts the loan from the preferential interest rate into the standard one. From 2013 through 2016, the default rate was quite low, approximately 1 % (Interview with a Former Minister of Agriculture, MoA, 11 December 2017). However, it should be noted that the number of beneficiaries monitored in the field was low as well.

6.2.2.3. Credibility and Trust

In the case of Preferential Agrocredit, the state is meeting the obligations defined in the framework of the programme. From 2013 through 2016, there were some changes in the programme ; however, these changes were implemented to improve the effectiveness of the programme and to improve the conditions of support for the beneficiaries. The state can credibly meet the financial obligations outlined by the programme ; however, the fact that Georgia has meagre tax rates in the face of increasing volumes of state programme support creates a perception, that without support limitations, state expenses and state revenue will not balance, and the state will face revenue defecits (interview with a beneficiary of the Preferential Agrocredit, 16 November 2017). The programme is a good starting point for accelerating investment; however, it is not viable for the long term, it is not stable, and no one knows how long it will be manageable (interview with a beneficiary of Preferential Agrocredit, 24 January 2018). Otherwise, in case of government change, the chance is low that power will be transferred to a political elite which will cease this programme (interview with a beneficiary of the Preferential Agrocredit programme, food processing, 16 November 2017).

Regarding the trust between the beneficiaries of the Preferential Agrocredit and bureaucrats involved in the programme as discussed in Section 6.2.2., the state, as well as projects are considered accessible to any agribusiness which meets the project criteria and administration of the project is fair (Interview with a beneficiary of Preferential Agrocredit, 15 December 2017). Loan is issued with a guarantee that even in case of government change, it will not cease, which creates a trust within the project (Interview with a beneficiary of Preferential Agrocredit, 24 January 2018). Between 2013 and 2016, bureaucrats assigned to specific projects within Preferential Agrocredit changed. The manager of the programme changed once, and management of the APMA several times, as well as the Minister of Agriculture. However, this change of policy officials affected neither the Preferential Agrocredit programme, nor its beneficiaries, as the beneficiaries have contracts directly with their lending banks (Interview with a beneficiary of Preferential Agrocredit, 15 December 2017). In this context, the interviewed beneficiary highlighted that if the state wants to harm a business, there are many other ways to do it, stating "if they want to kill a business, they do not necessarily need to use (withholding) credit to do it" (Interview with a beneficiary of Preferential Agrocredit, 15 December 2017). The bureaucrats who manage Preferential Agrocredit are easily accessible if needed via phone or for a meeting. There is no problem in gaining access to bureaucrats for sharing concerns. However, as stated by the local investor:

> Sharing problems does not make any sense. Ministers are frequently changing; you start sharing problems with one Minister, then he soon resigns and you have to start a new discussion about the same issue with the new Minister, who soon resigns as well. We have expressed our opinion once, twice, then a third time before we realized that stating the same opinion the fourth and fifth time does not make any sense (Interview with a beneficiary of the Preferential Agrocredit programme, 16 January 2018).

Since there is a lack of trust that information provided will be followed by relevant changes, in most cases, businesses are not willing to express their opinion.

6.2.2.4. *Feedback Mechanism*

In the framework of the Preferential Agrocredit programme , there is no formal mechanism for checks and balances. Hence, the state does not have a formalized obligation to seek feedback; and, there is no formal requirement to adopt rules, programmes, or policies based on the feedback. However, when financial organisations face difficulties in project implementation due to the existing rules, financial organisations address the manager of the programme informally. In this manner, a number of amendments have been added since the programme's initiation. For example, in late 2014, changes were applied that classified components of the programme according to purpose of production means (fixed or turnover assets) and financial instruments (loans or leasing). Before, components were divided based on the volume of support. Furthermore, new components were added to the programme in 2014. A new rule was applied to the programme in 2015 that obliges beneficiaries, if requested, to present a document that proves the loan is meeting its intended usage (Moiswrafishvili, 2017). According to a local investor, amendments to Preferential Agrocredit were apparently necessary. As a result the range of support as well as the duration of the support changed (Interview with a beneficiary of Preferential Agrocredit, 16 November 2017).

6.2.2.5. *Conclusion*

To sum up, some institutions of state-agribusiness relations are formal in the case of the Preferential Agrocredit programme , and some are informal. Regarding information exchange, there are no formal requirements that oblige the state and beneficiaries of the programme to meet regularly to exchange information regarding programme or sector-related issues. As the issuing of Preferential Agrocredit loans is delegated to commercial organizations, and field monitoring of the beneficiaries is conducted only for randomly selected cases, neither the programme manager of Preferential Agrocredit nor other representatives of the APMA or the Ministry of Agriculture of Georgia organizes regular meetings with beneficiaries of the programme to indetify obstacles and to get feedback on the programme implementation processes. There exists neither formal nor informal networks or platforms that unite all beneficiaries of the programme. However, there do exist informal institutions to access the state as needed via personal or professional networks. The APMA is accessible by all sizes of agribusinesses, and it is possible to reach a programme manager via phone to arrange meeting. As to the access to the representatives of the MoA, large agribusinesses and successful players in the sector can meet relevant representatives of the state at any level, up to the Ministerial,promptly, via phone, or using personal and professional networks in the sector. Small and medium-sized enterprises (SMEs) relay their concerns and needs to the state through industry-specific umbrella organizations or personal networks. The other informal institutions that connect the state and some of the beneficiaries of the programme (large agribusiness or successful/known agribusiness), are meetings initiated by industry-specific business associations, think tanks, or civil society organizations in the framework of specific, developmental organisation-funded projects. However, such meetings are not characterised by the exchange of detailed information, nor by solving sector-relevant obstacles. As the interviews illustrated, in most cases such meetings are conducted for the sake of making ticks in the agenda, and any issues raised are not followed up by action from the state, due to either the lack of will or feasibility.

One more informal institution for bringing state and agribusiness representatives together is to review a specific policy or programme -related amendments initiated by the state. These meetings are organized by the relevant state bodies. None of these type of meetings are characterised by open discussions or sharing a comprehensive information/feedback for a number of reasons. First fo all, as a constructive criticism on initiated policies or amandements is taken personally by policymaker(s), and impacts future relations with them. Therefore, representatives of private sector avoid to express their standpoint, being cautious to ruin its relationship with the policy makers. Besides, exchange of information is also limited, asthe state does not condition programme beneficiaries to regularly submit data on performanceof the supported projects. Morover, aprivate sector would not be willing to share business operations-related data even if the state requested it. To conclude, there is exchange of some information between the state an private sector actors, however, it is not the consultative collaboration, as characterised for the *strategic SBRs* discussed in Chapter II.

As for reciprocity in the case of Preferential Agrocredit, we observe formal institutions in the process of subsidizing agribusinesses. The rules of providing support are clear, transparent, and enforced. But there are neither formal nor informal institutions for defining performance indicators and disciplining beneficiaries. There are formal institutions for monitoring, but only randomly selected beneficiaries are monitored, to check the reasonability of the project at the initial stage. However, there are no formal institutions to monitor the success or the failure of the supported project. Consequently, there are no institutions to reward or punish Preferential Agrocredit beneficiaries. Hence, the state does not discipline agribusiness in the framework of the programme , which means that the state agribusiness relationship in Georgia in the framework of Preferential Agrocredit does not meet the reciprocity criteria of the institutions of *strategic SBRs*.

The state is credible in terms of meeting its obligations within the framework of the programme so far. There were changes of public officials at the APMA and the MoA. But these did not threaten the credibility of the state to meet its obligations to existing beneficiaries within the project, since the beneficiaries do not interact directly with the state. The beneficiaries consider that in the long term, there might be challenges for the state to cover programme -related some expenses if the provision of new subsidies is not stopped at some point. Moreover, there is a lack of trust by agribusiness that the state will follow up to solve the obstacles agribusiness raise. This is reflected in the fact that agribusiness is not motivated to share obstacles with the state, or express their attitude towards new policies and programmes, as they expect that the exchange of information will not be acted upon by state.

In the framework of the project, there are no formal institutions that oblige the state to establish feedback mechanisms. But there are informal institutions of providing feedback through informal, mostly individual meetings. As the interview data illustrate, beneficiaries address the programme manager when facing obstacles in implementing a project. Observations show that some feedback was followed by relevant changes. However, this is not a regular tendency.

To conclude, state-agribusiness relations within the framework of this programme lacks strategic consultation and does not meet the necessary conditions of reciprocity and trust, nor does it have a regular feedback mechanism.

6.3. The Case of Plant the Future

6.3.1. The Project Introduction

In 2015, the Ministry of Agriculture of Georgia initiated the Plant the Future programme through the Agriculture Project Management Agency (APMA) (Government of Georgia Decree N56, 2015). The programme design and conditions were developed in APMA. The programme aims to increase the utilization of agricultural land and to substitute old crops with new ones (Interview with Manager of Plant the Future, APMA, 15 December 2017). The programme has two components: perennial gardens and nursery gardens. The goal of the perennial gardens is to utilize Georgia's agricultural land by cultivating perennial crops. With this, the state aims to substitute imports, to increase the export potential, to simplify the supply of the primary production to the food processing enterprises and to improve living standards in rural parts of the country (Government of Georgia Decree N56, 2015). The goal of the nursery gardens component is to support the production of local, high-quality, phytosanitary clean planting material (seedlings), which will offer comparatively cheap local seeds and plants for cultivating gardens (Government of Georgia Decree N56, 2015).

APMA - currently [2020] restructured as the rural Development Agency (RDA)- provides financial support for both perennial gardens and nursery gardens. The instrument of financial support is co-financing investment. In addition to financial support, the state provides technical support, which includes training on plant pruning technologies in cultivated gardens, implementation of the Integrated Pest Management system (IPM), irrigation, and plant feeding issues. Participation in the training sessions is obligatory for beneficiaries and is outlined in their contracts (Government of Georgia Decree N56 Article 6).

The The programme - sets restrictions on the variety and quantity of crops that may be cultivated by a beneficiary. The restrictions differ between regions (Government of Georgia Decree N444, article 4). While the The programme sets restrictions on the variety of allowable crop types, the species within the types are not limited. The rationale behind this is that testing new species of crops requires the lengthy process of planting, waiting for the harvest, and observing how the harvest changes through time. "If APMA followed this way of permitting individual species, it would not be possible to implement the The programme - within the next 15 years" (Interview with Manager of the Plant the Future programme, APMA, 15 December 2017). For crop selection, APMA has not conducted field research, but has relied on Georgia's previous experience in crop cultivation (Interview with the Manager of Plant the Future, APMA, 15 December 2017). Most of the beneficiaries cultivate Chandler walnuts (1200 ha) and apples (800 ha) (Interview with the The Programme -'s Support Development Unit, APMA, 5 April 2017). Decisions on crop varieties are based on expert opinions and relevant sector literature (Interview with the Head of the Rural Development Coordination Division at the MoA, 4 December 2017). According to a local expert, this attitude conveys risks:

> Chandler walnut trees are characterised by high yields when they are cultivated in California, but will they give the same outcome in Georgia? In California, this crop yields 10–12 tonnes per hectare, while in Georgia the maximum volume per hectare so far reached only 2 tonnes. Are the orchards planted in the same conditions as they are in California, where they have high yields? Each of these details is crucial, as they influence the volume of yields, and whether they meet projected results (Interview with a local expert, 9 November 2017).

Since 2015, 691 projects have been approved through the Plant the Future programme. The majority (approximately 60 %) of the beneficiaries are investors who are living in the city, operating other businesses, and who own agricultural land or who have bought agricultural land and have invested in the sector. The remaining 40 % are those who already had fruit or vegetable gardens and applied for state support to extend their investment (Interview with the Head of the The Programme's Support Development Unit, APMA, 5 April 2017). These gardens are expected to yield the first harvest 4–5 years period after planting.

6.3.2. State–Agribusiness Relations

This section aims to illustrate research outcomes regarding the nature of the institutions of state–agribusiness relations in the case of the Plant the Future The programme -, and will discuss information exchange, reciprocity, credibility and trust, and feedback mechanism of the project in four respective subsections. The results rely on data gathered from interviews with relevant actors from April 2017 through February 2018 and the programme --related Decrees of the Government of Georgia.

6.3.2.1. Information Exchange

The interviews show that in the process of the The programme - elaboration there were meetings and discussions with agronomists with expertise in fruit crops (Interview with Head of the Rural Development Coordination Division, MoA, 4 December 2017). After the The programme -was initiated, the The programme - manager marketed and distributed information about it through regional information centres, and a formal presentation of the project was conducted in each region. Later, through the support of the APMA Marketing Department, a video presentation regarding fruit and nut garden cultivation was recorded and distributed to TV programmes (Interview with the Project Manager of Plant the Future, APMA, 15 December 2018). Also, the APMA maintains a very active call centre, with employees ready to respond to questions and clarify information regarding the requirements or procedures to get beneficiary of the the programme -.

As with the previous case, there are no formal rules for regular meetings or information exchange between the state and agribusiness involved in this programme, but the channel to set up informal meetings is open. Moreover, Plant the Future's programme manager can be reached easily if needed. In line with this, a local investor and beneficiary of the project stated:

> "When I learned about the programme, I went to the APMA directly. I did not have any personal network or contacts within APMA. When I stated the reason for my visit, the reception staff introduced me to the bureaucrats managing the project or involved in the other programme related activities. The programme manager explained to me in detail all related requirements and procedures to apply" (Interview with a beneficiary of the Plant the Future programme, 29 March 2017).

The state provides updates regarding the programme and information about new programme to its beneficiaries via email or phone, using the programme manager's database of beneficiaries' contact details (Interview with a beneficiary of the Plant the Future programme, 29 March 2017), however, there is a lack of knowledge and information how to care for the programme-specific crops. According to one of the beneficiaries:

> I could not find any books in Georgian on how to cultivate walnuts. I have access to the internet, and I know English, so I was able to access information on cultivation processes of similar crops in other countries; however, not all beneficiaries can do this (Interview with a beneficiary of Plant the Future, 16 November 2017).

The state does not have information regarding modern methods of cultivating and sustaining crops listed as targets of the programme (Interview with Performance Data Advisor on Public-Private Dialogue Tracking, USAID-G4G, 16 November 2017). Furthermore, the APMA has not conducted research on the demand for Plant the Future products nor on their potential export markets.

Most of the orchards give the first yield in 2019–2020. Beneficiaries are not obliged to regularly report investment performance to the APMA, nor must the APMA collect investment performance. However, the programme manager emphasized that he collects the data for personal interest by calling the beneficiaries to check the progress of their gardens (Interview with the Manager of Plant the Future programme, APMA, 15 December 2018).

6.3.2.2. *Reciprocity*

Plant the Future creates incentives for the private sector to invest in primary agriculture production in order to increase the utilization of agricultural land and increase potential primary agricultural production, to provide inputs to food processing businesses, to substitute imports, and increase exports. The support mechanism employed by this programme is co-financing investment for cultivating perennial crops, and for related nursery gardens. For perennial gardens, the state finances 70 % of the cost of seedlings, 50 % of the cost of installing a drip irrigation system. The maximum amount of support for each beneficiary is 100,000 GEL (38,461 USD), and the maximum area co-financed by the state is 20 hectares (Government of Georgia Decree N56 Article 4). In the case of nursery gardens, the state co-finances 50 % of total project costs, up to 150,000 GEL (57,692 USD) (Government of Georgia Decree N56 Article 4). The beneficiaries can participate multiple times; however, the total amount of support an single beneficiary can receive is limited to 100,000 GEL and the cultivated area to a maximum 20 ha.

Since inception, 693 investment projects were initiated through the incentives created by the Plant the Future in several regions of Georgia (The Annual Report of the Ministry of Agriculture, 2017). From all applications received for Plant the Future support, the APMA rejected only 15 (Interview with the Manager of Plant the Future, APMA, 15 December 2017). Financial support from the agency amounts to 22.3 million GEL, and a total cultivated area of 4,298 ha (The Annual Report of the Ministry of Agriculture, 2017). The project increased demand, and consequently price, for agricultural land in Georgia (Interview with the Manager of Plant the Future, APMA, 15 December 2017).

The eligibility of beneficiaries is assessed by the APMA, which maintains a standard list of requirements for all beneficiaries. The selection process of an applicant depends on the assessment of the requested documents. In order to qualify for support, a beneficiary must prove the ability to co-finance her/his share of the project costs (Interview with a Beneficiary of Plant the Future, 16 November 2017). In addition, an applicant must prove ownership of land, and provide a land analysis. The procedures to gain support are transparent. If the potential beneficiary meets these requirements, the state cannot refuse to provide support (Interview with a beneficiary of Plant the Future, 29 March 2017). Each beneficiary goes to APMA and meets the programme manager to review the documents before submitting them officially. Once the documents are submitted officially at APMA administration, the project is assigned to the programme manager, who distributes it among credit officers for processing. After assessment, a contract is prepared, then signed by the programme manager. After signing, it is reviewed by APMA's legal department. If everything is in good order, the beneficiary signs the contract (Interview with the Project Manager of Plant the Future, 15 December 2017). Thereafter, the money is transferred and the beneficiary starts the project-related activities. The beneficiary has a certain period for cultivation (Interview with the Manager of Plant the Future, APMA, 15 December 2017).

Within the framework of Plant the Future, there are no defined performance indicators in terms of production or export volumes. The only criterion tracked by the state is whether the support has been invested as intended. As long as investor beneficiary meets all preliminary conditions defined in the framewo rk of the programme and cultivates orchards, (s)he does not have any further obligation to APMA, and is even free to sell the orchards. For the state, the goal is to utilize agricultural land for orchards, and it does not matter who the owner is (Interview with Manager of Plant the Future, APMA, 15 December 2017).

Regarding initial conditions and programme performance standards, one of the beneficiaries emphasized that he considers it not necessary to plan market access or set 5-year production goals, saying "I cultivate walnuts. The general tendency is for demand for walnuts to increase, so if I make predictions based on current walnut prices, this should be a very profitable business" (Interview with the beneficiary of Plant the Future, 23 November 2018). However, concerning this, a local expert states that:

> As soon as the investment is made, the beneficiary should start planning the procedures for accessing markets (local or foreign) to realize profits from production. There are rules for exporting fruit […] however, there is no schematic as to how to do this profitably (Interview with a local expert, 9 November 2017).

According to the manager of the programme, the long term success indicators of the programme will be production volumes from the orchards cultivated within the framework of the programme . However, neither the project manager nor the MoA Department of Statistics has any obligation to collect corresponding data or track dynamics to assess the economic performance of the programme's outcome. As the programme manager emphasized, despite his lack of obligation to formally track the results of the programme , he does check progress by calling the benef iciaries occasionally, who are expected to show yields from their orchards (Interview with the Manager of Plant the Future, APMA, 15 December 2017).

APMA oversees the monitoring of Plant the Future, wh ich includes several phases. Initially, APMA monitors documents. The programme manager and team are in charge of the process at this stage. Later, after the designated cultivation time has passed, APMA conducts field monitoring through its monitoring unit. Representatives of the AMPA field monitoring unit visit each beneficiary, check the orchards or nurseries, count the plants, and write the conclusion about whether the support was spent reasonably or not (Interview with the Manager of the Plant the Future, APMA, 15 December 2017). After APMA concurs that proper crops are being cultivated and support has been used as intended, monitoring by APMA is finished. The beneficiaries of the programme mentioned in the interviews that their projects were monitored at the application and documentation stage, as well as in the field. After APMA's confirmation that the crops are being cultivated, even if the beneficiary stops taking care of the orchard, the state has no way of penalizing them. As stated by a programme beneficiary, the contract does not condition a beneficiary to produce (Interview with a beneficiary of Plant the Future, 23 November 2017). Given that economic performance is not monito red in the case of Plant the Future, with neither the APMA nor the MoA collecting production or export data, an accurate assessment of the programme 's economic performance or its contribution to the food and agricultural sector of Georgia is not possible.

As for Plant the Future as a programme, the state could cease the it at any time. The budget is approved annually, together with the budget of the MoA; however, this would not affect the current beneficiaries of the programme , who have already been funded by the state and have begun cultivation.

6.3.2.3. *Credibility and Trust*

In the case of Plant the Future, the state meets the obligations defined in the framework of the programme. According to a beneficiary of the programme , there have not been any obstacles created due to bureaucracy, obligations are being met by the state, with no delays of funding (Interview with a beneficiary of Plant the Future, 29 March 2017). The government encourages beneficiaries to make the best use of the investment. A beneficiary of the programme stated, "I had a three-month delay in the import of saplings from Greece. I wrote to APMA regarding this, and they understood and gave me more time" (Interview with a beneficiary of Plant the Future, 29 March 2017).

From 2015 through 2016, there had not been any significant changes in Plant the Future that might have affected beneficiaries. The manager of the programme has remained the same since its initiation in 2015. To reach the manager as well as other members of the project team is easy by telephone, or a visit to APMA. The scheme of the programme is simple, with information regarding requirements and related procedures available on the webpage of the project, as well as availability of the personnel designated to implement the programme .

The beneficiaries have trust in the programme , as well as its management. According to one beneficiary, the only reason for losing support from the state might be due to irresponsibility by not meeting the programme 's target or misusing funds (Interview with a beneficiary of Plant the Future, 23 November 2017). However, as mentioned by the programme manager of Plant the Future, there is a perception in certain regions that support is accessible only for investors who are related to representatives of the state or the government (Interview with the Project Manager of Plant the Future, APMA, 15 December 2017). The fact that APMA approved almost 98 % of the applications indicates that there is no nepotism.

6.3.2.4. Feedback Mechanism

In the framework of Plant the Future, there is no mechanism of getting feedback. The state does not have any formalized obligation to seek feedback on the programme ; thus, there can be no formal requirement to adopt feedback-based rules, programmes, or policies. According to the manager of the programme, it is difficult to maintain harmonic coordination among various agencies of the state while trying to adopt or implement programmes or projects quickly. The rhythm of the processes is slow because of so much bureaucracy. What is possible to be done in a commercial bank in one hour, it takes one month in state agencies. As the project manager of Plant the Future explained:

> One issue is that [agency] views are diverse, attitudes to the job are diverse, and responsibility is higher, so bureaucrats try to be very cautious and avoid taking responsibility for making decisions for fear of making a mistake. The second issue relates to lack of coordination […] no one enters into the processes fully; when you write an email you might get a response in two weeks, and the reaction to calls are delayed as well. Therefore, it is almost impossible to make fast changes (Interview with the Manager of Plant the Future, APMA, 15 December 2017).

Despite this, a number of amendments were made in the project. These were reflected in the Government of Georgia's Decrees No444 (2015), No159 (2015), No190 (2016), and in Amendments in Government of Georgia's Decree N 56 on Approval of the State Programme 'Plant the Future.' They were conceived to make procedures more accessible and feasible for businesses, and to make investment more effective. However, they do not utilise feedback mechanisms for assessment.

6.3.2.5. Conclusion

To sum up, in the case of Plant the Future, state-agribusiness relations are characterised by enforced formal and informal rules. There are no formal institutions that oblige state and agribusiness to collaborate on programme -related issues. However, there are informal channels for organizing meetings with programme managers if needed. The dissemination of programme information occurs via email or through municipal presentations. The state does not collect performance data from Plant the Future beneficiaries, nor is the agribusiness obliged to regularly report to the state regarding the subsidized projects' performance. Hence, information exchange, as a required feature of *strategic SBRs*, does not characterise this programme .

As to the reciprocity aspect of state-agribusiness relations within the programme framework, the subsidy's provision is based on formal institutions. The programme employs formal rules for monitoring all beneficiaries, however only at the initial documentation stage of the project, and confirming the programme goal of cultivating orchards. There are neither formal nor informal institutions for defining performance standards for the subsidized projects, and the state does not discipline the beneficiaries. Therefore, the SBRs of Plant the Future do not meet the reciprocity component of *strategic SBRs*.

The state can credibly meet its obligations to the programme , and it has the beneficiaries' trust. The beneficiaries are not vulnerable to administration changes as they interact with the state only at the beginning of their project. As long as the designated grove has been cultivated and the state has conducted its field monitoring, the programme beneficiaries have no further obligations to the state.

The programme employs neither formal nor informal institutions for feedback. Hence, the project does not meet the criteria of *strategic SBRs*, which implies feedback mechanisms on projects, programmes, and policies.

6.4. Co-Financing the Agriculture Products Processing and Storage Enterprises

6.4.1. Project Introduction

In 2014, the Ministry of Agriculture initiated the programme entitled Co-financing Agriculture Products Processing and Storage Enterprises (CAPPSE), and the Agriculture Project Management Agency (APMA)- currently [2020] RDA - implements it. The programme is intended to create new enterprises and rehabilitate existing ones in municipalities of Georgia (Government of Georgia

Decree N139, attachment 2, article 2, 2014). It consists of two components: one focused on co-financing agricultural products processing enterprises, and the other co-financing agricultural products storage enterprises. Co-financing agricultural product processing enterprises seeks to establish new, and rehabilitate old enterprises within the municipalities of Georgia, to enhance geographical diversification of processing enterprises, to improve the conditions for and facilitate creation of agricultural cooperatives, to develop the primary agriculture production base, and to increase the income of the rural population. Co-financing agricultural storage enterprises aims to support agricultural storage businesses, to raise the storage self-sufficiency rate with the perennial and annual plants, to assist storage enterprises to develop as future service providers, and to support standardization of the storage infrastructure.

APMA provides financial support for both components through grants and preferential agrocredit/leasing (Government of Georgia Decree N139, 2014). In addition to financial support, the state provides technical support for agribusinesses in the form of information on modern machinery and equipment, introduction to suppliers, importing and exporting information, training key personnel, supporting business plan preparation, and implementing international field safety management systems and standards.

From 2014 through 2016, support was provided to 46 enterprises—forty food processing and six storage enterprises. APMA received 1700 applications, but only 400 passed the first screening. The programme covers all regions of Georgia, except for five cities where the business is concentrated (Interview with the Manager of the Agriculture Products Processing and Storage Enterprises programme, APMA, 15 December 2017). The programme focuses on the processing and storage of already existing primary agricultural products, not on those that will eventually come via Plant the Future. According to the programme manager, APMA will not start building processing and storage enterprises today for Plant the Future beneficiaries, who will not harvest for 3–4 years (Interview with the Manager of the Co-financing Agriculture Products Processing and Storage Enterprises programme, APMA, 15 December 2017).

At the end of 2017, no more applications for agricultural product processing enterprises were being accepted. The government concluded that the quantity was already satisfactory (Interview with the Manager of the Agriculture Products Processing and Storage Enterprises, 15 December 2017).

6.4.2. State-Agribusiness Relations

This section illustrates research outcomes regarding state-agribusiness relations in the CAPPSE case. It is divided into four subsections, respectively. The results rely on data gathered from interviews with relevant participants and programme -related Decrees of the Government of Georgia.

6.4.2.1. Information Exchange

In the case of CAPPSE, there are no formal rules obliging the state and agribusiness to meet regularly. However, similar to the other cases, beneficiaries can meet and consult with a programme manager. The programme manager emphasized that there is frequent communication between the project team from APMA and the beneficiaries of the programme and that for either side, there are no obstacles to sharing information or arranging meetings upon request. However, the team from APMA, as well as representatives of other state organizations and agribusinesses, mostly meet at events such as product presentations or trade exhibitions (Interview with the Manager of Co-financing Agricultural Products Processing and Storage Enterprises programme, 15 December 2017). Although there are relatively few beneficiaries involved with this programme, roundtable meetings between state and agribusiness to discuss obstacles and opportunities are not being held.

There are no formal rules that require beneficiaries to regularly report data regarding their progress and performance to the state. However, upon request, they provide data regarding production categories, quantities, and employment (Interview with the Manager of the Agriculture Products Processing and Storage Enterprises programme, 15 December 2017). The state disseminates programme related information via a web page, television, announcements, as well as via information centres in the municipalities (Interview with the Manager of the Agriculture Products Processing and Storage Enterprises programme, 15 December 2017).

6.4.2.2. Reciprocity

CAPPSE creates incentives for the private sector to invest in creating new or rehabilitating old food processing and storage enterprises. The support mechanism employed is a grant comprising 40 % of the project's total value (not exceeding 600,000 GEL) and preferential agro-credit/leasing comprising 50 % of the value of the total project (not exceeding 1.5 million GEL). The remaining 10 % (minimum 250,000 GEL) should be contributed by the beneficiary (Annual

Report of MoA, 2017). With these subsidies as motivation, APMA hopes to initiate as many projects as possible.

The incentives created by the state through CAPPSE has led to an increase in food processing and storage enterprise investment. From 2014 to 2017, the government signed agreements with six investor for the food storage enterprise component, with a total investment in this component of 1.7 million USD and 4.1 million GEL. Of this, 689,468 USD and 1.7 million GEL was co-funded by the state. The state signed agreements with forty enterprises in the food processing component, with a total investment of 24.2 million USD and 4.2 million GEL, of which the state co-funded 8.7 million USD and 600 thousand GEL.

The Government of Georgia Decree N 139 (2014) defines the selection procedures of supported projects and covers the following phases: submitting an application, submitting a project, submitting a business plan, submitting proof that the potential beneficiary is eligible to receive CAPPSE support, and being able to contribute 10 % of the total cost (Government of Georgia Decree N139, 2014). The first filter is an online application, through which APMA determines the applicant's general eligibility for the programme. Applicants, who pass the first filter must complete and submit online a formal grant application using APMA's application template (Government of Georgia Decree N139, 2014). Once the grant application is uploaded, the grant-officers start an assessment of it. Currently, the programme involves two grant officers who receive many non-qualified grant applications, which are rejected directly. Some applications present good business ideas but do not present proper business plans (Interview with the Manager of the Co-financing Agriculture Products Processing and Storage Enterprises programme, APMA, 15 December 2017). After such an assessment, the APMA programme team prepares a list of questions for the potential beneficiary, calls him/her, and explains the additional required information. The preliminary discussion committee, selected by APMA, makes a preliminary selection of the project based on assessing the grant application (Government of Georgia Decree N139, 2014).

After the preliminary committee accepts the grant application, APMA sends the potential investors to business consulting companies hired by APMA to help them in business plan development. This is free of charge for the beneficiary during the decision process, and APMA is involved in the final stages of the business plan assesment. When the business plan is ready, the project is introduced to the grant committee, who then accepts or rejects the project. The committee consists of representatives from various ministries and business associations, selected by the APMA. A representative of the Ministry of Agriculture of Georgia attends the meeting as well, however, to avoid conflicts of interest it does not have the right to vote (Interview with the Manager of the Co-financing Agriculture Products Processing and Storage Enterprises programme, APMA, 15 December 2017). The grant committee discusses the project's feasibility, and if the project seems feasible, the committee approves it. If the project is accepted, APMA informs the beneficiary by official letter. With this letter, the applicant applies for preferential agro credit or leasing. The beneficiary has two months to finalize all procedures, including raising the necessary financial resources. APMA then signs the contract with the beneficiary, and the project starts (Interview with the Manager of the Co-financing Agriculture Products Processing and Storage Enterprises programme, APMA, 15 December 2017).

The key determinants for project selection are the existence of potential suppliers of primary products, experience in accessing markets, and the possession of the necessary equipment (Interview with the Manager of the Co-financing Agriculture Products Processing and Storage Enterprises programme, APMA, 15 December 2017). The requirements for approving the project include detailed information on production processes of final goods and presentation of desired machinery and its usage description. In addition, the potential beneficiary should present a business plan that includes detailed costs, information about potential suppliers, information regarding market access and production timeline, and export aspects of the applicant's production projections (Interview with the Manager of the Co-financing Agriculture Products Processing and Storage Enterprises programme, APMA, 15 December 2017). In line with this, the beneficiary of the project emphasized that while the application requires submission of a business plan that includes value chain information, no one provides a detailed analysis; the business plan is a total formality (Interview with a beneficiary of the Co-financing Agriculture Products Processing Enterprises programme, 24 January 2018).

One of the conditions for state support is that an enterprise that starts operations shall not change its shareholder profile structure without a negotiated agreement with APMA. Otherwise, as stated by the manager of the programme , "It is too early to talk about success indicators of the projects. At this stage, they must meet the purpose of the programme , function, and sustain it in the long term" (Interview with the Manager of the Co-Financing Agriculture Products Processing and Storage Enterprises project, APMA, 15 December 2017). The support is conditioned on the volume of the processed agricultural products at the end of the second year from starting the operation. According to one beneficiary of the co-financing food processing component, in the case of their enterprise, the support is conditioned to process 300 tonnes of fruit, but only processing is not an issue, as it needs realisation. However, there are no requirements in this regard (Interview with a beneficiary of the Co-financing Agriculture Products Processing Enterprises project, 24 January 2018). Hence, the only clearly defined performance indicator is a volume of processed primary agricultural products. Performance standards for realising the processed products, exports, and job creation, which are crucial metrics for determining successful economic performance, are not well-defined.

The CAPPSE project has a monitoring scheme (Interview with the Manager of the Co-financing Agriculture Products Processing and Storage Enterprises project, APMA, 15 December 2017), defined in the Government of Georgia Decree 139. APMA monitors the processes of enterprise creation, the usage of support in correspondence with the programme purpose, and maintains the enterprises' profile for two years (Government of Georgia Decree N139, 2014). After two years of operation, APMA ceases monitoring a beneficiary. The project manager mentioned that APMA cannot follow an enterprise's activities indefinitely (Interview with the Manager of the Co-Financing Agriculture Products Processing and Storage Enterprises project, APMA, 15 December 2017). The monitoring scheme does not include economic performance indicators, such as job creation, processed product sales, and exports.

The programme has a punishment clause, as well. If the beneficiary deviates from the support contract, the commercial bank and AMPA hold the real estate as collateral until all obligations to both the state and commercial bank are fulfilled (Interview with the Manager of the Co-Financing Agriculture Products Processing and Storage Enterprises, APMA, 15 December 2017). According to a programme beneficiary, should the enterprise not meet the processing quota of 300 tonnes of fruit by the designated time, the shareholders are not sure what sanctions the state will put on the business. However, they do not believe that APMA will stop supporting them during the initial phase:

> "When we submitted our updated application, we told the providers we made corrections to the projected outcomes of the loan. They said that applicant enterprises rarely meet all conditions, therefore I do not assume that AMPA will sanction us if we are not able to meet the target for processing" (Interview with a beneficiary of the Co-financing Agriculture Products Processing and Storage Enterprises programme, APMA, 15 December 2017).

In contrast, the CAPPSE manager said that in case of deviation from the conditions of the loan, investors must return the money to the state (Interview with the Manager of the Co-financing Agriculture Products Processing and Storage Enterprises project, APMA, 15 December 2017).

6.4.2.3. *Credibility and Trust*

In case of the CAPPSE programme, the state meets its obligations as defined in the framework of the programme. Between 2014 through 2016, the programme manager changed once in 2014. There were also changes in the management of APMA, as well as in the Ministry of Agriculture, including several changes of Ministers. However, these changes have not significantly affected the direction of the programme. The Manager as well as other members of the programme team are easy to reach by phone or by visiting APMA. The implementation of the project is comprehensive, as it includes several phases. Information regarding programme requirements and related procedures is available on the webpage; however, if needed, it is possible to get help from the officials assigned to the programme. In the CAPPSE framework, the roles of the programme manager as well as the programme team are crucial, as they help the applicants with the project and business plan development.

6.4.2.4. *Feedback Mechanism*

Within the CAPPSE framework, there are no formal institutions for feedback, nor does the state seek feedback on the programme. However, there were changes in the programme during the period of 2014–2017. One change extended the programme dimention geographically to all regions of the country. According to the programme manager, the rationale behind this was to allow regions lacking resources and business activities to benefit from the proGramme. The other change related to the minimum contributions from the applicant into the project. Initially, the contribution was set at 200 thousand USD. After the amendments, the amount declined to 100 thousand USD. According to the programme manager, APMA lowered this requirement to let comparatively low-budget projects benefit from this programme. Also, the programme added the storage enterprises component. According to the programme manager, initially the programme supported only the food processing industry component; and latery APMA added the storage enterprises component. Changes were made in terms of industry coverage as well. Initially, the programme did not cover wheat or alcoholic beverage processing, but later the state added these industries to the project framework for the twelve municipalities. The rationale behind this change was to enhance investment and economic activities in the municipalities where there were no economic activities (Interview with the Manager of the Co-financing Agriculture Products Processing and Storage Enterprises project, APMA, 15 December 2017).

6.4.2.5. Conclusion

State-agribusiness relations in this case employ a combination of formal and informal institutions, and several findings are revealed. First, even though the number of beneficiaries of the programme is not high (46 in total), there are neither formal nor informal institutions to set up regular meetings between relevant state and agribusiness actors for discussing obstacles and opportunities for food processing and storage enterprises. Moreover, there are no formally organised platforms or networks for information exchange. However, there are informal institutions that foster active communication between the APMA programme team and the programme applicants (who meet first-phase selection requirements), to advance their applications and business plans. There are no formal institutions that oblige the private sector to regularly report their business operations to the state; however, should the state need specific information, they request it from the agribusiness directly. Overall, the information exchange within this programme framework is not oriented toward sharing and addressing the obstacles and opportunities that affect the performance of food processing and storage enterprises. Hence the programme lacks the exchange of comprehensive information, one of the characteristics *of strategic SBR*.

Secondly, like the other two programmes, there is a formal, institutionalized subsidy provision process in the Co-financing Agriculture Processing and Storage Enterprises programme, with clearly defined procedures and criteria for beneficiary selection. The monitoring scheme of the programme is also formalized and relates to monitoring not only the documentation and proper application of the subsidy, but also production volumes at the end of the second year. However, the monitoring scheme does not set standards for the sales of the products, exports, or job creation. The programme also lacks a punishment scheme for disciplining errant businesses. Therefore, the programme does not meet the reciprocity criterium of *strategic SBRs*. Additionally, the programme employs neither formal nor informal institutions for feedback, hence, does not meet the feedback mechanism criterion, which is critical for *strategic SBRs*.

Conclusion

This chapter examined the nature of the institutions of the state-agribusiness relations in Georgia to understand whether or not state interventions in the food and agricultural sector of Georgia relies on *strategic SBRs*. It explored the rules of state-agribusiness relations in three cases, the state programmes Preferential Agrocredit, Plant the Future, and Co-financing of Agro Processing and Storage

Enterprises. These programmes aim to create incentives for businesses to invest in Georgia's food and agricultural sector to improve the economic performance of the sector to diversify production, export, and export markets.

State intervention in the food and agricultural sector of Georgia does not rely on the *strategic SBRs*. The research reveals several findings. First, because the country is small, there is no problem in reaching the representatives of the state via personal or professional networks; however, there are no organized, regular formal or informal meetings, which bring the state and agribusiness together for collaborative discussions on the obstacles and opportunities the private sector faces in the production process or accessing markets. Even in the rare cases when the information reaches the relevant state actors, there is a problem of follow up, either due to a lack of will or a lack of possibilities. The information exchange between the state and businesses needs to be *strategic*, i.e., aiming to understand the sector's obstacles and opportunities. However, this is not the case in Georgia.

Secondly, each of the programmes has well-defined, standardized criteria for selecting investment projects, and monitoring the implementation processes. However, they employ neither formal nor informal institutions for monitoring and evaluation the economic performance of the beneficiary projects. Consequently, enforcement schemes are also absent. Hence, none of the state support programmes satisfy the criteria of reciprocity, which is crucial for ensuring the maximum returns on subsidies.

Thirdly, within the frameworks of the programme, the state can credibly meet its obligations and promises as defined within each programme, despite changes of APMA programme managers and changes of the Ministers themselves. The beneficiaries trust that the state will not cease project support. However, they do not believe that expressing feedback on the programmes will result in relevant changes. The belief that there will not be follow up on expressed concerns distracts strategic dialogue between the state and the agribusinesses.

Finally, the programmes employ neither formal nor informal institutions for feedback. Enacting a feedback mechanism promotes the understanding of which interventions are fruitful and which are not. Hence, there is no formal feedback mechanism to monitor economic indicators, such as production, export, and job creation. Furthermore, the research findings show that there were some amendments to each programme. These amendments aimed to simplify the procedures to access credit and increase investment programmes in geography and size.

To conclude, in the cases of *strategic SBRs*, the states defined performance indicators to determine the success of the elaborated policies/programmes, monitored performance indicators, requested feedback from the private sector on state programmes and policies, and took into account feedback received for the adaptation of the policies or programmes. *Strategic* SBRs implies maintaining an ongoing dialogue between the state and agribusiness and strengthening the capacity to address selectively economic opportunities and obstacles identified through state-business dialogues. However, the research findings indicate that most of these criteria are absent in state-agribusiness relations in Georgia. The state provides support in accessing finances (carrots) for private actors to invest in the food and agricultural sector. These finances are directed to specific industries in the sector and specific activities, such as cultivating a new product or establishing new (or expanding old) food storage and food processing enterprises. As to enforcement, the state monitors whether the beneficiary started the activities for which financial support was provided. However, the state does not monitor the investment project's performance. Hence it does not discipline agribusiness. Considering that *strategic SBRs*, which maintain collaboration between the state and private sector, enhance policy experimentation and adaptation, and support market functions, are crucial for state intervention to overcome obstacles and support development, the key question is to understand why *strategic* state-business relations have not emerged in the food and agricultural sector of Georgia. The next chapter aims to address this question.

Chapter VII The Institutional Prerequisites for the Emergence of *Strategic SBRs*

Introduction

This chapter aims to explore why *strategic SBRs* have not emerged in the sector, despite the openness and high accessibility of the state for meetings with the private sector. The expectation is that the critical institutional prerequisites that maintain the emergence of *strategic SBRs* are absent in the sector. This study, based on the theoretical approaches discussed in Chapter III, argues that in order for *strategic* state–agribusiness relations to emerge, institutional prerequisites such as the existence of a pilot state agency, characterised by embeddedness and autonomy, a sufficient capability of the state, appropriate capability of umbrella organizations and agribusinesses are crucial. What is also crucial is an understanding of the importance of *strategic SBRs* and willingness to build these SBRs. Therefore, this chapter addresses the question: *Are there essential prerequisites for the emergence of strategic state–agribusiness relations in Georgia?* Finding the answer to this question will help to understand the reasons why *strategic SBRs* have not emerged in Georgia's food and agricultural sector.

The chapter is organized as follows: Section 7.1 discusses the structure of the state in relation to agribusiness and the capacity of the state. It discusses the Agriculture Project Management Agency (APMA) in terms of its functions and activities, embeddedness and autonomy, as well as the capability of the bureaucrats involved in the state–agribusiness relations from the Ministry of Environement Protection and Agriculture and the APMA . Section 7.2 sheds light on the structure of the private sector in relation to the state, and more specifically, the presence of umbrella organizations, their activities, capabilities and achievements and the capability of the agribusinesses. Section 7.3 reveals the research findings on the existing information exchange mechanisms in the sector. Section 7.4 offers a conclusion on the findings regarding the existence of the prerequisites for emerging *strategic SBRs* in the sector.

7.1. The Structure of the State in Relation to the Private Sector

The structure of the state in relation to the private sector is understood by the presence and length of the existence of a relevant pilot agency to promote investment and interact with businesses as well as to be the bridge between the government and business in terms of information provision (te Velde, 2006). The existence of such state agencies requires institutionalization of a complex set of political machinery (Evans, 1992, p. 141) because the polity specifies, implements and enforces the formal rules of economic exchange.

7.1.1. The Presence of the Pilot Agency: Agriculture Project Management Agency (APMA)

In 2012, under the umbrella of the Ministry of Agriculture of Georgia (MoA) - currently [2020] Ministry of Environmental Protection and Agriculture (MEPA) the state established the Agriculture Project Management Agency (APMA)-currently [2020] restructured as Rural Development Agency (RDA)-the pilot agency. The mission of APMA is to encourage the private sector to invest directly in Georgia's food and agricultural sector. The key responsibilities are to plan and manage the investment projects initiated by the MoA. The MoA gives the direction to APMA regarding the sub-sectors of the food and agricultural sector of Georgia that need intervention from the state. Based on the directions from the MoA, APMA plans a programme to promote investments that address the needs of the corresponding subsectors. The plan of a programme is discussed with the MoA in order to maintain coordination with all the relevant state agencies and to involve them in the process. Once the MoA accepts a programme, it is approved by the relevant Decree of the Government of Georgia (Interview with the Head of the Programme's Support Development, APMA, 5 April 2017). Then APMA starts the implementation of the approved project.

APMA is accountable to the Ministry of Agriculture of Georgia. It provides medium-term financial reports to the Ministry and reports quarterly regarding its activities (Interview with the Head of the Programmes Support Development Unit, APMA, 5 April 2017). APMA makes decisions regarding the daily activities independently from the MoA. But if the ongoing programmes require amendments, APMA has to discuss them with MoA. The MoA approves or rejects proposed amendments to programmes (Interview with the Manager of Plant the Future, APMA, 15 December 2017). APMA is not permitted to start new programmes independently from MoA. But the Ministry is open to suggestions from APMA on new programmes s addressing obstacles that prevent the development of the food and agricultural sector. APMA's expectation is that the MoA will meet new initiatives and suggestions from APMA with enthusiasm. The Plant the Future and Co-financing the Agriculture Processing and Storage Enterprises projects (Chapter VI) are examples of initiatives approved by the MoA (Interview with the Manager of the Preferential Agrocredit, APMA, 15 December 2017).

APMA's current [2018] activities are planning and managing programmes that create incentives for the private sector to invest in the food and agriculture sector. APMA's project portfolio currently includes programmes that offer interest rate subsidies on loans, provide grants and co-finances investments to create incentives for the private sector to invest in Georgia's food and agricultural sector. The primary goals of the programmes s are to facilitate investment in primary agricultural production as well as food processing and storage enterprises in the various regions of Georgia. Hence, the state agency in charge of creating incentives for investment in the food and agricultural sector is present, i.e. that one of the essential prerequisites for the emergence of the *strategic SBRs* is in place. However, APMA is not characterised by embeddedness of private actors, and does not serve as a bridge for information exchange between the political elite and agribusinesses, as investment promotion agencies in case of *strategic SBRs* did (see Chapter II). The sensible consultative part is absent from the process (Interview with a beneficiary of the Preferential Agrocredit, 15 December 2017). There is neither a platform where the APMA representatives meet the beneficiaries of the support programmes and exchange information regarding the progress and outcomes of the programmes , nor a comprehensive data warehouse where the indicators that are crucial for investment decisions are gathered. Even though both APMA and the MoA have a Division of Statistics and Analysis, none of them has a data portal that combines the information the private sector needs for an investment decision, such as the local and international market conditions, opportunities for specific sub-sectors, tariffs and labour market conditions. If a potential investor addresses the Statistics Division of MoA with an official letter, the public officials employed in the division prepare the requested data that is available and that they are allowed to share (Interview with the Head of the Division of Statistics and Analysis at the Department of the Policy Analysis, MoA, 4 December 2017). A general attitude from the experts, as well as from the public officials, is that the state should not prepare such a data portal, especially with information on market conditions, and that it is investors' duty to build networks, conduct research on local and export markets and to build a supply chain (Interview with the Head of the Rural Development Coordination Division, MoA, 4 December 2017).

Neither APMA nor the MoA has a comprehensive data warehouse of the economic performance indicators of the food and agricultural sector collected from the agribusinesses that are the beneficiaries of the state programmes. The state is not interested in collecting the data, and the evaluation is just about telling a good story (Interview with a beneficiary of Preferential Agrocredit, 15 December 2017). Currently, various indicators on the performance of the food and agricultural sector of Georgia are collected by various state agencies. For example, since 2006, the National Statistics Office of Georgia (Geostat) has conducted quarterly surveys of the agricultural sector. Since 2014, the Statistics and Analysis Division at MoA has collected data on the prices as well as on the yields of wheat, corn, apples and citrus fruits through the Regional Information Consulting Centres (Interview with the Head of the Division of Statistics and Analysis at the Department of Policy Analysis, MoA, 4 December 2017). The financial organizations record the data on the issued loans and grants for the beneficiaries of the state programmes and their regional distribution and provide it to APMA. The later is not available publicly online, but provided upon request (Interview with a Supply Chain Consultant, USAID-REAP, 29 November 2011). In addition, according to a public official from the MoA, the state started collecting information regarding the obstacles in the sector at a regional level from the Regional Information Consulting Centres. However, the information on the obstacles that the Regional Information Consulting Centres provide to the MoA is too general, and there is no added value from it. Similar information reaches the MoA faster through word of mouth, because the country is small and general information is distributed easily (Interview with the Head of the Division of Statistics and Analysis at the Department of Policy Analysis at the MoA, 4 December 2017).

7.1.2. State Capacity

The recruitment process at APMA and the MoA are similar. Once there is a job position available, employees normally rotate from one position to another, or from one department to the other. But the vacancy is still published online so the competition is formally announced publicly. There are formal institutions for selection: screening of the applications, (sometimes) examinations, and interviews (Interview with a public official, MoA, 4 December 2017). As revealed by one public official from MoA, the decision on hiring is not always based on just the merits of an applicant:

> "[…] I remember the case when the selection committee had to decide in the final phase of the competition between two candidates; one was an employee of MoA and the other a random applicant. Although the candidate from outside was excellent, we hired the insider […] I preferred the applicant from outside, the other members of the committee as well, but because we already knew the insider's working capabilities with the team, we selected him" (Interview with a public officer, MoA, 4 December 2017).

Besides, the MoA is ruling party-based, as the individuals who were in the Georgian Dream during the election campaign in 2012 are employed there. Hence, most of them have absolutely nothing to do with agriculture (Interview with an expert, 15 December 2017).

The salaries in the public sector are low in comparison to salaries in non-governmental organizations and the private sector. The highest position in the system, beyond management, is a chief specialist. A gross salary for this position is 1200 GEL (450 USD), which slightly exceeds the average salary (1124 GEL) in the country. It is around half the figure of the average salary in the private sector and three times lower than the average salary in the international developmental organizations operating in Georgia's food and agricultural sector (Interview with a public officer, MoA, 4 December 2017). The public sector can compete neither with NGOs nor with the private sector in terms of the conditions for its employees. Therefore, it is hard to attract qualified staff, or if already employed in the public sector, to motivate them to relate their long-term career goals to the sector (Interview with a Project Manager, EPRC, 20 November 2017). There are no performance assessment systems for public officials or bonus systems or remuneration attached to performance. The only reward attached to performance is the Certificate of Appreciation, which is awarded once a year to the best employee. Due to the low salary, it is hard to consider working in the sector in the long term. For a while, one can work with enthusiasm to serve the country. But the salary is quite low for this enthusiasm to last for a more extended period. The salary might not be the primary motivator; however, it should not be a discouraging one either (Interview with a public official, MoA, 4 December 2017). As a result, there is an outflow of staff from the public sector to the private sector, among them quite frequent changes of the Ministers. Since 2012, there have been four different Ministers of Agriculture. As a public official from the MoA mentioned:

> The individuals who moved from the MoA to the consulting firms earn more than the Minister does and have less responsibility […] (Interview with the Head of the Division of Statistics and Analytics at the Department of the Policy and Analysis, MoA, 4 December 2017).

Beyond enthusiasm, the only motivation for better performance in the public sector is the possibility to climb higher up the career ladder; however, the existing career ladder does not offer many opportunities (Interview with the Public Official, MoA, 4 December 2017).

The bureaucratic system is top down, with initiatives or assignments coming from management. Sometimes they ask for ideas; however, the question is whether these ideas are to be followed or not (Interview with a public official, MoA, 4 December 2017). There is a circle of a bureaucratic machine, and employees at a lower level have to follow the machine and do not have the opportunities to initiate ideas for development. As one former public official from the MoA revealed:

> […] "We were three or four employees; younger compared to the other staff members, who acquired education in Germany and the US. We had a passion for doing something important for changes in the sector, but we could not do anything, and there was no opportunity to use our knowledge. We always heard 'these inexperienced young employees.' The system is top-down. I have not done anything except writing bureaucratic letters [...] once individuals get into that bureaucratic machine, they should fit the situation and politics, and we get what we get" (Interview with a Supply Chain Consultant, USAID-REAP, 29 November 2017).

Bureaucrats from state agencies are freer in expressing opinions publicly than public officials from the MoA, as the messages or opinions expressed by the latter are interpreted as political ones. No public officials at the medium level of the bureaucracy machine attend public discussions on their own initiative. It only happens when there is agreement with the Minister or Deputy Minister, and mainly when the meeting is organized by an NGO (Interview with a Project Manager at the Economic Policy Research Centre, 20 November 2017). As stated by a local expert:

> There are cases that the MoA sends the chief specialist to attend the public discussions; however, these officials attend these meetings just for the sake of making a tick on the participant list that the representative of the MoA is attending the meeting. Even in cases of very heated discussions on food- and agriculture-related issues, they do not make comments on the discussed material (Interview with Project Manager, Think Tank, 20 November 2017).

Neither the MoA nor APMA has a systematic plan for building the capability of employees. The opportunities to participate in training and workshops are mostly offered by developmental organizations, which support the country's food and agriculture sector. The workshops take place in Georgia and abroad. It is up to the management to decide whom to offer the available training and workshop opportunities to. Whether the public officials at the lower level will have the chance to participate in training workshops depends on the head of the department or the manager. As a public official explained, based on experiences at the MoA, if an employee works hard and does overtime, opportunities for business trips are higher within the country as well as abroad (Interview with the Head of the Rural Development Coordination Division, MoA, 4 December 2017). However, many employees face language barriers to participating in international training due to a lack of knowledge of English and so do not take up these opportunities (Interview with the Head of Projects Support Development Unit, 5 April 2017).

To sum up, the pilot agency that is responsible for creating incentives for the private sector to invest in Georgia's food and agricultural sector has been present since 2014. However, this agency does not function as a bridge for information exchange between the state and agribusiness. The bureaucratic system is top-down and does not create any opportunities for the bureaucrats on the lower rungs of the ladder to initiate new ideas. Meritocracy does not characterize the selection criteria of public officials for the job positions. For hiring, there is competition in theory, but in practice what usually happens is that staff from inside the public sector are rotated from one position to another—it is rare for an outsider to be hired on the basis of merit. The remuneration is low. The system does not create motivation to have a long-term career in the public sector. This is reflected in the frequent changes of bureaucrats, including those in top positions. With these frequent changes, the institutional memory goes as well. Every new Minister wants to start from problem identifications in the sector, however the duration of their stay in the positions is so short, that even the problem identification process cannot be finished (Interview with the Agribusiness Project Coordination, EBRD, 30 January 2018). Thus, it is no wonder that the obstacles are not addressed.

7.2. The Private Sector in Relation to Public Sector

7.2.1. The Presence and Length of Existence of Umbrella Organizations

The findings from the interviews illustrate that the umbrella organizations under which enterprises from Georgia's food and agricultural sector are associated are diverse. The large enterprises are members of the Business Association of Georgia (BAG),. SMEs from the sector are members of the Georgian Small and Medium Enterprises Association (GSMEA). The SMEs from the food and agricultural sector, which are exporters as well, are members of the Export Development Association (EDA. The small and micro producers from the food and agricultural sector are associated with the Georgian Farmers' Association. In addition to the economy-wide and sector-specific umbrella organisations, there are sub-sector specific umbrella organisations as well, of which the relatively active ones include the Georgian Wine Association (GWA), the Hazelnut Exporters and Processors Association (HEPA), the Dairy Products Producers Association

(DPPA), the Milk Producers' Association (MPA) and the Georgian Shepherds Association (GSA) (Interview with a public officer, MoA, 4 December 2017).

Most of the umbrella organizations have existed for less than 10 years. The oldest ones are BAG (established in 2009), AGSME (established in 2010), and the Georgian Wine Association (GWA) (established in 2010). The majority have been set up since the state prioritized the sector. The reason behind their establishment was the needs of the sector as well as accessing financial support from international developmental organizations operating in the sector (Interview with a local expert, 9 November 2017). Since the prioritization of the sector in 2011, the Business Association of Georgia established the Agrarian Committee to study the obstacles that stymie the sector's development and to discuss these issues with the relevant decision makers and agribusiness, as well as to initiate reforms and necessary amendments in laws and regulations (Annual Report of BAG, 2017).

The umbrella organizations differ in the quantity and size (large, medium, small, and micro) of members, the targeted issues, activities, the institutions for membership, institutions for interaction with the state and financial sustainability. The Business Association of Georgia (BAG), , associates 70 enterprises, representing multiple sectors of the economy. Each member is a stakeholder and an integral part of BAG. Being a member is associated with some privileges. Firstly, because the association has a reputable status among the business elite and policy makers, being its member means that the business is developed and has a good network. Secondly, membership makes it more comfortable to organize individual meetings with representatives of the political elite if needed; hence, being a member is crucial for a business. Thirdly, BAG helps individual members to arrange meetings with the business elite when needed. Besides, each committee of BAG is provided with working and meeting space.

BAG has close relations with all branches of government, policy-makers and business elite, and informal but regular meetings with representatives of the state (Annual Report of BAG, 2017). It regularly organizes meetings with political elites. The meetings are closed so that the state and businesses can openly discuss the obstacles that businesses face. The process of organising meetings is as follows: first of all, BAG formulates the problem, then identifies the state body(ies) which the decision-making on the issue of interest concerns, and reaches the relevant public official(s) through the contacts BAG has in the relevant agency. Initially, the problem is introduced via a phone call and afterwards a problem statement is provided via email. Once the public officer prepares feedback on the problem, representatives of BAG and the state meet to discuss it (Interview with the Deputy Executive Director of BAG, 4 December 2017). As stated by the executive director of BAG:

> If the state cannot solve the problem the way we suggest, we request them to provide their suggestions for solving the problem. We sometimes succeed, sometimes not. It depends how ready the state is to make relevant changes [...] (Interview with the Deputy Executive Director of BAG, 4 December 2017).

BAG does not lobby the interest of any specific member, and it does not lobby if this lobbying could benefit some members but harm others. During the last two years BAG has held approximately 60 meetings with the political elite (Interview with the Deputy Executive Director of BAG, 4 December 2017). BAG is sustained financially, as its revenues are based on membership fees. It does not apply to any grant opportunities provided by the international developmental organisations, as according to the deputy executive director, these grants are given with certain conditions that limit the activities of the associations (Interview with the Deputy Executive Director of BAG, 4 December 2017).

The Georgian Small and Medium Enterprises Association (GSMEA) was founded by small and medium businesses and the business unions, such as the American Chamber of Commerce in Georgia, the EU–Georgia Business Council (EUGBC), the National Committee of the International Chamber of Commerce (ICC), and the Business Association of Georgia (BAG). Currently under the umbrella of GSMEA there are 4000 enterprises from various sectors of the economy, including the food and agricultural sector. Of these, approximately 3000 are actively involved in communications with GSMEA. The membership is open to any SME, it is free of charge and does not set any obligations for its members. At the initial stage the membership was fee-based, 20–30 GEL (8–12 USD) annually, but it did not work (Interview with the Head of the Economic Policy Associations Coalitions, USAID G4G, 1 December 2017). As stated by the Executive Director of GSMEA, when the membership size reaches around 20,000, GSMEA will set fee-based membership system again. Considering that 97 % of the enterprises in Georgia are SMEs, it is feasible to reach 20,000 members.

GSMEA requests its members to share their obstacles. Based on the provided information on the obstacles and needs, GSMEA prepares training sessions, seminars and qualification courses, and offers services to its members to overcome the obstacles they face. The SMEs buy the offered services. The revenue from selling the services is a financial source for the organisation in addition to the grants from the projects supported by the international donor organizations (Interview with the Executive Director of GSMEA, 15 December 2017). In addition, GSMEA offers its members advocacy and networking services, as well as opportunities to attend the public events it organises. Besides, it provides information on the requirements to comply with new laws and regulations. In case there are planned amendments in the law, GSMEA gets information via email formally, discusses it formally, and provides comments on the initiated amendments formally as well (Interview with the Executive Director of GSMEA, 15 December 2017). GSMEA is a member of the various councils established under the public agencies. The concern of interest is not sector-specific, but broad, economic level, to support improvement of the business environment. The key function of GSMEA, according to its Executive Director, is advocacy for improving the business environment in Georgia (Interview with the Executive Director of GSMEA, 15 December 2017).

The Export Development Association (EDA) was founded in 2012. It is a member-driven association, uniting up to 100 Georgian export-oriented producers and service providers. The majority of the members are from the food and agriculture sector, as it remains the leading sector in export (Interview with the Head of EDA, 1 February 2018). Membership of EDA is not fee-based. As stated by the head of EDA, because business does not understand the value and usage of the umbrella organizations, almost none of the enterprises pay the membership fee. However, all over the world, umbrella organizations are sustained financially by membership fees. In the case of EDA, members are obliged to participate in a survey conducted by the EDA twice a year. EDA offers services to Georgian exporters to develop an export-marketing plan, to manage export processes, to select markets for export and to break down barriers to trade.

EDA provides advisory service via an Export Helpdesk that is the first step to identify an interesting market and determine what potential it offers to exporters. The consulting services cover information regarding export documents, rules of origin, labelling, packaging, standards and certification, and tariff and non-tariff barriers. It also supports SMEs to find suitable markets, to observe trends and to set adequate expectations. The key source of revenue for EDA is the revenue from selling services, as well as projects supported by international development organizations or state-supported projects. If there were no projects from the international developmental organizations, the EDA would only depend on the revenue from the services they provided to the private sector and it would be hard to keep the permanent staff (Interview with the Head of EDA, 1 February 2017).

The Georgian Farmers Association (GFA), established in 2012, is an umbrella organization for 4000 small and micro-producers. GFA has close relations with the state bodies in the food and agricultural sector of Georgia. As the local expert stated, the director of GFA is very communicable, has a good network and active relationships with the state as well as with the developmental organizations in the country. The executive director of GFA is always present at the food and agricultural sector roundtables organized in the frameworks of the donor-supported projects (Interview with local expert, 24 November 2017). According to the deputy director of GFA, the organisation brings the obstacles of the small and micro producers to the state; however, these are individual- or small group-related micro problems rather than aggregated at the sectoral level. The key financial source for the association is revenue from the projects supported by the international donor organizations. Depending on international aid creates limitations in activities, as it is a top-down relationship and the beneficiary needs to meet the requirements of the donor organization (Interview with a Senior Researcher at the Private Sector Development Research Centre, 14 November 2017). It also creates a threat to the financial sustainability of the organization, as one day the developmental organizations may decide to leave the sector or the country (Interview with the Head of the Economic Policy Associations Coalitions, USAID G4G, 1 December 2017).

Since the sector became a priority, supporting creation of the umbrella organizations also became a priority for the international developmental organizations (Interview with a local expert, 9 November 2017). The research findings indicate the presence of the umbrella organizations at the sector or sub-sector levels in the food and agricultural sector. The MoA uses sub-sector specific associations as a bridge for sub-sector related businesses to provide information regarding the initiated regulations, changes in the law and exhibitions. The MoA sends this information to the relevant umbrella organizations, which distribute it among their members. Otherwise, it would be hard to distribute the information to all agribusinesses (Interview with a public officer, MoA, 4 December 2017). In order for the umbrella organizations to reach the state and be successful they need experience, personal contacts and networks with actors in the sector (Interview with a local expert, OXFAM, 6 November 2017). Most of the umbrella organizations lack professionalism and analytical skills(Interview with Project Manager, think tank, 20 November 2017). Besides, they avoid provision of critical feedback on initiated new regulations when they are presented in the public discussion. However, once a regulation is enforced, they start complaining that it is not manageable (Interview with Project Manager, think tank, 20 November 2017). According to a foreign expert in the field:

> The umbrella organizations in the food and agricultural sector of Georgia sometimes say sensible things and raise problems to discuss. However, they are not really fighting the war for addressing the initiated problems, but are simply money-making organizations, hunting for grants (Interview with a foreign expert, 24 November 2017).

However, there are exceptions as well. For example, from the Georgian Wine Association (GWA) there is a very positive process of consultations from the side of the wine industry and the state is very receptive to the ideas coming from them (Interview with a foreign expert, 24 November 2017). They manage to lobby the interests of their members well with the state (Interview with a former Minister of Agriculture, MoA, 11 December 2017). GWA, established in 2010, is the umbrella of thirty large and medium-sized wine producer and exporter enterprises. It was established with the goal of conducting a marketing campaign for Georgian wine and to popularize it (Interview with the Marketing Manager of the Georgian Wine Association, 1 December 2017). In the case of wine, the sector is well developed and the capability of the member enterprises is strong as well, which reflects the positive outcomes of GWA's activities. Members pay a membership fee, 1000–1500 USD annually.

The umbrella organizations need some stable financial sources to sustain themselves and to hire permanent staff with strong capacity. However, most of them rely on grants from developmental organizations, and face sustainability issues. The few that have membership fees have stricter requirements and demands from members to act to raise members' interests in discussions (Interview with the Head of EDA, 1 February 2018).

One of the key functions of the developmental umbrella organizations is gathering data on the performance of its members, as well as obstacles they face in the production process, aggregating it and disseminating the outcomes of the aggregate data with the relevant state agencies to initiate policy changes to overcome the obstacles the specific industries or the sector face. However, in the case of Georgia, as the research findings illustrate, even the strong umbrella organizations, like BAG or the GWA, do not fulfil such a function. BAG has some data for internal use to track the ongoing situation, but does not aggregate and provide it to the relevant agencies of the state for discussions. According to the executive director of BAG:

> If there is an interest, the state has the best data via access to the database of the Revenue Services and export and import. Hence, they can dedicate resources and analyse it. BAG provides feedback on the issues relevant to its members; however, they do not see the usefulness of sharing aggregate data of all problems together.

GWA puts effort into collecting some data, but it is very hard as its members do not have any obligations to report regularly. Even in cases when GWA requests some information regarding the markets in which the members are interested to export, the information is provided late (Interview with the Marketing Manager of GWA, 1 December 2017). The members of the Export Development Association have the obligation to participate in the EDA survey twice a year; however, none of the enterprises share data on business operations, turnover or financial statements. EDA gathers data on obstacles and analyses it (Interview with the Head of EDA, 1 February 2017). The Georgian Farmers Association gathers some type of data via a call centre, but they do not have the inhouse capability to organize and analyse it (Interview with the Deputy Head of GFA, 14 December 2017).

7.2.3. The Capacity of the Agribusiness

In addition to the presence and length of existence of umbrella organizations, the structure and the capability of the private sector are also crucial for the emergence of *strategic SBRs*. In the case of the food and agricultural sector of Georgia, the total number of the enterprises is 4249: 85 % (3621) small, 8 % (338) medium, and 7 % (290) large enterprises. Table 7.1 illustrates the distribution of the enterprises of the food and agricultural sector by size in primary production, food processing, as well as in sub-sectors of food and agriculture.

Tab. 7.1. Distribution of Agribusinesses by Size and Industries, 2016

	Small	Medium	Large
Primary Productions	900	98	37
Agro Product Processing (total)	2721	240	253
Among them:			
Meat production	166	24	20
Fish production	31	2	4
Vegetables	143	31	70
Diary	86	20	14
Wheat Cereal Production	8		
Bread and pastry for short-term storage	1509	66	32
Pastry for long-term storage	176	6	5
Pasta	58	10	5
Tea and coffee	70	9	5
Spirits	35	3	4
Wine	152	37	38
Beer	15	1	5
Mineral waters and non-alcoholic drinks	87	9	11
Others	185	22	38
Total	3621	228	290

Source: The Ministry of Agriculture of Georgia, 2017

The majority of these businesses are SMEs. The capacity of the businesses is meagre, especially in the case of SMEs. Most struggle even in the clear formulation of problems (Interview with the Project Manager at EPRC, 20 November 2017). According to the executive director of the Georgian SMEs Association, SMEs often do not even know that they have problems. Therefore, at first, GSMEA introduces them to the type of the problems they might have and help them to identify the problems they face (Interview with the Executive Director of GSMEA, 15 December 2017). In most cases, the problems stated by the private sector are on a micro level, rather than on sub-sectoral or sectoral leven, therefore there is a lack of interest from the state to discuss or to address them (Interview with Senior Researcher at the Private Sector Development Research Centre, 14 November 2017). Besides, the SMEs do not have the ambition to develop further and grow because they lack an understanding of the potential of their businesses. As stated by a local investor:

> The SME producers do not even assume that they can sell not only locally, but in other regions of the country and abroad as well. Therefore, providing information regarding the potentials of each subsector is crucial. There is a need for support from the state in this direction to raise awareness among the SMEs. The opportunities for participation in exhibitions may contribute to overcoming this information gap (Interview with a beneficiary of the Preferential Agrocredit, 24 January 2018).

In order to achieve success in agribusiness, there is a need for awareness and access to the knowledge of the existing opportunities and trends. However, in this sector, we observe only the knowledge inherited from the Soviet Union (Interview with local expert, OXFAM, 6 November 2018). The main constraint right now is access to knowledge, which is very complicated, as understanding exactly how to do something is not trivial at all (Interview with a beneficiary of Preferential Agrocredit, 15 December 2017). The sector has reached the stage that agribusiness has become unpredictable. There is a lack of knowledge in many realms starting from land cultivation and corn production to animal husbandry. The existing universities do not provide qualified education to fill the knowledge gap (Interview with a beneficiary of the Preferential Agrocredit project, 16 January 2018). It is hard to find labour that meets the requirements of the sub-sectors. As a local investor in the vegetable food processing industry explained, it was impossible to find an agronomist with required qualifications locally, so they had to hire one from Ukraine (Interview with a local investor, 7 December 2017). A local investor from the dairy industry conveys a similar message, mentioning that they had to invite a farm manager from Israel, as well as a veterinarian and agronomist (Interview with a beneficiary of the Preferential

Agrocredit programme, 16 November 2017). Because of the absence of the required expertise, in many cases, the investment in the sector is not based on useful predictions (Interview with local expert, 9 November 2017). According to a local expert:

> The SMEs cannot make feasible business plans. The plans are done in a very primitive manner, with a rough calculation of the costs and expectations about realization at a roughly calculated or estimated price, without taking into consideration the risks. Then the question is whether the beneficiaries of the programmes have a long-term operational plan or not (Interview with local expert, 14 November 2017).

Agribusiness is not the type of a business where employing a good manager is a sufficient condition to maintain the success of the business. The SMEs face systematic weaknesses, and liberalization of the markets is not sufficient to overcome those weaknesses. It might facilitate export, but cannot generate production and export itself, or if it does it generates it at the lowest quality in the markets because of the coordination difficulties. Therefore, there is a need for coordination and a roundtable where businesses and the state discuss these weaknesses. However, there is no such thing (Interview with a foreign expert, 24 November 2017).

To sum up, we observe the presence of umbrella organizations. Both sides are open for meetings in case of need. For the state, the umbrella organizations are more accessible sources of information distribution on policy changes, initiated amendments in the laws, and information on approaching exhibitions. However, the umbrella organizations do not collect and aggregate data from agribusinesses on their performance and on the obstacles they face in the process of operations. Hence, these umbrella organizations are not characterized by the critical functions of developmental umbrella organizations, which is to provide the state with aggregated data on the agribusiness performance and obstacles they face. Besides, most of the associations face financial sustainability issues, as they rely on developmental aid. As for the agribusiness, the majority (93 %) are SMEs, which have low capabilities and face many weaknesses.

7.3. Information Exchange Mechanisms

One more crucial element for the emergence of *strategic SBRs* is the existence of an active channel for state–business dialogue and information exchange (Doner and Schneider, 2000; te Velde, 2006). The literature suggests that such mechanisms bring together state and business actors to discuss and coordinate their actions, to accelerate reforms and make them more straightforward to implement, to promote transparency, and to build an atmosphere of mutual trust between the state and business (Herzberg and Wright, 2013). Neither the MoA nor APMA has a platform where agribusinesses and the state get together and discuss market and coordination-related obstacles. Hence, institutionalized public-private dialogue mechanisms, such as a public-private partnership council, deliberation council or regular forum, do not exist in this sector. However, it is still possible to initiate amendments to the law in the Parliament of Georgia, by writing a letter that explains the need for a change. According to the head of EDA:

> [...] as a rule, discussing certain changes and persuading the public sector regarding the necessity of those amendments for business happens via personal networks. Large as well as medium-size businesses have such close relations with the state that they can advocate specific ideas [...] The meetings with businesses happen in the framework of the projects basically [...] or in the pre- election period (Interview with the Head of the Export Development Association, umbrella organization, 1 February 2018).

When there is a need to share information with the private sector on the initiated amendments to the law, intended policy changes, or changes in strategy, the MoA sends it to umbrella organisations via email, which in turn distribute among their members (Interview with a public official, MoA, 4 December 2017). Besides, the MoA established Information and Consulting Service Centres (ICCs) in municipalities in 2013. In total, 59 ICCs have been established in all municipalities of Georgia, each of them employing 4–6 people (FAO, 2014). The ICCs are obliged to gather information regarding agriculture, regional food markets, and prices at the municipal level and timely inform the MoA regarding the sector's existing situation. They are responsible for providing information regarding the tax legislation and sector-specific regulations, government strategy, and state programmes to individual farmers, cooperatives, as well as enterprises (Interview with the Head of the project's Support Development, APMA. 5 April 2017). The ICCs are responsible for organizing training as well as information meetings. As the interviews revealed, the ICCs gather information for the MoA, but as for providing consultation to businesses, the capabilities of ICC employees are low. 'There is a lack of capacity in those centres; there is a lack of knowledge, so what can they teach others?' (Interview with the Project Manager at EPRC, 20 November 2017). According to a former Minister of Agriculture:

> With the establishment of ICCs, the 250 job positions were announced in the various regions of Georgia. For the announced job positions, 11,000 individuals applied; however, it was almost impossible to find candidates with the requiredskills. Therefore, the vacancies were announced for a second time, and in some regions, even a third time (Interview with a former Minister of Agriculture of Georgia, MoA, 11 December 2017).

The motivation of the employees at ICCs is low as well; the salary of the individuals employed in the ICCs is 50 % of the average salary in the country.

One more source of information provision from the state is the regular (monthly) newsletter 'Sofeli,' which has been published by MoA's Department of Public Relations since 2015. The newspaper publishes interviews with the representatives of the MoA and its subordinated agencies, which relates to the information regarding planned projects and their supporting activities. It also provides information on the new regulations and initiated amendments in the law. As mentioned during the interviews with public officials from the MoA and APMA, the only regularly planned meetings with the private sector as well as other actors in the food and agriculture sector of Georgia organized by the MoA is public discussions of the annual reports once a year. Besides, when any amendment in policy is initiated, the MoA distributes information regarding it via media sources, publishes it on the official webpage, distributes the draft document with the change to the targeted audience and organizes a public discussion around it as well. The state organizes meetings when necessary, but with the representatives of international organizations, umbrella organizations, and research organizations, as well as with some of the beneficiaries of the state programmes. These meetings are not regular but ad hoc, in response to a problem. In addition, under the Association Agreement with the EU, the MoA gets developmental aid with annual tranches upon meeting the conditions, which includes organizing a public-private dialogue twice a year. Therefore, the MoA meets the umbrella organizations and the other beneficiaries of the EU support programmes at least twice a year (Interview with the Deputy Head of the Farmers' Association, 14 November 2017).

To sum up, there is no mechanism, or body, which obliges the state and businesses to sit together regularly and discuss the coordination and market-related obstacles. As discussed in Chapter III, the existence of such a body is one of the criteria for the emergence of *strategic SBRs*, as it allows the state and businesses to get together, identify market obstacles and opportunities, anddiscuss the relevant issues to overcome market and coordination failures. As the interview results revealed, there is no information vacuum during policy initiation or planning amendments in the law. However, the exchanged information is not comprehensive during these meetings.

Conclusion

In case of the food and agricultural sector of Georgia, we observe some prerequisites for the emergence of *strategic SBRs*, which are, however, not sufficient to maintain this process. Institutionalized public–private dialogue mechanisms, such as a public-private partnership council, a deliberation council or regular forum, do not exist. Some other mechanisms for information exchange exist, but the exchanged information through these channels is not comprehensive and does not address overcoming coordination and market failures. We observe the presence of a pilot state agency, APMA – currently [2020] RDA, which creates incentives for investment in the sector, but it does not serve as an information exchange bridge between the state and agribusinesses in general, or the beneficiaries of the programmes in particular. The bureaucratic system is not merit-based. We observe the existence of the umbrella organizations at the economy, sector, and sub-sector levels, which are the sources of the information distribution to the private sector from the state. However, they do not gather the data on the obstacles and performance of the private sector, which is crucial to understand the obstacles provoking coordination and market failures in the food and agricultural sector of Georgia. The capacity of the agribusiness sector is low. Hence, the prerequisites which are necessary for the emergence of *strategic SBRs* are not sufficiently present in Georgia. Hence, it is no surprise that *strategic* state–agribusiness relations which facilitate effective state intervention in the sector do not emerge.

Chapter VIII Discussion and Conclusion

Since 2012, Georgia has experienced a shift from economic policies driven by the Washington Consensus to more interventionist ones. Since 2012, one of the critical targets of these interventionist economic policies has been Georgia's food and agricultural sector. The key argument of this book is that strategic coordination of activities between the state and agribusinesses is crucial for state intervention to address obstacles the food and agricultural sector faces and to utilize the sector's opportunities. Therefore, the nature of the institutions of state-agribusiness relations is critical in the process of state intervention in the sector. With this argument in mind, the research has addressed the following questions:

> *How has the state been intervening in the food and agricultural sector of Georgia? How does the state manage relationships with agribusinesses while intervening in the food and agricultural sector of Georgia? Why did strategic state–agribusiness relations fail to emerge in Georgia?*

To these ends, the study has thoroughly examined the instruments of state intervention in the sector and the nature of the institutional settings of state-agribusiness relations currently being applied; it has also explored reasons as to why *strategic SBRs* have not yet emerged.

The publication empirically addressed these questions in Chapters V, VI, and VII. Chapter V examined the instruments of state intervention in the food and agricultural sector of Georgia in 2004–2016 and the sector's performance since the state started active formalised intervention. Chapter VI examined the institutions of state-agribusiness relations. Chapter VII analysed prerequisites necessary for the emergence of *strategic SBRs*.

8.1. Main Findings

Chapter V explored *how the state has been intervening in Georgia's food and agricultural sector*, and *how its performance has changed since the state began an active intervention in 2013*. Thus, Chapter V examined state activities and instruments used to enhance the performance of Georgia's food and agricultural sector. The sector's performance is assessed via application of the UNIDO EQuIP toolbox, which proposes indicators for measuring the performance of economic sectors.

The research findings reveal that the role of the state and instruments of state intervention in the food and agricultural sector of Georgia has changed during the last decade. The sector lacked the state's attention until 2010 due to the political ideology of the ruling majority, representing the liberal economic school. The attitude was that the sector should survive independently in competition. The economy was growing in general, but the sector was lagging behind. The government did not favour the sector with development-oriented subsidies from the state budget, but it used its political power to force local investors—successful businesses in other sectors—to invest in the food and agricultural sector. The businesses invested, motivated either by fear of the reaction of state actors if they did not, or expectation that the government would reciprocate in the future. However, these investments showed a poor economic performance.

In 2011, the food and agricultural sector returned to being a development priority of the state, followed by elaborating on the first agricultural development strategy. The strategy focused on increasing the sector's competitiveness and productivity based on market principles, rather than providing direct subsidies. To increase competitiveness, the government focused on providing agribusiness with opportunities to participate in exhibitions and popularise Georgian products. The state saw its role as a supporter of the private sector in the modernization of production, as well as a provider of infrastructure and information regarding the markets and modern technological achievements. The state encouraged FDI flows through the policies, which improved the country's business environment; however, the volume of FDI in the sector remained low due to the unsolved core obstacles in the sector, including land fragmentation and incomplete land registration.

At the end of 2012, with a change of political power, agricultural development was declared a top priority. Prioritization of the sector was somewhat political, to fulfil pre-election promises on social programmes, rather than development-oriented. In 2014, after two years of planning, the MoA publicly presented an updated agricultural development strategy for 2015–2020. The broad goals highlighted in the updated strategy were similar to those stated in the previous strategy, i.e., investment growth, productivity and production growth, and export diversification and growth; however, the instruments to achieve them differed. State instruments to reach the goals included interest rate subsidies on agricultural loans, co-financing investment, and grants to create incentives for businesses to invest in Georgia's food and agricultural sector. The state intervenes in the sector and provides financial assistance to local agribusinesses through programmes such as Plant the Future, Preferential Agrocredit and Co-financing Agriculture Processing and Storage Enterprises. To manage investment projects incentivised through the state programmes, the MoA established the Agricultural Project Management Agency (APMA) in 2014. The state intervenes in the food and agricultural sector to increase and diversify production and export capabilities. However, increased state intervention has brought neither diversification of the domestic production and export dimensions of agricultural products nor a transformation of employment structures and value-added in the economy.

In successful cases of state interventions, the driver of the success has been the creation and maintenance of institutions that enable strategic coordination between the state and businesses. Even though the SBRs differed among the countries, the *strategic* ones featured the collaboration of political elites, businesses, and bureaucrats to address firm, industry, or sector-specific information and coordination failures that distract investment flows and growth. Chapter VI addressed the nature of the institutions of state-agribusiness relations in the process of state intervention in the food and agricultural sector of Georgia. It raised the question: *how does the state interact with agribusiness in the process ofstate intervention in the food and agricultural sector?* The analytical framework of the institutionalist approach of SBRs was applied to analyse the nature of state-agribusiness relations in Georgia. According to this analytical framework, the strategic SBRs are characterised by the information exchange, reciprocity, credibility and trust and enacted feedback mechanisms on state policies and state aid programmes to private sector. The analysis is presented in light of three state aid programmes, Preferential Agrocredit, Plant the Future, and the Co-financing Agricultural Processing and Storage Enterprises. The study examined the interactions between the state and agribusinesses in each selected case accounting for formal and informal institutional arrangements and their enforcement mechanisms.

Like many other transition countries, most aspects of the prevailed institutions of state-agribusiness relations are informal in Georgia. No formal rules oblige the state and agribusinesses to meet regularly, not even for the beneficiaries of the state programmes. Moreover, there are no public networks (webpage, forums, and regular meetings) dedicated to exchanging information between agribusiness, state, and other interested agents from the civil society organizations, developmental organizations, think tanks at state programmes, industries, or the sector levels. Despite this, meetings do occur between the state representatives and agribusinesses, but via personal or professional networks. The small size of the country simplifies getting access to the relevant representatives of the state or agribusiness actors through personal networks. If there are issues to discuss, arranging a meeting is easily manageable. Policymakers, as well as bureaucrats, are open for meetings. The Agriculture Project Management Agency (APMA) is open to all sizes of agribusinesses, and it is easy to reach programme managers via phone or to meet in-person. The Ministry of Agriculture of Georgia (currently [2020] the Ministry of Environmental Protection and Agriculture) is a very open body; even the Minister is reachable for a meeting. But, the criteria that determines the level of access to the state and the rank of a public official involved, depends on the size and success story of an agribusiness. Large agribusinesses and successful actors in the sector can reach state representatives up to the Ministerial level. SMEs convey their concerns and needs to the state through industry-specific umbrella organisations, however, these concern mostly individual agribusiness' specific and not generalizable problem at specific food industry or sector level.

The research findings illustrate that in Georgia, there are individual meetings initiated by agribusinesses in case of need. There are also various types of gatherings and meetings organized by the state, research organisations, international organisations, civil society organisations, or think tanks. However, the representatives of agribusinesses beyond the umbrella organisations are rarely invited or presented in these meetings. When the meetings are initiated from the state regarding the new policy or programme initiation or adapting existing ones, the state invites experts from whom they do expect agreement/ acceptance of the initiated amadements or programmes. In such meetings, it happens often that most participants support the initiative or prefer not to oppose it. Even if the representatives of agribusinesses are invited in such meetings, they lack the willingness to share information. They have expectations that there will not be a follow-up from the state on their shared concerns. On the one hand, agribusinesses' motivation to express openly constructive criticism is diminished due to public officials' ongoing attitude, taking personal offence at critical feedback on their programmes and policies. Such an attitude raises fear among agribusinesses that critical feedback might negatively affect their future relationships with state actors. Also, representatives of the state tend to maintain the idea that policymakers know better than the private sector. On the other hand, the state lacks interest in getting information on obstacles the private sector faces, as they are sceptical of the possibility of making relevant changes. Thus, many of these meetings are pointless, as they do not yield any usable information exchange. Even in cases when concerns are shared, public officials' frequent resignations and slow bureaucratic decision-making distract the follow-up process of shared concerns at such meetings. Furthermore, due to frequent changes of designated public officials, institutional memory is not preserved, which distracts the state agribusiness meetings to contribute to building long-term relationships and trust.

The findings show that even though both APMA and the MoA have a Division of Statistics and Analysis, none of them has a data portal with information on local and international market conditions, opportunities for specific sub-sectors, tariffs, and labour market conditions, all of which the private sector needs from the state to make sound investment decisions. Moreover, the state is not even collecting data on the performance of agribusinesses, which are supported through state programmes. The lack of relevant resources explains this.

The second critical feature of *strategic SBRs*, reciprocity, is absent from state-agribusiness relations in Georgia. The state does provide subsidies, and each state support programme has a formalised selection process for subsidy provision. The decision is based on the beneficiary's credibility to repay the loan or ability to co-finance investment rather than the investment project's long-term economic performance. The state programmes have already supported 30,599 investment projects. The state is motivated to increase the number of supported projects, as their quantity is informally used as an indicator of success. The subsidies provided are not tied to performance indicators for success or failure. The state believes it is too early to define performance assessment criteria at the initial stages of a subsidised project. APMA does not have a formal obligation to monitor the beneficiaries' economic performance; subsequently, APMA does not collect data on the performance of agribusiness to assess the beneficiaries' economic performance. Hence, the state does not monitor the economic performance of the subsidised projects; accordingly, neither can identify the beneficiaries, who deviate from the conditions of subsidy nor punish them in case of deviation. In Georgia, like failed cases of state interventions discussed in Chapter II, the state provides subsidies but does not provide disciplinary regulation for subsidized businesses. Therefore, there is a threat that the unproductive subsidies will not be identified and ceased.

Credibility within the framework of projects is one more feature aspect of *strategic SBRs*. In the food and agricultural sector of Georgia, the state remains credible within the state support programmes. There were some changes to each of the case study programmes. However, these changes sought to improve support conditions for the beneficiaries rather than enhance subsidised projects' economic performance. The fact that Georgia has meagre tax rates in the face of rising volumes of state support programmes creates the perception that the state will eventually have to cease financial support for agribusinesses, as state expenses are not balanced by state revenue.

Another credibility related key component of *strategic SBRs* is trust between agribusinesses and the state. On the one hand, in case of Georgia, the fact that the projects' administration is considered to be fair and that the state has not deviated from its obligations within the frameworks of the programmes, creates trust for these state programmes. However, agribusiness does not have trust that in case of need, expressing feedback on the programmes will be followed by the relevant changes. Lack of trust, on its turn, distracts strategic dialogue between the state and agribusiness actors. Hence, the credibility in state commitments has built trust for the programmes; however, not considering feedback provided by the private sector eroded trust in information exchange between the state and agribusiness actors. The latter distracts strategic dialogue between the state and agribusinesses.

Enacted feedback mechanisms are one more component of *strategic SBRs*. In Georgia, the state programmes that provide support to agribusiness do not employ formal or informal institutions for feedback provision to check economic indicators such as the realisation of production, exports, and job creation. Hence, the state does not track which interventions work and which do not. In Georgia's case, the state does not determine performance indicators for success or failure and does not seek feedback on implemented programmes. The findings of this study reveal that state intervention in Georgia's food and agricultural sector is not facilitated by *strategic SBRs* between the state and agribusiness actors. Thus, the strategic state agribusiness relations failed to emerge in Georgia so far.

Chapter VII addressed the question *why strategic SBRs failed to emerge in the food and agricultural sector of Georgia.* According to the institutionalists approach to *strategic SBRs*, establishing *strategic SBRs* that maintain information exchange, reciprocity, credibility, and trust between the players, requires specific institutional prerequisites. These specific institutional prerequisites include the existence of the state agency, which creates incentives for investing in economic sectors and is a bridge for information exchange between the state and businesses, and its capability; the existence of the umbrella organisations, which associate businesses at industry or sector level and their capability, and the existence of an information exchange mechanisms.

In terms of the structure of the public sector in relation to the private sector, this study found that the *pilot agency*, Agriculture Project Management Agency (APMA), which is responsible for creating incentives for the private sector to invest in the food and agricultural sector, has been present since 2014. The agency is accountable to the Ministry of Agriculture of Georgia. APMA is autonomous in its daily activities; however, it does not have the decision-making power to start new programmes or implement amendments in existing ones. Regular interactions with agribusinesses do not characterise APMA. It does not gather data at programmes or sector level and does not involve agribusinesses in the programme elaboration processes. Hence, AMPA does not serve as a bridge for information exchange between decision-makers and agribusinesses, one of the key prerequisites for the emergence of *strategic SBRs*.

The state employs a formal recruitment system for public officials and bureaucrats, including vacancy announcements, application screening, exams (in some cases), and interviews. However, hiring decisions have not always been based solely on an applicants' merits, but also networks. The bureaucratic system is top-down, and salaries in the public sector are low compared to those in non-governmental organisations and the private sector. Therefore, it is hard to retain qualified staff to the public sector in a long-term. There are neither performance assessment systems nor performance-based salary bonus systems for public officials. As a result, there is an outflow of staff from the public sector to the private sector, including frequent changes of ministers.' Frequent resigning of policymakers directs resources toward short-term problems that require more straightforward solutions and offer quick, visible results. The core obstacles that distract the sector's development, such as lack of knowledge, education, and relevant skills, remain a low priority for years, as overcoming them requires long-term dedication from policymakers. Those who expect a short stay in their position tend not to be interested in seeking to address the problems, which require long-term dedication and consistency for solutions.

The private sector's interaction with the state is facilitated by influential *umbrella organisations*, which bring together businesses at the economy, sector, or industry levels. Since the sector became a priority, supporting the creation of the umbrella organizations also became a priority for the developmental organizations. The research highlights that those *umbrella organisations* under which enterprises from the food and agricultural sector are associated are diverse in Georgia. The *umbrella organisations* differ not only in terms of the quantity and size (large, medium, small, and micro) of member businesses, but also in terms of their targets, activities, rules for membership, relations with the state (methods and frequency), and financial sustainability. The large enterprises are members of the Business Association of Georgia (BAG), which is the umbrella for seventy large enterprises from various sectors of the economy. The Small and Medium Size Enterprises (SMEs) are members of the Georgian Small and Medium Enterprises Association (GSMEA), the umbrella of 4000 SMEs, representing multiple economy sectors. The SMEs from the food and agricultural sector of Georgia, which are exporters as well, are members of the Export Development Association (EDA), which is the umbrella of 100 exporters from various sectors of the economy. The small and micro-producers are associated with the Georgian Farmers Association, which currently has approximately 4000 members from the food and agricultural sector. In addition to the economy-wide and sector-specific *umbrella organisations*, there are sub-sector specific *umbrella organisations*. Comparatively active ones include the Georgian Wine Association

(GWA), the Hazelnut Exporters and Processors Association (HEPA), Dairy Products Producers Association (DPPA), Milk Producers Association (MPA), and the Georgian Shepherds Association (GSA). Most of these umbrella organisations were established after the state prioritized the sector.

Umbrella organisations contribute to information exchange between the state and agribusiness. For the state, the umbrella organisations are the most accessible means of information distribution on the policy changes, pending amendments to laws, and information on approaching exhibitions. However, for *umbrella organisations* to maintain effective communications with the state experience, personal contacts and networks are necessary. Most of the umbrella organizations lack analytical skills. They need some stable financial sources to sustain themselves and to hire permanent staff with strong capabilities. However, most of them rely on grants from developmental organizations, and face sustainability issues. The few that have membership fees have stricter requirements and demands from members to act to raise members' interests in discussions, and their actions are limited to talks. Sometimes they raise problems to discuss. However, they are not fighting the war for addressing the initiated problems. Besides, they avoid making political comments or criticising new regulations when they are introduced in the public discussion. However, once a regulation is enforced, they start complaining that it is not manageable to be met by agribusinesses.

One of the key functions of the developmental umbrella organizations is gathering data on the performance of its members, as well as obstacles they face in the production processes, aggregating it and disseminating the outcomes of the aggregate data with the relevant state agencies to initiate policy changes to overcome the obstacles the specific industries or the sector face. However, in the case of Georgia, as the research findings illustrate, even the strong umbrella organizations, like BAG or the GWA, do not accomplish such a function.

As to the structure and the capability of agribusiness in Georgia, research findigs reveal that 85 % (3621) of agribusinesses are small, 8 % (338) are medium, and 7 % (290) are large enterprises. The capacity of agribusinesses is meagre, especially in the case of SMEs. Most of them have difficulties defining the business operation related obstacles they face. Besides, SMEs mostly do not have the ambition to grow, as they lack an understanding of their business development potentials.

As for information exchange mechanisms, in the case of the food and agricultural sector of Georgia, no mechanism or body obliges the state and business actors to sit together regularly to identify coordination and market-related failures. Institutionalised state-business dialogue mechanisms, such as public-private partnership councils, deliberation councils, or other regular forums, do not exist. Even though there are some information exchange meetings through personal or professional networks or meetings organized by the civil society organisations or think tanks in the frameworks of developmental organisation-funded projects, they do not serve exchange of the comprehensive information on the coordination and market failures.

To conclude, in Georgia's food and agricultural sector, we observe some elements of the prerequisites for the emergence of *strategic SBRs;* nevertheless, they are not sufficient to foster the emergence of *strategic SBRs*. The *pilot agency*, APMA (currently [2020] RDA) that creates incentives for investment in the sector exists; however, it does not serve as an information exchange bridge between the state and agribusinesses. We do observe *umbrella organisations* at the economy, sector, and sub-sector levels, which are the sources of the information distribution to the private sector from the state; however, they gather data neither on the economic performance of agribusiness nor on obstacles the agribusinesses face, which is crucial to understanding the causes of coordination and market failures in the food and agricultural sector of Georgia. Also, agribusiness has low production and export capability. Hence, the prerequisites necessary for the emergence of *strategic SBRs* are not fully present in Georgia. Therefore, it is no wonder that the *strategic SBRs* that maintain effective state intervention in the sector have not emerged.

8.2. Research Contribution

Chapters II and III of the thesis discussed the empirical research and theoretical considerations on the role of state-business relations in the process of state intervention in economic activities, the institutional settings of *strategic SBRs*, and institutional prerequisites that maintain the emergence of *strategic SBRs*. Much of the earlier discussions in literature on state-led economic activities focused on ideological questions whether intervene or not, rather than on the design of interventions. Therefore, empirical studies on the design of interventions, the role of SBRs in the process of state interventions, and on the institutions of *strategic SBRs* have evolved more recently. The research started in the mid-1990s, further developed in the 2000s, and gained more general acceptance in the 2010s. This study contributes to the renewed debates on state-led economic activities with specific focus on the role of the institutions of SBRs in catalysing this process.

The study contributes to regional studies as it explores the case of Georgia, small open economy in the post-Communist region. The empirical evidence on the SBRs has been undertaken mostly in East Asia, Latin America, and in some

Sub-Saharan African countries; however, in post-Communist transition countries, the role of institutions for economic development, and among them, the institutions of SBRs have been mostly neglected in the empirical analysis. Thus, this research fills a gap in the literature regarding the regional dimensions of empirical studies on the institutions of SBRs.

Likewise, by studying the case of institutions of the state agribusiness relations in Georgia, which is a transition economy, this study contributes in the literature of transition studies. Like many transition economies (Steer and Sen, 2008), informal institutions of SBRs are prevailed in Georgia, and professional and business networks are essential for building these relations. On the one hand, the personal and professional ties are determinant for the state agribusiness relations. On the other hand, we observe limited institutional memory in the state due to frequent changes of assigned public officials; therefore, it is not feasible for businesses to build long term relations with the state. As the explored cases of Georgia's food and agricultural sector revealed, the lack of trust distracts the strategic dialogue between the state and agribusinesses. Yet, the strategic dialogue between state and agribusiness actors is crucial to identify the obstacles the private sector faces in the production processes and address with interventionist policies to eliminate the sector's key distractions, coordination and market failures.

In addition, the thesis contributes to the empirical studies of the state interventions, as it explores the state intervention instruments in the food and agricultural sector of Georgia and the sector's performance before and after the intervention. As it is discussed in Chapters II and III of this book, state intervention to drive development requires the existence of a long-term development strategy (Reich, 1982; UNCTAD, 2016), as in the short term, only populist interests raised by ordinary politics may be politically feasible (Haggard, 2004, p. 60). The research outcome of this thesis concludes analogous. Georgia's Agricultural Development Strategy targets five years, 2015–2020, which is not sufficient for addressing the core obstacles of the sector's development. These core obstacles include agricultural land registration, lack of coordination between suppliers of primary production and producers, broken value chains between suppliers of primary productions and food processors, lack of access to local and international markets, lack of coordination within various branches of bureaucracy, lack of knowledge, education, and relevant skills to produce high-quality products. Consequently, addressing these obstacles remains beyond priority, as overcoming them requires long-term strategy with specific action plans and long-term dedication from policymakers. The thesis also confirms that the institutions that enable strategic coordination between the political elites and agribusinesses are crucial for the state intervention to target the obstacles that distract the sector's development and utilize the sector's opportunities at its maximum.

Moreover, the study contributes to the cutting-edge, controversial, and policy-relevant academic debates about the role of institutions of state-business relations in the process of state intervention in economic activities. The research provides a comprehensive analysis of the nature of institutions of state agribusiness relations by exploring the state and businesses actors' behaviors, the rules behind the behavior, and their enforcement in the three cases of state intervention in the food and agricultural sector of Georgia. As discussed in Chapters II and III, in cases of strategic SBRs, the principal purpose of meetings between the state and businesses is to engage in collaborative dialogue and maximize the potential benefit of information exchange (Herzberg and Wright, 2013). In Georgia, however, though state-agribusiness meetings do happen, these meetings do not serve to maximize the potential of information exchange. Based on the findings from the exploring the case of the food and agricultural sector of Georgia, for the state agribusiness meetings to be meaningful, the primary prerequisite is the willingness of the businesses to share their problems and the willingness of the state to gather information on existing obstacles and address them with elaborating and implementing the relevant policies and programmes. In the case of Georgia, agribusinesses lack the willingness to share information. They have expectations that there will not be a follow-up from the state on their shared concerns. Furthermore, representatives of the state tend to maintain the idea that policymakers know better than the private sector. The state also lacks interest in getting information on obstacles the private sector faces, as they are sceptical of the possibility of making relevant changes due to lack of relevant capability. Hence, the study results coincide the theory statements (see Chapter III), that information exchange between state and business depends on the state's capability to collect and analyse information and data from businesses, and businesses' willingness to provide information and data to the state (Maxfield and Schneider, 1997; te Velde, 2013).

Furthermore, the thesis explores the institutional prerequisites for the emergence of *strategic SBRs*. In addition to the core prerequisites discussed in the literature, which includes the existence of the pilot agency, which creates incentives for the private sector to invest and functions as a bridge for information exchange between the state and businesses, umbrella organisations, the capability of the state and capability of the businesses, information exchange mechanisms, as the findings from Georgia indicate, one more core prerequisite for the emergence of the strategic SBRs is the prevailed believe among the actors regarding the role of institutions of SBRs for economic development. In Georgia, it is prevailed to neglect the role of institutions of SBRs. In case of Georgia, the mental models /believes of the representatives of the state and agribusinesses determine this attitude to SBRs. On the one hand, among the state actors the prevailed believe is that the state knows better than businesses. Also, constructive criticism is taken personally by policy makers, who elaborated the programmes. On the other hand, agribusinesses believe that providing information to state will no make any difference, as they do not expect follow up actions from the state to address the shared concerns. Hence, these believes are also constraints for emergence of *strategic SBRS.*

This research contributes to developmental studies literature as well. The case of Georgia reveals that the bureaucratic system is crucial for addressing the core obstacles for developing the food and agricultural sector. Firstly, it is hard to attract qualified staff, or if already employed in the public sector, to motivate them to relate working in the public sevtor to their long-term career goals. Prevailed informal institution of frequent resigning of policymakers directs resources towards short-term problems that require more straightforward solutions and offer quick, visible results. However, the core obstacles of the sector that distract development require long term dedication from policymakers. Those who expect a short stay at their office tend not to be interested in seeking to address the issues which need long-term dedications. Secondly, there is a circle of a bureaucratic machine, and employees at a lower level have to follow the machine. They do not have the opportunities to initiate ideas for development. The prevailed system does not allow to utilise the employees' knowledge and skills to its fullest to contribute to the sector's development. Thirdly, a systematic plan for building the capability of the state bureaucracy is absent.

Studying the case of Georgia reveals some interesting contributions also from the theoretical perspective. The case studies explored in this book highlight that informal institutions determine the nature of state agribusiness dialogue in Georgia. The small size of the country and mental models, which are the heritage of the culture (North, 1995, p. 7), make it possible to reach economic actors through personal networks easily. However, the ease of reaching public officials, informal institutions of information exchange and dialogue between the representatives of the state and business do not contribute to building long term relationships and trust. For the later, meetings are necessary conditions, however not sufficient. Also, a follow up of shared concerns is crucial for motivating the actors from the private sector to share the feedback on the policies and programmes, as well as information regarding the obstacles they face. Besides, in case of information exchange, preserved institutional memory is crucial. But in Georgia, due to the frequent resignation of assigned public officials, we observe limited institutional memory. Therefore, informal institutions of information exchange do not contribute to building trust, as trust depends on the length of the relationship between the state and business actors and is sensitive to personnel changes. Furthermore, in Georgia, a large number of members in an umbrella organisation do not contribute to collecting sector level, representative data. The high membership distracts from the interaction between all members; hence, information gathered is limited to a tiny group of producers and not available to the industry, sector, or business levels. Hence, existence of umbrella organisations does not contribute much in overcoming information-related imperfections in the food and agricultural sector of Georgia.

The research also contributes to the empirical studies of agricultural economics in the post-Communist region. It provides a comprehensive analysis of the sector's potential and obstacles that distract the process for development. Moreover, the thesis provides an analysis of the sector's performance in 2004–2016 to observe the changes in the sector's performance since the state started active intervention.

8.3. Implications and Recommendations

"Give a Man a Fish, and You Feed Him for a Day. Teach a Man To Fish, and You Feed Him for a Lifetime" (Chinese Proverb)

The empirical chapters of this book explored attention-grabbing insights on the state-led economic activities and the nature of the institutions of the state agribusiness relations in Georgia. This section intends to draw research-based policy implications and recommendations for the Ministry of Environmental Protection and Agriculture (MEPA), Agricultural Project Management Agency (APMA) (currently [2020] restructured as Rural Development Agency), and umbrella organisations (UO) for the emergence of the strategic state agribusiness relations. The emergence of the strategic state agribusiness relations is crucial for state intervention in Georgia's food and agricultural sector to target overcoming the obstacles the sector faces and utilizing the opportunities.

8.3.1. The Recommendations to the Ministry of Environmental Protection and Agriculture (MEPA)

The research findings revealed that the Agriculture Development Strategy 2015–2020 has several shortcomings. First, the strategy elaboration process was not based on the collaborative interaction with private sector to share comprehensive information to identify the obstacles the private sector faces in the production processes and a development potential of the sector. The strategy targets a short term, during which the sector's key obstacles, which include absence of coordination between suppliers of primary production and food producers, broken value chains, obstacles of testing and processing/packaging/branding primary products to be ready for retail stores, obstacles to access to local and international markets, lack of knowledge and relevant skills to produce high-quality primary and secondary products, absence of relevant education programs in the field and shortage of skilled labor, is not feasible to be addressed. Furthermore, the strategy does not present measurable performance indicators for success and failure of against which the effectiveness of taken activities and programmes can be measured. Hence, both the process of strategy elaboration and the content of the strategy requires improvements.

To improve the strategy elaboration process, we recommend MEPA to engage in a collaborative dialogue with agribusinesses and maximize potential benefit of information exchange. For this reason, we recommend the Division of Statistics and Analytics representatives at the Department of the Policy and Analysis at MEPA to organize two types of meetings with the private sector, sectoral and functional. The sectoral meetings should get together the state representatives and the food and agricultural sector industries to collect information from the actors in the specific sub-sector, more specifically, obstacles the suppliers and producers face in the product cultivation and realisation processes. We recommend the Division of Statistics at MEPA to prepare a report depicting the findings from the meetings to follow up them . We recommend incorporating the findings in a draft strategy. We recommend functional meetings to target getting together the representatives of state, agribusinesses, research organisations, think tanks, NGOs, consulting organisations, academia, and international development organisations, intending to collect an expert opinion on the draft strategy and incorporate it in the strategy elaboration process. We recommend identifying measurable performance indicators for success and failures and monitoring plans to regularly track the outcomes of the implemented activities, to identify which interventions work and which does not and to improve and update the strategy's content. Also, to create institutions (formal and informal rules that can be enforced) for getting feedback on the enacted strategy action plan.

As the research outcomes revealed, even though increasing export volume, diversifying export products and markets is one of the state's key priorities, the state does not have an export development strategy for agricultural products. The state intervention mechanisms to support export promotion are limited to creating incentives for agribusinesses to participate in exhibitions. However, agribusinesses' exporting capability is low; the export dimensions of products are limited and scarce in scale. The principal obstacle is finding qualified exporters who have qualified products ready for export. To address this shortcoming, we recommend the MEPA to develop a very targeted export development strategy of the food and agricultural products. For this reason, the recommendation to MEPA is to organise active consultations with potential exporters, exporters, and product suppliers. Also, to formulate performance indicators for the export targets, get feedback from agribusinesses on the feasibility of the targets, and update it based on the provided feedback. In addition, we recommend the MEPA to identify the market demand at the potential trade partner countries (at the initial stage for inquary can be taken the countries with which Georgia has signed Free Trade Agreements) and local food processors and to target the local investment, which is subsidised through state programmes, to cultivate the products that meet the targeted market needs.

The findings revealed that even though both APMA and the MEPA have a Division of Statistics and Analysis, none of them has a data portal with information on local and international market conditions, labour market conditions, opportunities for specific sub-sectors, tariffs, all of which the private sector needs from the state to make sound investment decisions. Therefore, one more recommendation for the MEPA is to create a data warehouse, incorporating information on investment opportunities, labor market conditions, tax policy, local and international markets, suppliers, producers, and exporters.

As in Georgia prevailed believe is that state business relations serve only large businesses or those who have personal contacts with high ranked officials, creating formal institutions for state business dialogue might contribute to building trust. Thus, to establish a mechanism or body where the representatives of the state and private sector get together and discuss the relevant issues to overcome market and coordination failures in the sector. This body should be open to all and be autonomous of state intervention in its decision-making. It can be wide-ranging or focus on specific issues (Herzberg and Wright, 2013). The literature suggests that such mechanisms bring together state and business actors to discuss and coordinate their actions to accelerate reforms and make implementing them more straightforward, promote transparency, and build an atmosphere of mutual trust between the state and business actors (Herzberg and Wright, 2013).

8.3.2. The Recommendations to the Pilot Agency-APMA (RDA)

As the research findings reveal, the state intervention in Georgia's food and agricultural sector is not based on the strategic state agribusiness relations. Page and Tarp (2017, p. 19) argue that in the process of state intervention, without a strategic dialogue with businesses, the state will remain ignorant of the constraints faced by the private sector. It will also lack an understanding of new opportunities and, hence, be unable to offer the means to build consensus around a long-term development strategy. From the private sector, constructive engagement with the state offers the chance to help the state shape public policy to address the most severe constraints to success. Such coordination offers the prospect of greater policy certainty for both sides. Thus, this subsection provides some recommendations to the APMA (RDA). The recommendations target APMA (RDA) to develop institutions that support the emergence of strategic state agribusiness relations in the framework of state support programmes, which are initiated by the MEPA and implemented by the APMA (RDA).

We recommend APMA (RDA) to develop institutions that support the exchange of comprehensive information between beneficiaries of the state programmes and the state. Thus, we recommend the statistics division of APMA (RDA) to collect and process data on the performance of the subsidized projects and the obstacles the beneficiaries face in product cultivation, product processing, or realising procedures. To maintain the regular provision of the data from the beneficiary, APMA (RDA) is recommended to put it as one of the conditions for subsidy provision. AMPA (RDA) should also define punishment criteria in case the beneficiary will not report the data regularly. Also, APMA (RDA) is recommended that in the framework of each state support programme, to organise sub sectoral meetings with the representatives of programme beneficiary agribusinesses, relevant umbrella organisations, and state, including the Ministry of Economy and Sustainable Development, Ministry of Environmental Protection and Agriculture, and APMA (RDA). These meetings should target from agribusinesses side to provide feedback on the state support programmes, also on the shortcomings they face in the project implementation process, and from the state side to provide information on the potential of the supporting industries in terms of demand at local or external markets, also regarding the export-related procedures, labor market conditions, tax policy. What is important is that these meetings to maintain a exchange of comprehensive information and feedback that will be incorporated in the state's and private actors future activities.

The research findings indicate that one of the key obstacles of the food and agricultural sector is coordination failure between the suppliers of the primary agricultural products and food processors. The research findings showed that food processors faced production obstacles because of supply constraints in local primary products. Due to insufficient volumes and quality of primary products, successful food processors in the related industries produce at a suboptimal level.

Therefore, they can neither satisfy local market demand nor produce sufficient scale for export. There are also breaks in the value chain between comparatively larger food processors, distributors, and suppliers, due to the deviation from supply or payment requirements. We recommend to APMA (RDA) to institutionalise the relationship between those primary agricultural product suppliers and food processors, who are beneficiaries of the state support programmes. For this reason, we suggest the Statistical Division of APMA to generate a database of the suppliers and food processors. Access to this database should be open for all beneficiaries of the state programmes. Also, we advocate APMA (RDA), at least once a year to organize meeting of suppliers of primary productions and food processors in the framework of state support programmes discussed in this publication. Such meetings might contribute to building trust between product suppliers and food processors. Also, it might contribute to a process of sustained value chain building.

The research findings indicate that state-agribusiness relations in the framework of the state support programmes face shortcomings in terms of the absence of reciprocity conditions. The state is motivated to increase the number of supported projects, as their quantity is informally used as an indicator of success of the programme. Economic theory states that when subsidies are available, investors will seek to acquire them (Mueller, 1989). However, economic theory also states that the hard part of subsidy provision is to ensure their strategic usage (Mueller, 1989). Theories, as well as cases of *strategic SBRs*, indicate that disciplining subsidy provision and usage is crucial in order for state intervention to promote development. Therefore, we recommend APMA (RDA) to be very explicit at the initial stage of the programme about the performance criteria (employment, production, productivity, export) and assess the performance of the subsidies. We suggest while providing aid to focus on the quality of the projects rather than quantity. We recommend to support less but very targeted, development oriented projects. We suggest devoting resources to monitoring the subsidies and applying rewards or punishments based on subsidies' performance to achieve maximum returns from the subsidised investment. Thus, we advocate APMA (RDA) to acquire a subsidy monitoring plan and punishment clause in case of deviations or rewards in case of success. Also, to maintain the enforcement of punishment and reward. Considering the importance of disciplining subsidies, we recommend APMA (RDA) to develop clear performance measures for success and failure and conditions of subsidy provision based on the ability to repay the loans and the feasibility of meeting the performance conditions.

One more shortcoming of the state agribusiness relations in the framework of subsidised programmes is the absence of the feedback mechanism on implemented programmes. The existence of viable feedback mechanisms, which maintain the flow of feedback on the rules and norms of behaviour, is crucial (Pelikan, 1986), as they help economic actors learn from failures to correct organisational errors. Feedback mechanisms also help policy makers enhance policy adaptability. The adaptability of interventionist policies and programmes encourages trials and experiments and provides for elimination or adjustment of programmes, policies, or rules of the game that fail to achieve targeted goals. In cases of *strategic SBRs*, the state identified policies/programmes with appropriate local context, defined performance indicators to measure the success of implemented policies/programmes, monitored the previously defined performance indicators, requested feedback from the private sector, and considered their feedback when adapting the policies or programmes (Page and Tarp, 2017). Enacting a feedback mechanism provided the opportunity to understand which interventions worked and which did not. The feedback mechanisms monitored economic performance regarding the job growth rate, output, and exports (Kim, 2014). In case of failure, the policies or programmes were either modified or abandoned. Therefore, we advocate APMA (RDA) to develop the institutions for getting regular feedback on state support programmes. Also, to be committed, that feedback will be incorporated to make the state programmes more targeted.

8.3.3. The Recommendations to the Umbrella Organisations

Umbrella organizations (UOs) may serve as a bridge for information provision between the state and the private sector. The research findings reveal that in the cases of *strategic SBRs*, umbrella organisations encompassed and represented businesses' interests to the state and monitored and sanctioned their members (Doner and Schneider, 2000). In Georgia, the umbrella organisations are sources for information dissemination from the state to agribusiness. The disseminated information includes updates on planned policy changes, amendments to the law, investment opportunities, and market conditions to their members. Though, the umbrella organisations do not gather and aggregate the data from the private sector on the performances, obstacles they face in product cultivation, realization, or export processes. One recommendation to umbrella organisations is to collect data from their members and aggregate it at a sub-sector level. We also recommend umbrella organisations to condition their members to report data on their performance in exchange for membership. The other recommendation to UOs is to contribute in exchange of comprehensive information between the state and agribusiness actors. Therefore we recommend UOs to collect the information on obstacles and interests their members face, aggregate them on sub-sector or sector level, and voice the generalized obstacles of the sector to the relevant representatives of the state.

The research findings illustrate that agribusinesses' capability in Georgia is low, especially in the case of SMEs, most of which have difficulties even in determining and formulating obstacles they face in the cultivation and product realisation processes. Besides, the SMEs lack knowledge on existing market opportunities and do not have the ambition to grow further. The SMEs also face problems of coordination in building value chains. Considering the systemic weaknesses small and medium-sized agribusinesses face, we recommend the umbrella organisations to elaborate targeted training and workshop plan and train their members. This can become source for sustained financial inflow for UOs, contribute in capability building of SMEs and help to enforce industry quality standards.

8.4. Limitations and Future Research

This study has thoroughly examined the instruments of state intervention in Georgia's food and agricultural sector and the nature of the institutional settings of state-agribusiness relations. The publication has also explored why *strategic SBRs* have not yet emerged. The principal argument of this research is that strategic coordination of activities between the state and agribusinesses is crucial for state intervention to address obstacles the food and agricultural sector faces and utilize the sector's opportunities. However, the importance of the institutional setting of the state agribusiness relations has been neglected in the process of state interventions from both policymakers and the private actors. Therefore, there is a lack of academic and policy research on this issue in the context of Georgia. On the one hand, the lack of literature studying the state interventions or institutions of the state business relations in Georgia created a limitation for this research, as the literature review section of this publication does not include evidence from Georgia. On the other hand, this allows the research to contribute substantially to academic debates and policy debates in Georgia, as the study is the only research that comprehensively explores the issue in the context of Georgia, post Communist transition economy.

One more limitation the research faces is related to the time frame explored in the research. As interviews and research analysis for the study were conducted in April 2017–February 2018, the study assesses the sector's economic performance for 2004–2017. Hence, it includes only a 5-year period of state intervention in the sector. The short time frame does not put limitations on a comprehensive study of the instruments of the state intervention and institutional setting of the state agribusiness relations. However, it puts limitations on assessment of the success or the failure of the intervention in terms of economic performance. Considering that the state expects the outcomes of some of the investment projects in 2020–2021, it will be interesting to assess the investment projects' economic performance in a more extended period.

For future research, it will be interesting to explore the institutions of SBRs in other countries in the post—Communist region. For comparison analysis, it would be interesting to observe the state business relations in Ukraine's food and agricultural sector. Politically, the country has gone a similar path to Georgia, like the Orange Revolution, military conflict with Russia, and association agreement with the EU. On the one hand, studying Ukraine's case will allow a chance to understand if the nature of SBRs is path-dependent on the Soviet legacy in the post-Communist region. On the other hand, it will help to understand if the differences in size and geography make in differences in SBRs.

One more interesting issue for future research is to explore the role of digital governance in the emergence of *strategic SBRs.* In most of the unsuccessful cases of SBRs, we observe that the state could not monitor and discipline the subsidies due to a lack of resources. It will be interesting to study if digitalisation of subsidy monitoring improves the reciprocity feature of SBRs. For this reason a comperative analaysis with the case of Estonia, which has digitalised monitoring schemes of agriculture subsidies, will be interesting.

Furthermore, the research findings show that the mental models of state and business actors, and preserved informal institutions, which are the heritage of culture or past experiences, are determinants of the existing nature of SBRs in the case of Georgia. Therefore, it would be interesting to explore the role of culture for emerging strategic SBRs, specifically if there are differences like SBRs between countries with different cultures.

Appendix 1.

The List of Interviewees

	Position	Date
1.	Former Minister of Finance of Georgia (2005–2007)	18.01.18
2.	Deputy Executive Director at Business Association of Georgia	04.12.17
3.	Economic Policy Expert, the Parliament of Georgia	01.12.17
4.	Foreign Expert	24.11.17
5.	Deputy Director, Georgian Farmers' Association	14.12.17
6.	Vocational Education Expert, Georgian Farmers Association	14.12.17
7.	Beneficiary of the Preferential Agrocredit and Co-financing Agriculture Processing and Storage Enterprises programme	24.01.18
8.	Senior Researcher at Private Sector Development Research Centre at ISET Former Deputy Head of the Department of the Agricultural Development at the Ministry of Agriculture (2011–2013)	14.11.17
9.	Beneficiary of the Plant the Future programme	29.03.17
10.	Head of the Division of Statistics and Analysis, at the Department of Policy and Analysis, MoA (currently [2020] MEPA)	04.12.17
11.	Agribusiness, not a beneficiary of any state programmes	07.12.17
12.	Expert/economist, PMC Research Centre	20.11.18
13.	Performance Data Advisor, Public Private Dialogue Tracking, Governing for Growth in Georgia, USAID Beneficiary of state programme Plant the Future	16.11.17
14.	Agribusiness, a beneficiary of the Preferential Agrocredit programme	15.12.17
15.	Head of the Georgian SMEs Association	15.12.17
16.	Head of the Programmes' Support Development Unit, APMA (2014–2017)	05.04.17
17.	Public Finance Expert, Transparency International in Georgia (2011–2016)	22.11.17
18.	Professor of Business and Economics, Tbilisi State University	29.01.18
19.	Expert of Agricultural Economics	09.11.17
20.	Expert of Monitoring and Evaluation of the Economic Development Projects (with a focus on food and agriculture), APRC	24.11.17
21.	Expert in Agricultural Economics, APRC	09.11.17
22.	Minister of Agriculture of Georgia (May 2013–January 2014) Deputy Minister of Agriculture of Georgia (November 2012–May 2013)	11.12.17

	Position	Date
23.	Supply Chain Consultant in the USAID/REAP project Former employee at the Division of Sectoral Development at MoA Former employee at Agro Development Group at TBC Bank	29. 11.17
24.	Beneficiary of the Plant the Future and the Preferential Agrocredit Programmes	23.11.17
25.	Marketing Manager, Georgian Wine Association	01.12.17
26.	Project Manager, the Institute for Development of Freedom of Information (IDFI)	14.11.17
27.	Chief Specialist, Department of International Relations and International Trade, Ministry of Economy and Sustainable Development	28.11.17
28.	Project Manager, EPRC Experience working on food and agriculture-related research and project since 2002	20.11.17
29.	Agribusiness, beneficiary of the Preferential Agrocredit programme	16.11.17
30.	Agribusiness, beneficiary of the Preferential Agrocredit programme	16.01.18
31.	Manager of the Preferential Agrocredit and Plant the Future programmes, APMA	15.12.17
32.	Expert, FAO-ENPARD	27.12.17
33.	Head of the Rural Development Coordination Division, MoA	05.12.17
34.	Advocacy and Civil Society Strengthening Component Lead, USAID_G4G	01.12.17
35.	Manager of the Co-financing Agriculture Storage and Processing Enterprises programme, APMA	15.12.17
36.	Expert, OXFAM	06.11.17
37.	Agribusiness Project Coordinator, EBRD	30.01.18
38.	Founder and Head of the Export Development Association of Georgia	01.02.18
39.	Head of Targeted Projects Unit, ACDA	12.12.17

Bibliography

Acemoglu, D., Johnson, S., & Robinson, J. A. (2005). Institutions as the Fundamental Cause of Long-Run Growth. In P. Aghion and S. Durlauf (Eds.), *Handbook of Economic Growth*, 1st ed., Vol. 1, pp. 386–472, [online]. Available from: https://economics.mit.edu/files/4469 (Accessed 02.18.2020).

Acemoglu, D., & Robinson, J. A. (2012). *Why Nations Fail the Origins of Power, Prosperity, and Poverty*, 1st ed. New York: Crown Business Publishing.

Ackah, C., Aryeetey, E., & Clottey, E. (2013). State–Business Relations and Firm Performance in Ghana. In K. Sen (Ed.), *State-Business Relations and Economic Development in Africa and India.* London: Routledge.

Adcock, R., & Collier, D. (2001). 'Measurement Validity: A Shared Standard for Qualitative and Quantitative Research.' *The American Political Science Review*,95 (3), pp. 529–246.

Adly, A. (2010). 'Politically-Embedded Cronyism: The Case of Post-Liberalization Egypt.' *Business and Politics*, 11 (4), pp. 1–26, [online]. Available from https://www.researchgate.net/publication/46555438_PoliticallyEmbedded_Cronyism_The_Case_of_Post-Liberalization_Egypt (Accessed 02.02.2020).

African Development Bank. (2012). *Assessing the Impact of Presidents Investors' Advisory Council: Country Case Studies.* Tunis: African Development Bank.

Ahrens, J. (2002). *Governance and Economic Development. Comparative Institutional Approach.* Cheltenham: Edward Elgar Publishing.

Ahrens, J. (2010). 'The Politico-Institutional Foundation of Economic Transition in Central Asia: Lessons from China.' *Economic and Environmental Studies*, 10 (2), pp. 161–188, [online]. Available from https://www.researchgate.net/publication/228695767_The_politicoinstitutional_foundation_ofeconomic_transition_in_Central_Asia_Lessons_from_China (Accessed 01.04.2020).

Ahrens, J. (2011). Governance, Development, and Institutional Change in Times of Globalization. In J. Ahrens, R. Caspers, and J. Weingarth (Eds.), *Good Governance in the 21st Century: Conflict, Institutional Change and Development in the Era of Globalization*. Cheltenham: Edward Elgar Publishing.

Ahrens, J., & Hoen, H. W. (Eds.). (2013). *Institutional Reform in Central Asia. Politico-Economic Challenges.* New York: Routledge.

Ahrens, J., & Stark, M. (2014). 'Emulating East Asian Developmental States? The Institutional Foundations of Economic Transition in Central Asia, Critique Internationale.' *Revue Comparative de Sciences Sociales*, 63 (Avril–Juin), pp. 95–110.

Amsden, A. (1989). *Asia's Next Giant: South Korea and Late Industrialization.* New York: Oxford University Press.

Amsden, A. H. (1991). 'Diffusion of Development: The Late-Industrializing Model and Greater East Asia.' *American Economic Review*,81 (2), pp. 282–286, [online]. Available from http://www.jstor.org/stable/2006870 (Accessed 05.07.2019).

Anderson, K. (2013). 'Is Georgia the Next "New" Wine-Exporting Country?' *Journal of Wine Economics*, 8 (1), pp. 1–28, [online]. Available from https://www.semanticscholar.org/paper/IsGeorgia-the-next-%27new%27-wine-exporting-country Anderson/36845560c44c8a87943d1a613c108a61004354a4?p2df (Accessed 05.07.2020).

Aoki, M. (2007). 'Endogenizing Institutions and Institutional Change.' *Stanford University*, [online]. Available from http://ebour.com.ar/pdfs/Aoki%20Endogenizing%20Institutions.pdf (Accessed 03.12.2019).

Aryeetey, E., & Owoo, N. (2015). *Ghana's Experiments with Business-Government Coordination*, [online]. World Institute for Development Economics Research. Available from https://www.wider.unu.edu/sites/default/files/wp2015-099.pdf (Accessed 11.12.2019).

Asian Development Bank. (2008). *Samoa: Consolidating Reform for Faster Economic Growth*. Manila: Asian Development Bank.

Athukorala, P. (2014). 'Growing with Global Production Sharing: The Tale of Penang Export Hub, Malaysia.' *Competition and Change*, 18 (3), 221–245, [online]. Available from https://journals.sagepub.com/doi/abs/10.1179/1024529414Z.00000000058 (Accessed 07.08.2019).

Aumann, R. J. (1976). 'Agreeing to Disagree.' *The Annals of Statistics*, 4 (6), pp. 1236–1239, [online]. Available from http://www.ma.huji.ac.il/raumann/pdf/Agreeing%20to%20Disagree.pdf (Accessed 04.05.2019).

Axelrod, R. (1984). *The Evolution of Cooperation*. New York, NY: Basic Books.

Babakholov, S., Kim, K. R., & Sanaev, G. (2018). 'Economic and Agricultural Development after Transition in CIS Countries.' *Journal of Agricultural, Life and Environmental Sciences*, 30 (3), pp. 200–225, [online]. Available from http://www.jales.org/articles/article/ARQW/#References (Accessed 06.01.2020).

Banfield, E. C. (1958). *The Moral Basis of Backward Society*. New York, NY: Free Press.

Bardhan, P. (2005). 'Institutions Matter, but Which Ones?' *Economics of Transition*, 13 (3), pp. 499–532, [online]. Available from http://web.stanford.edu/~avner/Greif_228_2005/Bardhan.%202005%20Institutions%20Matter,%20but%20which%20one.pdf (Accessed 05.05.2019).

Bardhan, P. (2016). 'State and Development: The Need for a Reappraisal of the Current Literature.' *Journal of Economic Literature*, 54 (3), 862–892, [online]. Available from https://ideas.repec.org/a/aea/jeclit/v54y2016i3p862-92.html (Accessed 01.04.2019).

Batcha, S. (2012). 'Evaluation of the Impact of State Business Relationship on the Economic Growth of Togo.' *Economia*. Seria Management, 15 (2), pp. 380–391, [online]. Available from www.management.ase.ro/reveconomia/2012-2/13.pdf (Accessed 09.08.2019).

Baumann, E. (2012). 'Post-Soviet Georgia: It's a Long, Long Way to "Modern" Social Protection.' *Economies et Socihes*,Serie « Developpement, croissance et progres,» 46 (2), pp. 259–285, [online]. Available from https://horizon.documentation.ird.fr/exl-doc/pleins_textes/divers12-07/010056159.pdf (Accessed 07.07.2019).

Beach, D., & Pedersen, R. B. (2013). *Process Tracing Methods. Foundations and Guidelines.* Ann Arbor: University of Michigan Press.

Beck, T., & Laeven, L. A. (2005). *Institution Building and Growth in Transition Economies.* World Bank Policy Research Working Paper, 3657, pp. 1–51, [online]. Available from https://openknowledge.worldbank.org/bitstream/handle/10986/8203/wps3657.pdf?sequence=1&isAllowed=y (Accessed 12.12.2019).

Bhagwati, J. (1993). *India in Transition: Freeing the Economy*. Oxford: Clarendon Press.

Bhagwati, J. N. (1982). 'Directly Unproductive, Profit-Seeking Activities.' *Journal of Political Economy*, 90 (5), pp. 988–1002, [online]. Available from https://www.journals.uchicago.edu/doi/10.1086/261104 (Accessed 09.09.2019).

Biddle, J., & Vedat, M. (1995). *Institutional Influences on Economic Policy in Turkey: A Three Industry Comparison*. World Bank Occasional Paper no. 3, [online]. Available from http://documents1.worldbank.org/curated/en/673301468779346200/pdf/multi0page.pdf (Accessed 03.05.2020).

Birdsall, N., & Fukuyama, F. (2011). 'The Post-Washington Consensus: Development after the Crisis.' *Foreign Affairs* 90 (2), pp. 45–53, [online]. Available from https://www.foreignaffairs.com/articles/2011-02-16/post-washington-consensus (Accessed 09.02.2019).

Bissonnette, J. F. (2013). 'Development through Large-Scale Oil Palm Agribusiness Schemes. Representations of Possibilities and the Experience of Limits in West Kalimantan.' *Journal of Social Issues in Southeast Asia*, 28 (3), pp. 485–511, [online]. Available from https://www.jstor.org/stable/43186978?read-now=1&seq=1#page_scan_tab_contents (Accessed 19.11.2018).

Bluashvili, A., & Sukhanskaya, N. (2015). *Country Report: Georgia*. Georgian Center for Agribusiness Development, [online]. Available from http://docplayer.net/11445346-Country-report-georgia.html (Accessed 23.03.2017).

Boehnke, K., Lietz, P., Schreier, M., & Wilhelm, A. (2011). Sampling: The Selection of Cases for Culturally Comparative Psychological Research. In D. Matsumoto and F. F. van de Vijver (Eds.), *Cross-Cultural Research Methods in Psychology*,pp. 101–129. Cambridge: Cambridge University Press.

Booth, D. (Ed.). (2015). *Developmental Regimes in Africa: Synthesis Report*,[online]. Available from https://openaccess.leidenuniv.nl/bitstream/handle/1887/32028/ASC-075287668-3612-01.pdf;jsessionid=66948CB4277F9391B-CF1BF3E5486C824?sequence=1 (Accessed 10.10.2017).

Bourdieu, P., & Coleman, J. S. (Eds.). (1991). *Social Theory for a Changing Society*. Boulder, CO: Westview Press.

Box-Steffensmeister, J. M., Brandy, E. H., & Collier, D. (2010). Chapter 28: Case Selection for Case Study Analysis: Qualitative and Quantitative Techniques. In J. M. Box-Steffensmeister, E. H. Brandy, and D. Collier (Eds.), *The Oxford Handbook of Political Methodology*. With the assistance of J. Gerring: Oxford University Press.

Boyd, R., & Richerson, P. J. (1985). *Culture and the Evolutionary Process*. Chicago, IL: University of Chicago Press.

Bräutigam, D., & Diolle, T. (2009). *Coalitions, Capitalists, and Credibility: Overcoming the Crisis of Confidence at Independence in Mauritius*. Developmental Leadership Program Research Paper No. 4, [online]. Available from https://res.cloudinary.com/dlprog/image/upload/ucuWdOkawhjuHiFoHjClYWhz-5waxKraQ7cxrlaVG.pdf (Accessed 06.04.2020).

Bräutigam, D., Rakner, L., & Taylor, S. (2002). 'Business Associations and Growth Coalitions in Sub-Saharan Africa.' *Journal of Modern African Studies*, 40 (4), pp. 519–547 [online] https://www.researchgate.net/publication/231884290_Business_associations_and_growth_coalitions_in_Sub-Saharan_Africa (Accessed 07.12.2019).

Buur, L., Kjer, A. M., Therkildsen, O., & Whitfield, L. (2015). *The Politics of African Industrial Policy. A Comparative Perspective*. Cambridge: Cambridge University Press.

Buur, L., & Whitfield, L. (2013). Industrial Policy and State-Business Relations: Towards a Heuristic Approach. In D. W. te Velde (Ed.), *State-Business Relations and Industrial Policy: Current Policy and Research Debates*,[online]. Available from https://degrp.squarespace.com/s/DEGRP-Policy-Essays-State-business-relations-and-industrialpolicy.pdf (Accessed 07.10.2018).

Bwalya, S., Phiri, E., & Mpembamoto, K. (2011). 'How Interest Groups Lobby to Influence Budget Outcomes in Zambia.' *Journal of International Development*, 23, pp. 420–442, [online]. Available from https://onlinelibrary.wiley.com/doi/abs/10.1002/jid.1778 (Accessed 11.11.2017).

Cali, M., & Sen, K. (2012). 'Do Effective State-Business Relations Matter for Economic Growth? Evidence from Indian States.' *World Development*, 39 (9), pp. 1542–1557, [online]. Available from http://www.sciencedirect.com/science/article/pii/S0305750X11000234 (Accessed 10.05.201).

Cammett, M. (2007). 'Business Government Relations and Industrial Change: The Politics of Upgrading in Morocco and Tunisia.' *World Development*, 35 (11), pp. 1889–1903, [online]. Available from http://dx.doi.org/10.1016/j.worlddev.2007.01.003 (Accessed 10.12.2017).

Campos, J. E., & Root, L. H. (1996). *The Key to the Asian Miracle. Making Shared Growth Credible.* Washington, DC: The Brookings Institution.

Caselli, F. (2005). Chapter 9: Accounting for Cross-Country Income Differences. In P. Aghion and S. N. Durlauf (Eds.), *Handbook of Economic Growth*, 1A, pp. 679–742. New York: Elsevier.

Chang, H.-J. (1993a). 'Interpreting Korean Experience: Heaven or Hell?' University of Cambridge Research Paper 42, Faculty of Economics and Politics, The University of Cambridge.

Chang, H.-J. (1993b). 'The Political Economy of Industrial Policy in Korea.' *Cambridge Journal of Economics*, 17 (2), pp. 131–157, [online]. Available from https://www.jstor.org/stable/23599704?seq=1 (Accessed 06.04.2020).

Chang, H.-J. (1994). *The Political Economy of Industrial Policy.* New York, NY: St. Martin's Press.

Chang, H.-J. (1999). The Economic Theory of the Developmental State. In M. Woo-Cumings (Ed.), *The Developmental State*, pp. 182–199. Ithaca, NY and London: Cornell University Press.

Chang, H.-J. (2006). *The East Asian Development Experience: The Miracle, the Crisis, and the Future.* London: Zed Books.

Cheng, T.-J. (1988). Business Interests Associations in Export Oriented Industrializing Economies. Paper presented at the meetings of the APSA, Washington, DC.

Chingaipe, H. (2013). Chapter 8: Particularistic Concertation: State-Business Relations and State Formation in Colonial Malawi. In K. Sen (Ed.), *State-Business Relations and Economic Development in Africa and India*. London: Routledge.

Chingaipe, H., & Leftwich, A. (2007). *The Politics of State–Business Relationships in Malawi*. IPPG, discussion paper series number 7, [online]. Available from https://assets.publishing.service.gov.uk/media/57a08bebe5274a31e0000e94/IPPGDP7.pdf (Accessed 01.02.2020).

Cimoli, M., Dosi, G., & Stiglitz, J. E. (2008). 'The Future of Industrial Policies in the New Millennium: Toward a Knowledge-Centered Development Agenda.' LEM Working Paper Series 2008/19, Laboratory of Economics and Management (LEM), Sant'Anna School of Advanced Studies, Pisa, Italy, [online]. Available from https://www.econstor.eu/bitstream/10419/89549/1/640462014.pdf (Accessed 01.02.2020).

Coase, R. (1937). 'The Nature of the Firm. '*Economica*, 4 (16), pp. 386–405, [online]. Available from https://onlinelibrary.wiley.com/doi/full/10.1111/j.1468-0335.1937.tb00002.x (Accessed 01.02.2020).

Collier, D. (2011). 'Understanding Process Tracing.' *APSC*, 44 (04), pp. 823–830, [online]. Available from https://polisci.berkeley.edu/sites/default/files/people/u3827/Understanding%20Process%20Tracing.pdf (Accessed 01.02.2020).

Collier, D., & Mahoney, J. (1996). 'Insights and Pitfalls: Selection Bias in Qualitative Research.' *World Politics*,49 (1), pp. 56–91, [online]. Available from https://www.cambridge.org/core/journals/world-politics/article/insights-and-pitfalls-selection-bias-in-qualitative-research/B11DD5ACD-114BC493F2294F2B889CBB6 (Accessed 01.02.2020).

Congleton, R. D. (2015). The Nature of Rent-Seeking. In R. D. Congleton and A. Hillman (Eds.), *Companion to the Political Economy*. Cheltenham: Edward Elgar Publishing.

Cooper, D. R., & Schindler, P. S. (2003). *Business Research Methods*. 8th ed. Boston, MA: McGraw-Hill/Irwin.

Corbin, J., & Strauss, A. (2008). *Basics of Qualitative Research: Techniques and Procedures for Developing Grounded Theory*, 3rd ed. Thousand Oaks, CA: SAGE Publications, Inc.

Corvi, R. (1997). *An Introduction to the Thought of Karl Popper*. London: Routledge.

Creswell, J. W. (2009). *Research Design. Qualitative, Quantitative, and Mixed Methods Approaches* (3rd ed.). Thousand Oaks, CA: SAGE.

Davis, L., & North, D. C. (1971). *Institutional Change and American Economic Growth*. Cambridge: Cambridge University Press.

De Long, J. B. (2003). India Since Independence: An Analytical Growth Narrative. In D. Rodrick (Ed.), *In Search of Prosperity: Analytical Narratives on Economic Growth*. Princeton, NJ: Princeton University Press.

Denzau, A. T., & North, D. C. (1994). 'Shared Mental Models: Ideologies and Institutions.' *Kyklos*, 47, pp. 3–31, [online]. Available from https://onlinelibrary.wiley.com/doi/abs/10.1111/j.1467-6435.1994.tb02246.x (Accessed 01.02.2020).

Dey, I. (1993). *Qualitative Data Analysis. A User-Friendly Guide for Social Scientists.* London: Routledge.

Dinh, H. T. (2017). Case Studies of Decentralized Coordination in China. In J. Page and F. Tarp (Eds.), *The Practice of Industrial Policy*, pp. 145–166. Oxford: Oxford University Press.

Doner, R., & Schneider, B. (2000). 'Business Associations and Economic Development: Why Some Associations Contribute More than Others.' *Business and Politics*, 2 (3), 261–288, [online]. Available from https://www.cambridge.org/core/journals/business-and-politics/article/business-associations-and-economic-development-why-some-associations-contribute-more thanothers/80BFA7537971DEE48B0143A253103BB4 (Accessed 10.08.2020).

Eggertsson, T. (1990). *Economic Behaviour and Institutions.* Cambridge: Cambridge University Press.

Eggertsson, T. (1998). 'Limits to Institutional Reforms.' *Scandinavian Journal of Economics*, 100 (1), 335–357, [online]. Available from https://onlinelibrary.wiley.com/doi/abs/10.1111/1467-9442.00105 (Accessed 01.02.2020).

Eggertsson, T. (2005). *Imperfect Institutions: Possibilities and Limits of Reform.* Ann Arbor: University of Michigan Press.

Engvall, J. (2012). *Against the Grain: How Georgia Fought Corruption and What It Means*, [online]. Available from https://www.silkroadstudies.org/resources/pdf/SilkRoadPapers/2012_09_SRP_Engvall_Georgia-Corruption.pdf (Accessed 01.03.2020).

ENPARD. (2016). *Analysis of Preferential Agrocredit Project in Georgia*, [online]. Available from http://enpard.ge/en/wp-content/uploads/2015/05/Analysis-of-Preferential-Agro-Credit-Project_ENG.pdf (Accessed 09.09.2019).

Evans, P. (1992). The State as Problem and Solutions: Prediction, Embedded Autonomy, and Structural Change. In S. Haggard and R. Kaufman (Eds.), *The Politics of Economic Adjustment*. Princeton, NJ: Princeton University Press.

Evans, P. (1995). *Embedded Autonomy: States and Industrial Transformation.* Princeton, NJ: Princeton University Press.

Evans, P. (1997). State Structures, Government–Business Relations, and Economic Transformation. InS. Maxfield and B. R. Schneider (Eds.), *Business and the State in Developing Countries*. Ithaca, NY: Cornell University Press.

Evans, P. (1998). 'Transferable Lessons Re-Examining Institutional Prerequisites of East Asian Economic Policies.' *Journal of Development Studies*,34 (6), pp. 66–86, [online]. Available from https://econpapers.repec.org/article/tafjdevst/v_3a34_3ay_3a1998_3ai_3a6_3ap_3a66-86.htm (Accessed 01.02.2020).

Evans, P. (2010). *The Challenge of the 21st Century Development: Building Capability Enhancing States.* UNDP, Global Event Working Paper, [online].

Available from http://www.sfb597.uni-bremen.de/download/de/publikationen/ohts/EvansChallenge_21st_century.pdf (Accessed 02.02.2020).

Evans, P. (2012). What Will the 21st Century Developmental State Look Like? Implications of Contemporary Development Theory for the State's Role. In S. W. Chiu and S. Wong (Eds.), *Repositioning the Hong Kong Government: Social Foundations and Political Challenges*. Hong Kong: Hong Kong University Press.

Evans, P. (2013). Human Development, State Transformation and the Politics of the Developmental State. In S. Leibfried, E. Huber, M. Lange, J. Levy, F. Nullmeier, and J. D. Stephens (Eds.), *The Oxford Handbook of the Transformations of the State*. Oxford: Oxford University Press.

Fernandez, R., & Rodrik, D. (1991). 'Resistance to Reform: Status Quo Bias in the Presence of Individual Specific Uncertainty.' *American Economic Review*, 85 (5), pp. 1146–1155, [online]. Available from https://dash.harvard.edu/bitstream/handle/1/37927057/Resistance%20to%20Reform%20rodrik%20VOR.pdf?sequence=2&isAllowed=y (Accessed 02.02.2020).

Food and Agriculture Organization of the United Nations. (2012). *Assessment of the Agriculture and Rural Development Sectors in the Eastern Partnership Countries*,Georgia, [online]. Available from http://enpard.ge/en/wp-content/uploads/2015/05/Georgia_Assesment_FINAL_en.pdf (Accessed 30.01.2019).

Food and Agriculture Organization of the United Nations. (2014). *Review and Assessment of the Ministry of Agriculture of Georgia Information and Consultation Service Centres*, [online]. Available from http://enpard.ge/en/wp-content/uploads/2015/05/Review-MoA-Information-Consulting-Service_120514.pdf (Accessed 30.01.2019).

Food and Agriculture Organization of the United Nations. (2017). *The Future of Food and Agriculture: The Trends and Challenges*, [online]. Available from http://www.fao.org/3/a-i6583e.pdf (Accessed 02.03.2019).

Frieden, J. A. (1991). *Debt Development and Democracy: The Political Implications. In Debt and Democracy in Latin America 1965–1985*. Princeton, NJ: Princeton University Press.

Furubotn, G. E., & Richter, R. (2005). *Institutions & Economic Theory*. Ann Arbor: The University of Michigan Press.

Gebreeyesus, M., & Iizuka, M. (2012). 'Discovery of Flower Industry in Ethiopia: Experimentation and Coordination.' *Journal of Globalization and Development*, 2 (2), pp.1–27, [online]. Available from https://econpapers.repec.org/article/bpjglobdv/v_3a2_3ay_3a2012_3ai_3a2_3an_3a5.htm (Accessed 04.04.2019).

George, A. L., & Bennett, A. (2005). *Case Studies and Theory Development in the Social Sciences.* BCSIA Studies in International Security. Cambridge, MA: MIT Press.

Gerring, J. (2001a). Concepts: General Criteria. In *Social Science Methodology: A Criterial Framework*, pp. 35–64. Cambridge: Cambridge University Press.

Gerring, J. (2001b). Research Design: General Criteria. In *Social Science Methodology: A Criterial Framework*, pp. 155–199. Cambridge: Cambridge University Press.

Gerring, J. (2001c). Methods. In *Social Science Methodology: A Criterial Framework*, pp. 200–229. Cambridge: Cambridge University Press.

Gerring, J. (2004). 'What Is a Case Study and What Is It Good for?' *The American Political Science Review*,98 (2), pp. 341–354, [online]. Available from https://fekmekci.files.wordpress.com/2014/11/gerring-case-study.pdf (Accessed 08.04.2020).

Gerring, J. (2006). 'Single-Outcome Studies: A Methodological Primer.' *International Sociology*,21 (5), pp. 707–734, [online]. Available from http://people.bu.edu/jgerring/papers/Single_Outcome_Studies.pdf (Accessed 06.04.2020).

Gerring, J. (2007). *Case Study Research. Principles and Practices.* 2nd ed. New York: Cambridge University Press.

Gibbs, G. R. (2007). Analysing Qualitative Data. In U. Flick (Ed.), *The Sage Qualitative Research Kit*. London: Sage.

Gillham, B. (2000). *The Research Interview.* London: Continuum.

Goddard, D. (1973). 'Max Weber and the Objectivity of Social Science.' *History and Theory*, 12 (1), pp. 1–22, Wiley for Wesleyan University, [online]. Available from https://www.jstor.org/stable/2504691?seq=1 (Accessed 02.03.2019).

Goldstein, A. (2002). 'EMBRAER: From National Champion to a Global Player.' *CEPAl Review*, 77, pp. 97–115, [online]. Available from https://www.academia.edu/1911425/EMBRAER_From_national_champion_to_global_player (Accessed 06.04.2020).

Gollin, D., Lagakos, D., & Waugh, M. E. (2014). 'Agricultural Productivity Differences across Countries.' *The American Economic Review*, 104 (5), pp. 165–170, [online]. Available from https://www.aeaweb.org/articles?id=10.1257/aer.104.5.165 (Accessed 06.04.2020).

Gómez-Mera, L., Kenyon, T., Margalit, Y., Guilherme Reis, J., & Varela, G. (2014). *New Voices in Investment: A Survey of Investors from Emerging Countries*. Washington, DC: World Bank, [online]. Available from http://www.worldbank.org/content/dam/Worldbank/document/Trade/New_Voices_in_Investment.pdf (Accessed 02.03.2019).

Gorton, W. A. (2006). *Karl Popper and the Social Sciences.* New York: The State University of New York Press.

Granovetter, M. (1985). 'Economic Action and Social Structure: The Problem of Embeddedness.' *American Journal of Sociology*, 91 (3), pp. 481–510, [online]. Available from https://www.jstor.org/stable/2780199?seq=1#metadata_info_tab_contents (Accessed 02.03.2019).

Guba, E. G. (1990). The Alternative Paradigm Dialog. In E. G. Guba (Ed.), *The Paradigm Dialog*, pp. 17–30. Newbury Park, CA: Sage.

Haggard, S. (2004). 'Institutions and Growth in East Asia.' *Studies in Comparative International Development*, 38 (4), pp. 53–81, [online]. Available from https://www.researchgate.net/publication/240357408_Institutions_and_Growth_in_East_Asia (Accessed 02.03.2019).

Haggard, S., Maxfield, S., & Schneider, B. R. (1997). Theories of Business and Business-State Relations. In S. Maxfield and B. R. Schneider (Eds.), *Business and the State in Developing Countries.* Ithaca, NY: Cornell University Press.

Hallward-Driemeier, M., & Pritchett, L. (2015). 'How Business Is Done in the Developing World: Deals Versus Rules.' *The Journal of Economic Perspectives*, 29 (3), pp. 121–140, [online]. Available from https://www.aeaweb.org/articles?id=10.1257/jep.29.3.121 (Accessed 06.04.2020).

Hampwaye, G., & Jeppesen, S. (2014). 'The Role of State-Business Relations in the Performance of Zambia's Food Processing Sub-Sector.' *Bulletin of Geography*, Socioeconomic series, 26 (26), pp. 83–92, [online]. Available from https://content.sciendo.com/view/journals/bog/26/26/article-p83.xml (Accessed 06.04.2020).

Handley, A. (2008). *Business and the State in Africa: Economic Policy-Making in the Neo-Liberal Era.* Cambridge: Cambridge University Press.

Harriss, J. (2006). *Institutions and State-Business Relations: Improving Institutions for Pro-Poor Growth.* IPPG, [online]. Available from https://assets.publishing.service.gov.uk/media/57a08c2f40f0b652dd00117c/IPPGBP2.pdf (Accessed 06.04.2020).

Hausmann, R., & Rodrik, D. (2002). Economic Development as Self-Discovery. NBER Working Papers, 8952, [online]. Available from https://econpapers.repec.org/paper/nbrnberwo/8952.htm (Accessed 06.04.2020).

Hausmann, R., & Rodrik, D. (2003). 'Economic Development as Self-Discovery.' *Journal of Development Economics*, 72 (2), pp. 603–633, [online]. Available from https://www.sciencedirect.com/science/article/abs/pii/S030438780300124X (Accessed 06.04.2020).

Hawkes, C. (2006). 'Uneven Dietary Development: Linking the Policies and Processes of Globalization with the Nutrition Transition, Obesity, and Diet-

Related Chronic Diseases.' *Globalization and Health*, 2 (4), pp. 1–18, [online]. Available from https://globalizationandhealth.biomedcentral.com/articles/10.1186/1744-8603-2-4 (Accessed 06.04.2020).

Hawkes, C. (2010). The Influence of Trade Liberalisation and Global Dietary Change: The Case of Vegetable Oils, Meat, and Highly Processed Foods. In C. Hawkes, C. Blouin, S. Henson, N. Dragen, and L. Dube(Eds.), *Trade, Food Diet, and Health: Perspectives and Policy Options*. Oxford: Blackwell.

Herzberg, B., & Wright, A. (2013). *The PPD Handbook. Public-Private Dialogue*, [online]. Available from http://siteresources.worldbank.org/INTEXPCOMNET/Resources/PPD_Handbook.pdf (Accessed 06.04.2020).

Iootty, M., Kilroy, A., Onugha, I., & Palmade, V. (2013). *Georgia Competitive Industries Preliminary Sector Diagnostic*. World Bank Other Operational Studies, 16069, [online]. Available from http://documents1.worldbank.org/curated/en/363001468249708789/pdf/792770ESW0P1440ox0377371B00PUBLIC0.pdf (Accessed 08.07.2020).

Jackson, P. T. (2011). *The Conduct of Inquiry in International Relations: Philosophy of Science and Its Implications for the Study of World Politics*. New York: Routledge.

Janesick, V. J. (1994). The Dance of Qualitative Research Design: Metaphor, Methodology, and Meaning. In N. K. Denzin and Y. S. Lincoln (Eds.), *Handbook of Qualitative Research*, pp. 209–219. Thousand Oaks, CA: Sage.

Jarvis, L. S. (1994). Changing Private and Public Roles in Technological Development: Lessons from the Chilean Fruit Sector. In J. R. Anderson (Ed.), *Agricultural Technology: Policy Issues for the International Community*. Wallingford: CAB International.

Jick, D. T. (1979). 'Mixing Qualitative and Quantitative Methods: Triangulation in Action. Qualitative Methodology'. In *Administrative Science Quarterly*, 24 (4), pp. 602–611, [online]. Available from https://www.jstor.org/stable/2392366?seq=1 (Accessed 06.04.2020).

Jobelius, M. (2011). *Economic Liberalism in Georgia: A Challenge for E.U. Convergence and Trade Unions*. Fridrich Ebert Stiftung, Tbilisi, [online]. Available from http://library.fes.de/pdf-files/id/08135.pdf (Accessed 07.25.2016).

Johnson, C. (1982). *MITI and the Japanese Miracle. The Growth and Industrial Policy, 1925–1975*. Stanford, CA: Stanford University Press.

Johnson, C. (1987). Political Institutions and Economic Performance: The Government-Business Relation in Japan, South Korea, and Taiwan. In F. Deyo (Ed.), *The Political Economy of the New Asian Industrialism*. Ithaca, NY: Cornell University Press.

Kathuria, V., Rajesh, R., & Sen, K. (2013). State-Business Relations and Productivity in Indian Industry. In K. Sen (Ed.), *State-Business Relations, and Economic Development in Africa and India*. London, UK: Routledge.

Khan, M., & Blankenburg, S. (2009). The Political Economy of Industrial Policy in Asia and Latin America. In M. Cimoli, G. Dosi, and J. E. Stiglitz (Eds.), *Industrial Policy and Development: The Political Economy of Capabilities Accumulation*. Oxford: Oxford University Press.

Kim, E. M. (2015). *Korea'sEvolving Business-Government Relationship*. Wider working paper, 103 [online]. Available from https://www.econstor.eu/bitstream/10419/126322/1/837303117.pdf (Accessed 08.08.2020).

Kim, E. Y. (1993). 'The Developmental State and the Politics of Business Interest Associations: The Case of the Textile Industry in South Korea.' *Pacific Focus*, 8 (2), pp. 31–60.

Kim, W. (2011). *Korea's State–Business Partnership and the Growth of Chaebols*. Rochester, NY: Social Science Research Network.

Kohli, A. (2007). 'State, Business, and Economic Growth in India.' *Studies in Comparative International Development*, 42 (1), pp. 87–114, [online]. Available from https://www.researchgate.net/publication/227293787_State_Business_and_Economic_Growth_in_India (Accessed 06.04.2020).

Kohli, A. (2009). 'States and Economic Development.' *Revista de Economia Política*, 29 (2), pp. 212–227, [online]. Available from https://www.researchgate.net/publication/262544706_States_and_Economic_Development (Accessed 08.03.2020).

Krueger, A. O. (1974). 'The Political Economy of the Rent-Seeking Society.' *American Economic Review*, 64 (3), pp. 291–303, [online]. Available from https://www.jstor.org/stable/1808883?seq=1#metadata_info_tab_contents (Accessed 06.04.2020).

Kuckartz, U. (2014). *Qualitative Text Analysis. A Guide to Methods, Practice & Using Software*. Los Angeles, CA: SAGE.

Kvale, S. (2007). *Doing Interviews*. Thousand Oaks, CA: Sage.

Lall, S. (1992). 'Technological Capabilities and Industrialization.' *World Development*, 20 (2), pp. 165–186, [online]. Available from https://econpapers.repec.org/article/eeewdevel/v_3a20_3ay_3a1992_3ai_3a2_3ap_3a165-186.htm (Accessed 06.04.2020).

Land, D. V. (2013). *Green Grass: Reality and Potential of Georgian Agriculture*. Discussion Paper Series Private Sector and Development. The National Parliamentary Library of Georgia.

Laothamatas, A. (1992). *Business Associations and New Political Economy of Thailand: From Bureaucratic Polity to Liberal Corporatism*. Boulder, CO: Westview.

Latif, A., & Schmitz, H. (2009). *State–Business Relations and Investment in Egypt*. Institute of Development Studies, University of Sussex, Research Report 61, [online]. Available from http://www2.ids.ac.uk/gdr/cfs/pdfs/RR61.pdf (Accessed 06.04.2020).

Leftwich, A. (2009). *Analysing the Politics of State-Business Relations: A Methodological Concept Note on the Historical Institutionalist Approach*. IPPG Discussion Paper, 23A, [online]. Available from https://assets.publishing.service.gov.uk/media/57a08b3c40f0b64974000a54/IPPGDP23.pdf (Accessed 06.04.2020).

Leibfried, S., Huber, E., Lange, M., Levy, J. D., Nullmeier, F., & Stephens, J. D. (2015). *The Oxford Handbook of the Transformations of the State*. Oxford: Oxford University Press.

Lemma, A., & te Velde, D. W. (2017). Chapter 4: State–Business Relations as Drivers of Economic Performance. In J. Page and F. Tarp (Eds.), *The Practice of Industrial Policy*, pp. 1–24, [online]. Available from http://www.oxfordscholarship.com/view/10.1093/acprof:oso/9780198796954.001.0001/acprof-9780198796954-chapter-4?print=pdf (Accessed 06.04.2020).

Lewis, D. (1969). *Conventions: A Philosophical Study*. Cambridge: Harvard University Press.

Lin, J. Y. (2009). *Economic Development and Transition*. Cambridge: Cambridge University Press.

Lin, J. Y. (2011). 'New Structural Economics: A Framework for Rethinking Development.' *The World Bank Research Observer*, 26 (2), pp. 194–221, [online]. Available from https://academic.oup.com/wbro/article-abstract/26/2/193/1642270 (Accessed 10.07.2020).

Lin, J. Y., & Chang, H. J. (2009). 'Should Industrial Policy in Developing Countries Conform to Comparative Advantage or Defy It?' *Development Policy Review Debate*,27 (5), pp. 483–502, [online]. Available from https://www.comfama.com/contenidos/servicios/Gerenciasocial/html/Cursos/Columbia-2015-ll/Lecturas/2.pdf (Accessed 06.04.2020).

Lin, J. Y., & Monga, C. (2010). *Growth Identification and Facilitation: The Role of the State in the Dynamics of Structural Change*. World Bank Policy Working Paper, 5313, [online]. Available from http://documents.worldbank.org/curated/en/438321468164948980/pdf/WPS5313.pdf (Accessed 06.04.2020).

Lin, J. Y., & Nugent, J. B. (1995). Institutions and Economic Development. In H. Chenery and T. N. Srinivasan (Eds.), *Handbook of Development Economics*, 1st ed., Vol. 3, pp. 2301–2370. Amsterdam: Elsevier Science.

Lupia, A., & McCubbins, M. (1998). *Political Credibility and Economic Reform, Part 1: Do Politicians Intend to Keep the Promises They Make*. A Report for the

World Bank. [online] available at https://www.researchgate.net/publication/252146681_Political_Credibility_and_Economic_Reform (Accessed 20.09.2020)

Lusztig, M. (1998). 'The Limits of Rent Seeking: Why Protectionists Become Free Traders.' *Review of International Political Economy*, 5 (1), pp. 38–63, [online]. Available from www.jstor.org/stable/4177256 (Accessed 06.04.2020).

Mackie, J. L. (1965). 'Causes and Conditions.' *American Philosophical Quarterly*,2 (4), 245–264 [online]. Available from https://www.jstor.org/stable/20009173?seq=1#metadata_info_tab_contents (Accessed 06.04.2020).

Mahoney, J. (2012). 'The Logic of Process Tracing Tests in the Social Sciences.' *Sociological Methods & Research*,41 (4), pp. 570–597, [online]. Available from https://econpapers.repec.org/article/saesomere/v_3a41_3ay_3a2012_3ai_3a4_3ap_3a570-597.htm (Accessed 06.04.2020).

Marangos, J. (2009). 'The Evolution of the Term "Washington Consensus."' *Journal of Economic Surveys*, 23 (2), pp. 350–384, [online]. Available from https://www.researchgate.net/publication/46541285_The_evolution_of_the_term'Washington_Consensus (Accessed 06.04.2020).

Maxfield, S., & Schneider, B. R. (Eds.). (1997). *Business and the State in Developing Countries*. Ithaca, NY: Cornell University Press.

Maximov, A. (2017). *Unlocking the Export Potential of Georgian Agriculture*, German Economic Team-Georgia, Policy Paper Series, [online]. Available from http://www.get-georgia.de/wp-content/uploads/2017/04/PP_01_2017_en.pdf (Accessed 07.07.2020).

Maxwell, J. A. (2009). Designing a Qualitative Study. In L. Bickman and D. J. Rog (Eds.), *The Sage Handbook of Applied Social Research Methods*, 2nd ed., pp. 214–253. Thousand Oaks, CA: Sage.

Mehta, P. B., & Walton, M. (2014). *Ideas, Interests, and the Politics of Development Change in India*. ESID Working Paper, 36, [online]. Available from https://assets.publishing.service.gov.uk/media/57a089ef40f0b652dd000498/esid_wp_36_mehta_walton.pdf (Accessed 06.04.2020).

Miles, M. B., & Huberman, A. M. (1984). *Qualitative Data Analysis: A Sourcebook of New Methods*. Thousand Oaks, CA: SAGE Publications Inc.

Mody, A. (1993). 'Learning through Alliances.' *Journal of Economic Behaviour and Organisations*,20 (2), pp. 151–170, [online]. Available from https://www.sciencedirect.com/science/article/abs/pii/0167268193900887 (Accessed 06.04.2020).

Moistsraphishvili, I. (2017). *The Assessment of Preferential Agrocredit Program*. RAPDI, Tbilisi, [online]. Available from http://www.bridge.org.ge/uploads/

files/docs/9365Assessment-of-Preferential-Agro-Credit-Programme_GEO.pdf (Accessed 06.04.2020).

Moore, M., & Schmitz, H. (2008). *Idealism, Realism, and the Investment Climate in Developing Countries.* IDS Research Summary, 307, [online]. Available from https://www.ids.ac.uk/publications/idealism-realism-and-the-investment-climate-in-developing-countries/ (Accessed 06.04.2020).

Mueller, D. C. (1989). *Public Choice II.* Cambridge: Cambridge University Press.

Mummert, U. (1999). *Informal Institutions and Institutional Policy-Shedding Light on the Myth of Institutional Conflict.* Jena, Max-Planck-Inst. zur Erforschung von Wirtschaftssystemen.

Nabli, M. K., & Nugent, J. B. (1989a). 'The New Institutional Economics and Its Applicability to Development.' *World Development*, 17 (9), pp. 1333–1347, [online]. Available from https://www.sciencedirect.com/science/article/abs/pii/0305750X89900764?via%3Dihub (Accessed 06.04.2020).

Nash, J. (1953). 'Two-Person Cooperative Game.' *Econometrica*, 21 (1), pp. 128–140, [online]. Available from https://www.jstor.org/stable/1906951?seq=1#metadata_info_tab_contents (Accessed 06.04.2020).

Nattrass, N., & Seekings, J. (2010). *State, Business, and Growth in Post-Apartheid South Africa.* IPPG discussion paper series, 34, [online]. Available from https://citeseerx.ist.psu.edu/viewdoc/download?doi=10.1.1.850.3460&rep=rep1&-type=pdf[T1] (Accessed 06.04.2020).

Naylor, R. L., Liska, A. J., Marshall, B. B., Walter, P. F., Gaskell, J. G., Scott, D. R., & Cassman, G. K. (2007). 'The Ripple Effect: Biofuels, Food Security, and the Environment.' *Environment: Science and Policy for Sustainable Development*, 49 (9), pp. 30–43, [online]. Available from https://www.tandfonline.com/doi/abs/10.3200/ENVT.49.9.30-43 (Accessed 08.04.2020).

Nelson, R., & Winter, S. (1982). *An Evolutionary Theory of Economic Change.* Cambridge: Harvard University.

Neuman, W. L. (2000). *Social Research Methods: Qualitative and Quantitative Approaches*, 4th ed. Boston, MA: Allyn & Bacon.

Newnham, R. E. (2015). 'Georgia on My Mind? Russian Sanctions and the End of the "Rose Revolution."' *Journal of Eurasian Studies*, 6 (2), pp. 161–170, [online]. Available from https://www.sciencedirect.com/science/article/pii/S187936651500010X (Accessed 08.04.2020).

North, D. C. (1978). 'The Structure and Performance: The Task of Economic History.' *The Journal of Economic Literature*,16 (3), pp. 963–978, [online]. Available from https://www.jstor.org/stable/2723471?seq=1 (Accessed 08.04.2020).

North, D. C. (1984). 'Government and the Cost of Exchange.' *Journal of Economic History*, 44 (2), pp. 255–264.

North, D. C. (1990). *Institutions, Institutional Change and Economic Performance.* Cambridge: Cambridge University Press.

North, D. C. (1991). 'Institutions.' *The Journal of Economic Perspectives*, 5 (1), pp. 97–112, [online]. Available from https://www.jstor.org/stable/1942704?seq=1 (Accessed 08.04.2020).

North, D. C. (1992). 'Institutions, Ideology, and Economic Performance.' *Cato Journal*, 11 (3), pp. 477–488, [online]. Available from https://www.cato.org/sites/cato.org/files/serials/files/cato-journal/1992/1/cj11n3-11.pdf (Accessed 08.04.2020).

North, D. C. (1993). 'Institutions and Credible Commitment.' *Journal of Institutional and Theoretical Economics*, 149 (1), pp. 595–619, [online]. Available from https://www.jstor.org/stable/40751576?seq=1 (Accessed 08.04.2020).

North, D. C. (1995). *Some Fundamental Puzzles in Economic History/Development.* St. Louis, MI: Mimeo.

North, D. C. (2005). *Understanding the Process of Economic Change.* Princeton, NJ: Princeton University Press.

North, D. C., & Thomas, R. P. (1973). *The Rise of the Western World: A New Economic History.* Cambridge: Cambridge University Press.

North, D. C., & Weingast, B. W. (1989). 'Constitutions and Commitment: Evolution of Institutions Governing Public Choice in Seventeenth Century England.' *Journal of Economic History*, 49 (4), pp. 803–832, [online]. Available from https://www.jstor.org/stable/2122739?seq=1 (Accessed 08.04.2020).

Ocampo, J. A., Rada, C., & Taylor, L. (2009). *Growth and Policy in Developing Countries: A Structuralist Approach.* New York, NY: Columbia University Press.

Olson, M. (1982). *The Rise and Decline of Nations: Economic Growth, Stagflation, and Social Rigidities.* New Haven, CT: Yale University Press.

Onuf, N. G. (1989). *World of Our Making: Rules and Rule in Social Theory and International Relations.* Columbia: University of South Carolina Press.

Onugha, I., Lootty, M., Kilroy, A., & Plmade, V. (2013). *Georgia Competitive Industries Preliminary Sector Diagnostic.* The World Bank, [Online] Available from http://researchgeorgia.ge/userfiles/admin_files/147.pdf (Accessed 08.04.2020).

Organization for Economic Co-operation and Development (OECD). (2009). *Agricultural Policies in Emerging Economies: Monitoring and Evaluation*, [online] Available from https://www.oecd.org/tad/agricultural-policies/42347206.pdf (Accessed 08.04.2020).

Ostrom, E. (1986). 'An Agenda for the Study of Institutions.' *Public Choice*, 48 (1), pp. 3–25, [online]. Available from https://www.jstor.org/stable/30024572?seq=1 (Accessed 08.04.2020).

Page, J. (2014). *Industrial Policy in Practice: Africa's Presidential Investors' Advisory Councils.* UNU-WIDER, Working Paper, 117, [online]. Available from http://www.wider.unu.edu/publications/working-papers/2014/en_GB/wp2014-117/ (Accessed 08.04.2020).

Page, J., & Tarp, F. (Eds.). (2017). *The Practice of Industrial Policy*. Oxford: Oxford University Press.

Patton, M. Q. (2002). *Qualitative Research and Evaluation Methods*, 3rd ed. Saint Paul, MN: Sage Publications.

Peiffer, C. (2012a). *The Politics of State Business Relations in the Pacific: What Is Already Documented and What Do We Need to Know?* DLP Background Paper, 13. Australia: DLP.

Peiffer, C. (2012b). *Reform Coalitions. Patterns and Hypotheses from a Survey of the Literature.* In Coalitions in the Politics of Development, Development Leadership Program, Concept Paper, 5, [online]. Available from http://www.mspguide.org/sites/default/files/resource/dlp_coalitions_in_the_politics_of_development.pdf (Accessed 08.04.2020).

Pelikan, P. (1986). *The Formation of Incentive Mechanisms in Different Economic Systems.* Research Institute of Industrial Economics, Working Paper Series, 155, [online]. Available from https://www.ifn.se/wfiles/wp/wp155.pdf (Accessed 08.04.2020).

Pindyck, R. S. (1991). 'Irreversibility, Uncertainty, and Investment.' *Journal of Economic Literature*, 29 (3), pp. 1110–1148, [online]. Available from http://www.samsi.info/sites/default/files/Pindyck91.pdf (Accessed 08.04.2020).

Pindyck, R. (1993). 'A Note on Competitive Investment under Uncertainty.' *American Economic Review*, 83 (1), pp. 273–77, [online]. Available from http://web.mit.edu/rpindyck/www/Papers/CompetitiveInvestUncertAER1993.pdf (Accessed 08.04.2020).

Polanyi, K. (1967). *The Tacit Dimension.* Garden City: Doubleday-Anchor.

Popper, K. R. (1959). *The Logic of Scientific Discovery.* London: Hutchinson & Co.

Priewe, J. (2015). Even Strategies for Development in Comparison. In A. Calcagno, S. Dullien, A. Marquez-Valazquez, N. Maystre, and J. Priewe (Eds.), *Rethinking Development Strategies after the Financial Crisis*, 1, [online]. Available from https://unctad.org/en/PublicationsLibrary/gdsmdp20151_en.pdf (Accessed 08.04.2020).

Pritchett, L., & Werker, E. (2012). *Developing the Guts of GUT (Grand Unified Theory): Elite Commitment and Inclusive Growth.* Effective States and Inclusive Development Research Centre (ESID), University of Manchester, Working Paper, 16, [online]. Available from https://assets.publishing.service.

gov.uk/media/57a08aaded915d3cfd00089e/esid_wp_16_pritchett_werker.pdf (Accessed 08.04.2020).

Przeworski, A. (2004). 'Institutions Matter.' *Government and Oppositions*, 39 (4), pp. 527–650, [online]. Available from https://www.cambridge.org/core/journals/government-and-opposition/article/institutions-matter-1/670E3CA05B9E684BF918205D06203454 (Accessed 08.04.2020).

Qureshi, M., & te Velde, D. W. (2012). 'State-Business Relations, Investment Climate Reform, and Firm Productivity in Sub-Saharan Africa.' *Journal of International Development*, 25 (7), pp. 912–935, [online]. Available from https://www.researchgate.net/publication/264369266_State-business_relations_investment_climate_reform_and_firm_productivity_in_sub-Saharan_Africa (Accessed 08.04.2020).

Qureshi, M. S., & te Velde, D. W. (2013). State-Business Relations and Firm Performance in Zambia. In K. Sen (Ed.), *State Business Relations, and Economic Development in Africa and India*. London: Routledge.

Rabionet, S. E. (2011). 'How I Learned to Design and Conduct Semi-Structured Interviews: An Ongoing and Continuous Journey.' *The Qualitative Report*, 16 (2), pp. 563–566, [online]. Available from https://nsuworks.nova.edu/cgi/viewcontent.cgi?article=1070&context=tqr (Accessed 08.04.2020).

Reich, R. B. (1982). 'Making Industrial Policy.' *Foreign Affairs*, 60 (4), pp. 852–881, [online]. Available from https://www.foreignaffairs.com/articles/1982-03-01/making-industrial-policy (Accessed 08.04.2020).

Restuccia, D., Yang, T. D., & Zhu, X. (2008). 'Agriculture and Aggregate Productivity: A Quantitative Cross-Country Analysis.' *Journal of Monetary Economics*, 55 (2), pp. 234–250, [online]. Available from https://ideas.repec.org/a/eee/moneco/v55y2008i2p234-250.html (Accessed 08.04.2020).

Richter, R. (2005). 'The New Institutional Economics: Its Start, Its Meaning, Its Prospects.' *European Business Organization Law Review*, 6 (2), pp. 161–200, [online]. Available from https://www.researchgate.net/publication/228261489_The_New_Institutional_Economics_Its_Start_Its_Meaning_Its_Prospects (Accessed 08.04.2020).

Richter, R. (2015). *Essays on New Institutional Economics*. Switzerland: Springer International Publishing.

Rimple, P. (2012). *Who Owned Georgia 2003–2012*? Transparency International, [online]. Available from http://www.transparency.ge/sites/default/files/post_attachments/Who%20Owned%20Georgia%20English.pdf (Accessed 08.04.2020).

Ritchie, J., & Lewis, J. (2003). *Qualitative Research Practice: A Guide for Social Science Students and Researchers*. London: SAGE.

Rodrigues, T. E. (2009). 'Agricultural Explosion in Brazil: Exploring the Impacts of Brazilian Agricultural Development Over the Amazon.' *International Journal of Sociology of Agriculture and Food*, 16 (1), pp. 1–12, [online]. Available from https://www.semanticscholar.org/paper/Agricultural-Explosion-in-Brazil%3A-Exploring-the-of-Rodrigues/473794cdab5b4f5cadf8af7c1f3cdfdcdecf0e70 (Accessed 08.04.2020).

Rodrik, D. (1989). 'Promises, Promises: Credible Policy Reform via Signalling.' *Economic Journal*, 99 (397), pp. 756–772, [online]. Available from https://www.jstor.org/stable/2233769?seq=1 (Accessed 08.04.2020).

Rodrik, D. (1991). 'Policy Uncertainty and Private Investment in Developing Countries.' *Journal of Development Economics*, 36 (2), 229–243, [online]. Available from https://www.sciencedirect.com/science/article/abs/pii/030438789190034S (Accessed 08.04.2020).

Rodrik, D. (1998). 'Has Globalization Gone Too Far?' *Challenge*, 41 (2), pp. 81–94, [online]. Available from https://www.jstor.org/stable/40721822?seq=1 (Accessed 08.04.2020).

Rodrik, D. (2003). *In Search of Prosperity: Analytic Narratives on Economic Growth.* Princeton, NJ: Princeton University Press.

Rodrik, D. (2004). *Industrial Policy for the 21st Century.* John F. Kennedy School of Government, Harvard University, [online]. Available from https://drodrik.scholar.harvard.edu/publications/industrial-policy-twenty-first-century (Accessed 08.04.2020).

Rodrik, D. (2008). 'Second-Best Institutions.' *American Economic Review*, 98 (2), pp. 100–104 [online]. Available from https://econpapers.repec.org/paper/nbrnberwo/14050.htm (Accessed 08.04.2020).

Rodrik, D. (2009). 'Industrial Policy: Don't Ask Why, Ask How.' *Middle East Development Journal*, 1 (1), pp. 1–29, [online]. Available from https://www.tandfonline.com/doi/abs/10.1142/S1793812009000024 (Accessed 08.04.2020).

Rojid, S., & Seetanah, B. (2013). State–Business Relations and Economic Growth: The Case of Ghana. In K. Sen (Ed.), *State–Business Relations and Economic Development in Africa and India.* London: Routledge.

Rojid, S., Seetanah, B., & Shalini, R. (2010). *Are State–Business Relations Important to Economic Growth? Evidence from Mauritius.* IPPG Discussion Paper Series, 36, [online]. Available from https://assets.publishing.service.gov.uk/media/57a08b2aed915d3cfd000b94/dp36.pdf (Accessed 08.04.2020).

Russell, B. (1954). *Human Society in Ethics and Politics.* New York: Simon & Schuster.

Sabry, M. (2018). 'Could Formalized State Business Relations Lead to Economic Growth? Business Participation, Government Representation, and

Institutions.' *International Journal of Social Economics*, 45 (7), pp. 1010–1029, [online]. Available from https://www.researchgate.net/publication/325578288_Could_formalized_State_Business_Relations_lead_to_economic_growth_Business_participation_government_representation_and_institutions (Accessed 08.04.2020).

Schmitter, P. (2008). The Design of Social and Political Research. In D. D. Porta and M. Keating (Eds.), *Approaches and Methodologies in the Social Sciences: A Pluralist Perspective*, pp. 263–295. Cambridge: Cambridge University Press.

Schmitter, P. C. (2016). 'The Design of Social & Political Research.' *Chinese Political Science Review*, 1 (4), pp. 577–609, [online]. Available from https://www.researchgate.net/publication/309303190_The_Design_of_Social_and_Political_Research (Accessed 08.04.2020).

Schneider, B. R. (1993). 'The Career Connection: A Comparative Analysis of Bureaucratic Preferences and Insulations.' *Comparative Politics*, 25 (3), pp. 101–122, [online]. Available from https://www.jstor.org/stable/422249?seq=1(Accessed 08.04.2020).

Schneider, B. R. (2013). *Institutions for Effective Business-Government Relations.* Inter-American Development Bank, Working Paper, 418, [online]. Available from https://www.econstor.eu/bitstream/10419/115417/1/IDB-WP-418.pdf (Accessed 08.04.2020).

Schreier, M. (2012). *Qualitative Content Analysis in Practice.* London: SAGE.

Sen, K. (2010). *From Collusion to Collaboration: State Business Relations and Economic Performance in India.* Manchester: IPPG.

Sen, K. (2013a). *Institutions and Governance in Developing Countries.* Cheltenham, UK: Edward Elgar Publishing.

Sen, K. (Ed.). (2013b). *State–Business Relations and Economic Development in Africa and India.* London: Routledge.

Sen, K. (2013c). 'The Political Dynamics of Economic Growth.' *World Development*, 47, pp. 71–86, [online]. Available from https://www.sciencedirect.com/science/article/abs/pii/S0305750X13000685?via%3Dihub (Accessed 08.04.2020).

Sen, K. (Ed.). (2013d). *State Business Relations and Economic Development in Africa and India.* London: Routledge.

Sen, K. (2015). *State-Business Relations.* GSDCR, topic guide, [online]. Available from http://www.gsdrc.org/wp-content/uploads/2015/10/State-BusinessRels.pdf (Accessed 10.04.2020).

Sen, K., & te Velde, D. W. (2009). 'State–Business Relations and Economic Growth in Sub-Saharan Africa.' *The Journal of Development Studies*, 54 (8), pp. 1267–1283, [online]. Available from https://www.tandfonline.com/doi/abs/10.1080/00220380902863307 (Accessed 08.04.2020).

Seperteladze, Z., Davitaia, E., Lamparadze, S., Memarne, G., Gaprindashvili, G., & Aleksidze, T. (2015). 'Agro-Landscape Zoning of West Georgia for Spreading New Varieties of Tangerine in Order to Reveal Optimal Natural Conditions.' *International Journal of Geosciences*, 6 (12), pp. 1339–1352, [online]. Available from https://www.scirp.org/journal/paperinformation.aspx?-paperid=62338 (Accessed 10.06.2020).

Shepsle, K. A. (1991). Discretion, Institutions, and the Problem of Government Commitment. In P. Bourdieu and J. Coleman (Eds.), *Social Theory for a Changing Society*, pp. 245–265. Boulder, CO: Westview Press.

Shergelashvili, T., & Tokmazashvili, M. (2012). *Agriculture Transformation of Georgia, 20 Years of Independence.* European Initiative Liberal Academy Tbilisi, [online]. Available from http://www.ei-lat.ge/images/doc/20%20Years%20of%20IndependenceTransformation%20of%20Georgian%20Agricultural%20System.pdf (Accessed 10.04.2020).

Shubik, M. (1970a). 'On Different Methods for Allocating Resources.' *Kyklos*, 23 (2), pp. 332–337,[online]. Available from https://onlinelibrary.wiley.com/doi/abs/10.1111/j.1467-6435.1970.tb02562.x (Accessed 08.08.2020).

Shubik, M.(1970b). 'Game Theory, Behaviour, and the Paradox of the Prisoner's Dilemma: Three Solutions.' *The Journal of Conflict Resolution*, 14 (2), pp. 181–193, [online]. Available from https://www.researchgate.net/publication/249727971_Game_theory_behavior_and_the_paradox_of_the_Prisoner' s_Dilemma_Three_solutions (Accessed 10.04.2020).

Silagadze, A. (2014). 'Priorities for the Economy of Post-communist Georgia in the Context of the World Financial Crisis.' In *Problems of Economic Transition*,56 (8), pp. 3–16, [online]. Available from https://www.tandfonline.com/doi/abs/10.2753/PET1061-1991560801 (Accessed 10.04.2020).

Small, M. L. (2009). 'How Many Cases Do I Need?' *Ethnography*, 10 (1), pp. 5–38, [online]. Available from https://journals.sagepub.com/doi/10.1177/1466138108099586 (Accessed 10.04.2020).

Smith, A. (1776). *An Inquiry into the Nature and Causes of the Wealth of Nations.* McMaster University Archive for the History of Economic Thought, [online]. Available from https://socialsciences.mcmaster.ca/econ/ugcm/3ll3/smith/wealth/wealbk01 (Accessed 10.01.2020).

Sohal, A., & Ferme, B. (1996). 'An Analysis of the South Korean Automotive, Shipbuilding and Steel Industries.' *Benchmarking for Quality Management and Technology*, 3 (2), pp. 15–30, [online]. Available from https://www.emerald.com/insight/content/doi/10.1108/14635779610118678/full/html (Accessed 10.04.2020).

Stake, R. (1995). *The Art of Case Study Research.* Thousand Oaks, CA: SAGE.

Steer, L., & Sen, K. (2008). *Informal Institutions in Transition. How Vietnam's Private Sector Boomed without Legal Protection*. IPPG, discussion paper, 19, [online]. Available from http://www.ippg.org.uk/PDF/Vietnam%2019.pdf (Accessed 10.04.2020).

Stiglitz, J. E. (1996a). 'Some Lessons from the East Asian Miracle.' *World Bank Research Observer*, 11 (2), pp. 151–177, [online]. Available from https://www.semanticscholar.org/paper/SOME-LESSONS-FROM-THE-EAST-ASIAN-MIRACLE Stiglitz/e5002ca3d0e2655d9558589bbb264f1785108d65 (Accessed 10.04.2020).

Stiglitz, J. E. (1996b). *Whither Socialism*. Cambridge, MA: The MIT Press.

Sutton, J. (2004). 'The Auto-Component Supply Chain in China and India. A Benchmarking Study.' *LSE*, [online]. Available from https://core.ac.uk/download/pdf/93091.pdf (Accessed 10.04.2020).

Syrquin, M. (1988). Chapter 7: Patterns of Structural Change. In H. Chenery and T. N. Srinivasan (Eds.), *Handbook of Development Economics*, Vol. 1, pp. 203–273. Amsterdam: North-Holland Publishing.

Te Velde, D. W. (2006). *Measuring State–Business Relations in Sub Saharan Africa*. IPPG, [online]. Available from: https://www.odi.org/sites/odi.org.uk/files/odi-assets/publications-opinion-files/6116.pdf (Accessed 10.04.2020).

Te Velde, D. W. (Ed.). (2010). *Effective State–Business Relations, Industrial Policy and Economic Growth*. IPPG, [online]. Available from https://www.odi.org/sites/odi.org.uk/files/odi-assets/publications-opinion-files/6126.pdf (Accessed 10.04.2020).

Te Velde, D. W. (2012). Measuring State–Business Relations in Sub-Saharan Africa. In K. Sen (Ed.), *State–Business Relations and Economic Development in Africa and India*. London: Routledge.

Te Velde, D. W. (Ed.). (2013). *State–Business Relations and Industrial Policy: Current Policy and Research Debates*. Growth Research Programme, [online]. Available from https://static1.squarespace.com/static/5167f6a2e4b0f1cbdee8d1c0/t/520bbceee4b0835de583c34f/1376500974972/DEGRP+Policy+Essays+State-business+relations+and+industrial+policy.pdf (Accessed 10.04.2020).

The Annual Report of Business Association of Georgia. (2017). BAG, [online]. Available from https://bag.ge/file.helix?i=a729ae92-c229-4f3d-9dd8-6c5cbf78b07a&r=P (Accessed 10.04.2020).

The Annual Report on Entrepreneurship in Georgia. (2017). The National Statistics Office of Georgia, [online]. Available from https://www.geostat.ge/media/13741/Mewarmeoba-sakqrtveloshi-2016.pdf (Accessed 04.03.2019).

The Annual Report of the Ministry of Agriculture of Georgia. (2017). MOA, [online]. Available from http://www.moa.gov.ge/Ge/Public/Annual/1014 (Accessed 10.04.2020).

The Georgian Law on Entrepreneurship. (1994). The Parliament of Georgia, [online]. Available at https://matsne.gov.ge/ka/document/view/28408?publication=63 (Accessed 10.04.2020).

The Government of Georgia Decree N 2144. (2013). On Transfer of Money to the Non-Entrepreneurial (Non-Commercial) Legal Entity – Agriculture Project Management Agency. The Government of Georgia, [online]. Available from http://gov.ge/files/275_39600_600578_214423.12.13.pdf (Accessed 10.04.2020).

The Government of Georgia Decree No.139. (2014). On the Measures to Be Taken under the Co-Financing of the Preferential Agro-Credit and Agricultural Food Processing and Storage Enterprises. The Government of Georgia, [online]. Available from https://www.matsne.gov.ge/document/view/2237341?publication=0 (Accessed 10.04.2020).

The Government of Georgia Decree No.444. (2015). On the Amendments to the Government of Georgia Decree No/ 56 On Approval of the State Programme' Plant the Future'. The Government of Georgia, [online]. Available from http://apma.ge/files/documents/LdCAitrepMov.pdf (Accessed 10.04.2020).

The Government of Georgia Decree No. 56. (2015). On Approval of the State Programme 'Plant the Future.' The Government of Georgia, [online]. Available from http://apma.ge/files/documents/7wm6dQyUyqdU.pdf (Accessed 10.04.2020).

The Government of Georgia Decree No 159. (2015). On the Amendments to the Government of Georgia Decree No. 56 on Approval of the State Programme 'Plant the Future'. The Government of Georgia, [online]. Available from http://apma.ge/files/documents/3TujJPq4PXFd.pdf (Accessed 10.04.2020).

The Government of Georgia Decree No 190. (2016). On the Amendments to the Government of Georgia Decree No. 56 on Approval of the State Programme' Plant the Future'. The Government of Georgia, [online]. Available from http://apma.ge/projects/read/plant_future/2:parent (Accessed 10.04.2020).

The SME Members Registration Form. Georgian Small and Medium Enterprise Association, [online]. Available from https://docs.google.com/forms/d/1IgUl297evfDx_OBUaDnOyCFFwPF2sENDxebqSxi17II/viewform?edit_requested=true (Accessed 10.04.2020).

Timm, C. (2013). *Economic Regulation and State Interventions. Georgia's Move from Neoliberalism to State-Managed Capitalism.* PFH, Working Paper, [online]. Available from http://www.econstor.eu/obitstream/10419/75297/1/749922974.pdf (Accessed 10.04.2020).

Timm, C. (2014). *A Liberal Developmental State in Georgia? State Dominance and Washington Consensus in the Post-Communist Region*. PFH, Research Paper, [online]. Available from https://www.pfh-university.com/fileadmin/Content/PDF/forschungspapiere/a-liberaldevelopmental-state-in-georgia_timm.pdf (Accessed 10.04.2020).

Timm, C. (2016). Legitimacy and State-Led Economic Policy in Georgia. In M. Brusis, J. Ahrens, and M. S. Wessel (Eds.), *Politics and Legitimacy in Post-Soviet Eurasia*. London: Palgrave Macmillan.

Timmer, C. P. (2007). *The Structural Transformation and the Changing Role of Agriculture in Economic Development: Empirics and Implications*. American Enterprise Institute, working paper, [online]. Available from https://fse.fsi.stanford.edu/publications/the_structural_transformation_and_the_changing_role_of_agriculture_in_economic_development (Accessed 10.04.2020).

Timmer, C. P., & Akkus. S. (2008a). *The Structural Transformation as a Pathway Out of Poverty: Lessons from Global Patterns and Divergent Country Paths*. Center for Global Development, working paper, 150, [online]. Available from https://www.files.ethz.ch/isn/91306/wp150.pdf (Accessed 10.04.2020).

Tollison, R. D. (1982). 'Rent-Seeking: A Survey.' *Kyklos*, 35 (4), pp. 575–602, [online]. Available from https://onlinelibrary.wiley.com/doi/abs/10.1111/j.1467-6435.1982.tb00174.x (Accessed 10.04.2020).

Tollison, R., & Congleton, R. (1995). *The Economic Analysis of Rent-Seeking*. Aldershot, UK: Elgar.

Torri, T. (2003). 'The Mechanism for State-Led Creation of Malaysia's Middle Classes.' *The Developing Economies*, XLI-2, pp. 221–242, [online]. Available from https://www.ide.go.jp/library/English/Publish/Periodicals/De/pdf/03_02_06.pdf (Accessed 10.04.2020).

Trubek, D. M. (2010). *The Developmental States and the Legal Order. Towards a New Political Economy of Development and Law* [online]. University of Wisconsin Legal Studies Research Paper, 1075, [online]. Available from https://papers.ssrn.com/sol3/papers.cfm?abstract_id=1349163 (Accessed 10.04.2020).

Tullock, G. (1975). 'The Transition Gains Trap.' *BellJournal of Economics*, 6 (2), pp. 671–678, [online]. Available from https://www.jstor.org/stable/3003249?seq=1 (Accessed 10.04.2020).

UNCTAD. (2016). *The Structural Transformation and Industrial Policy*. United Nations, [online]. Available from https://vi.unctad.org/stind/indpolfull.pdf (Accessed 10.04.2020).

UNIDO (United Nations Industrial Development Organization). (2009). *Industrial Development Report. Breaking in and Moving Up: New Industrial Challenges for the Bottom Billion and the Middle-Income Countries*. UNIDO, [online]. Available from https://www.unido.org/sites/default/files/2009-02/IDR_2009_print_0.PDF (Accessed on 10.04.2020).

Uzzi, B. (1996). 'The Sources and Consequences of Embeddedness for the Economic Performance of Organizations.' *American Sociological Review*, 61 (4), pp. 674–698, [online]. Available from https://www.jstor.org/stable/2096399?seq=1 (Accessed 10.04.2020).

Vakulchuk, R. (2014). *Kazakhstan's Emerging Economy. Between State and Market*, [online]. Available from https://www.researchgate.net/publication/299731455_Kazakhstan%27s_emerging_economy_Between_state_and_market (Accessed 10.04.2020).

Vu-Thanh, T. A. (2014). The Political Economy of Industrial Development in Vietnam: Impact of State–Business Relationship on Industrial Performance 1986–2012. World Institute for Development Economics Research (UNU-WIDER), Working Paper, 158, [online]. Available from https://ideas.repec.org/p/unu/wpaper/wp2014-158.html (Accessed 10.04.2020).

Wade, R. (1990). *Governing the Market: Economic Theory and the Role of Government in East Asian Industrialization*. Princeton, NJ: Princeton University Press.

Warwick, K. (2013). 'Beyond Industrial Policy. Emerging Issues and New Trends.' *OECD Science, Technology and Industry Policy Papers*, 2, [online]. Available from https://www.oecd-ilibrary.org/science-and-technology/beyond-industrial-policy_5k4869clw0xp-en (Accessed 10.04.2020).

Weber, M. [1968/1922]. *Economy and Society.* In G.Roth and C. Wittich (Eds.), (1978) *Economy and Society: An Outline of Interpretive Sociology*. London: University of California Press , [online]. Available from https://openlibrary.org/books/OL5071877M/Economy_and_society (Accessed 08.08.2020).

Weingast, B. R. (1993). 'Constitutions as Governance Structures: The Political Foundations of Secure Markets.' *Journal of Institutional and Theoretical Economics*, 149 (1), pp. 286–311, [online]. Available from https://www.jstor.org/stable/40751603?seq=1 (Accessed 04.10.2020).

Weiss, R. S. (1994). *Learning from Strangers. The Art and Method of Qualitative Interview Studies.* New York: Free Press, a Division of Macmillan, Inc.

Whitfield, L., & Buur, L. (2014). The Politics of Industrial Policy: Ruling Elites and Their Alliances. *Third World Quarterly*, 35 (1: New Actors and Alliances in Development), pp. 126–144, [online]. Available from https://www.tandfonline.com/doi/abs/10.1080/01436597.2014.868991 (Accessed 10.04.2020).

Whitfield, L., Buur, L., Therkildsen, O., & Kjer, A. M. (2015). *The Politics of African Industrial Policy. A Comparative Perspective*. Cambridge: Cambridge University Press.

Wiggins, S. N. (1991). 'The Economics of Firm and Contracts: A Selective Survey.' *Journal of Institutional and Theoretical Economics*, 147 (4), pp. 603–661, [online]. Available from https://www.jstor.org/stable/40751451?seq=1 (Accessed 10.04.2020).

Williamson, J. (1990). *Latin American Adjustment: How Much Has Happened?* Institute for International Economics, Conference Volume. Washington, DC.

Wittgenstein, L. (1953). *Philosophical Investigations*. Oxford: Blackwell.

World Bank. (1993). *The East Asian Miracle: Economic Growth and Public Policy*. New York: Oxford University Press.

World Bank. (2002). *World Development Report 2002: Building Institutions for Markets*,[online]. Available from http://documents.worldbank.org/curated/en/850161468336075630/World-development-report-2002-building-institutions-for-markets (Accessed 10.04.2020).

World Bank. (2008). *World Development Report 2008: Agriculture for Development*, [online]. Available from https://openknowledge.worldbank.org/handle/10986/5990 (Accessed 10.04.2020).

World Bank. (2012a). *Fighting Corruption in Public Services: Chronicling Georgia's Reforms*, [online]. Available from http://documents.worldbank.org/curated/en/518301468256183463/Fighting-corruption-in-public-services-chronicling-Georgias-reforms (Accessed 10.04.2020).

World Bank. (2012b). *World Development Report 2013: Jobs*, [Online]. Available from https://openknowledge.worldbank.org/handle/10986/11843 (Accessed 10.04.2020).

Yardley, L. (2009). Demonstrating Validity in Qualitative Psychology. In J. A. Smith (Ed.), *Qualitative Psychology: A Practical Guide to Research Methods* (pp. 235–251). Los Angeles, CA: Sage.

Yin, R. K. (2011). *Qualitative Research from Start to Finish*. New York, NY: The Guilford Press.

Zahari, Z., Barlow, C., & Gondowarsito, R. (2006). 'Oil Palm in Indonesia Socio-Economic Improvement – A Review of Options.' *Oil Palm Industry Economic Journal*, 6 (1), pp. 18–29, [online]. Available from https://www.researchgate.net/publication/5223969_Oil_Palmin_ Indonesian_SocioEconomic_Improvement_A_Review_of_Options (Accessed 10.04.2020).

www.ingramcontent.com/pod-product-compliance
Ingram Content Group UK Ltd.
Pitfield, Milton Keynes, MK11 3LW, UK
UKHW021832100926
8556IPUK00004B/295

9 783631 846780